Dislocating Labour

Journal of the Royal Anthropological Institute Special Issue Series

The Journal of the Royal Anthropological Institute is the principal journal of the oldest anthropological organization in the world. It has attracted and inspired some of the world's greatest thinkers. International in scope, it presents accessible papers aimed at a broad anthropological readership. We are delighted to announce that from 2014 the annual special issues will also be available from the Wiley Blackwell books catalogue.

Previous special issues of the JRAI:

DISLOCATING LABOUR

ANTHROPOLOGICAL RECONFIGURATIONS

EDITED BY PENNY HARVEY and
CHRISTIAN KROHN-HANSEN

This edition first published 2018
© 2018 Royal Anthropological Institute

Registered Office
John Wiley & Sons Ltd, The Atrium, Southern Gate, Chichester, West Sussex, PO19 8SQ, UK

Editorial Offices
350 Main Street, Malden, MA 02148-5020, USA
9600 Garsington Road, Oxford, OX4 2DQ, UK
The Atrium, Southern Gate, Chichester, West Sussex, PO19 8SQ, UK

For details of our global editorial offices, for customer services, and for information about how to apply for permission to reuse the copyright material in this book, please see our website at www.wiley.com/wiley-blackwell.

The right of Penny Harvey and Christian Krohn-Hansen to be identified as the authors of the editorial material in this work has been asserted in accordance with the UK Copyright, Designs and Patents Act 1988.

Library of Congress Cataloging-in-Publication Data

CIP data requested

9781119508380

A catalogue record for this book is available from the British Library.

Journal of the Royal Anthropological Institute.
Incorporating MAN
Print ISSN 1359-0987
All articles published within this special issue are included within the ISI Journal Citation Reports® Social Science Citation Index. Please cite the articles as volume 24(Supp) of the Journal of the Royal Anthropological Institute.

Cover image: 'Tourism Labour', copyright Penny Harvey

Cover design by Ben Higgins

Set in 10 on 12pt Minion by Aptara Inc.

Printed in Singapore by C.O.S. Printers Pte Ltd

1 2018

Contents

Shifting relations between state, capital, and place

Notes on contributors

Ben Campbell is Senior Lecturer in Anthropology at Durham University. He has worked for over three decades on transformations in indigenous agro-pastoralist communities in the Nepal Himalayas, and the interactions of local knowledge practices with institutions of environmental protection and political economic change. He joined the interdisciplinary Durham Energy Institute, integrating anthropological perspectives in research on sustainability matters, leading to implementation of a biogas renewable energy system at the yak cheese factory mentioned in his essay. His recent publications include 'Communities of energy' (with Jon Cloke and Ed Brown), *Economic Anthropology* (2016); *Living between juniper and palm: nature, culture and power in the Himalayas* (Oxford University Press, 2013); and 'Low-carbon yak cheese: transition to biogas in a Himalayan socio-technical niche' (with Paul Sallis), *Interface Focus* (2013). *Department of Anthropology, University of Durham, Durham DH1 3LE, UK. ben.campbell@durham.ac.uk*

Alanna Cant is a Postdoctoral Research Fellow at the School of Anthropology and Conservation, University of Kent. She holds a Marie Skłodowska-Curie grant from the European Commission for her current research, which looks at the restoration of religious architectural and artistic heritage in rural Mexico. Her recent publications include 'The art of indigeneity: aesthetics and competition in Mexican economies of culture', *Ethnos: Journal of Anthropology* (2016); and 'The allure of art and intellectual property: artisans and industrial replicas in Mexican cultural economies', *Journal of the Royal Anthropological Institute* (2015). *School of Anthropology and Conservation, Marlowe Building, University of Kent, Canterbury CT2 7NR, UK. A.Cant@kent.ac.uk*

Jan Grill is Assistant Professor of Sociology at the Universidad del Valle, Colombia, and an Honorary Fellow at the University of Manchester. He is also Research Associate at the Department of Social Anthropology at the University of Manchester. He has conducted extensive ethnographic research among Slovak, Czech, and Hungarian Roma/Gypsy groups, exploring issues related to different forms of migration from Central Eastern Europe to the United Kingdom and Canada. His central research interests are migration, ethnicity, racialization, marginality, labour, and the ethnography of the state. His recent publications include '"In England, they don't call you black!" Migrating racialisations and the production of Roma difference across Europe', *Journal of Ethic and Migration Studies* (2017); and 'Struggles for the folk: politics of culture in Czechoslovak ethnography, 1940s-1950s', *History and Anthropology* (2015). *Department of Social Sciences, Faculty of Social Sciences and Economy, Universidad del Valle, Ciudad Universitaria Meléndez, Calle 13 #100-00, Cali, Colombia. jan.grill@correounivalle.edu.co*

Penny Harvey is Professor of Social Anthropology at the University of Manchester and also holds a position as Professor II at the University of Oslo. She has conducted ethnographic fieldwork in Peru, Spain, and the United Kingdom, and published on language and communication, state practice, technology, expertise, infrastructure, and material politics. She is the co-author (with Hannah Knox) of *Roads: an anthropology of infrastructure and expertise* (Cornell University Press, 2015) and co-editor (with Caspar Bruun Jensen and Atsuro Morita) of *Infrastructures and social complexity* (Routledge, 2016). *Department of Social Anthropology, University of Manchester, Manchester M13 9PL, UK. penny.harvey@manchester.ac.uk*

Ingjerd Hoëm is Professor of Social Anthropology at the Department of Social Anthropology, University of Oslo. For twenty years she has carried out ethnographic research in the Pacific, especially in Tokelau. Her research focuses on the politics of communication. She is the author of *Languages of governance in conflict: negotiating democracy in Tokelau* (John Benjamins, 2015), *Theatre and political process: staging identities in Tokelau and New Zealand* (Berghahn, 2004), and *A way with words: language and culture in Tokelau society* (Orchid Press, 1995). *Department of Social Anthropology, University of Oslo, PO Box 1091, Blindern, NO-0317 Oslo, Norway. ingjerd.hoem@sai.uio.no*

Christian Krohn-Hansen is Professor of Anthropology at the University of Oslo. He is the author of *Making New York Dominican: small business, politics, and everyday life* (University of Pennsylvania Press, 2013) and *Political authoritarianism in the Dominican Republic* (Palgrave Macmillan, 2009), and co-editor (with Knut G. Nustad) of *State formation: anthropological perspectives* (Pluto Press, 2005). He is currently working on a book on Santo Domingo's popular economy. *Department of Anthropology, University of Oslo, PO Box 1091, Blindern, NO-0317 Oslo, Norway. christian.krohn-hansen@sai.uio.no*

Keir Martin is Associate Professor in Social Anthropology at the University of Oslo. He completed his Ph.D. in 2006 after two years of fieldwork in East New Britain province, Papua New Guinea, working among the Matupi community in the aftermath of the volcanic eruptions of 1994. He is the author of a monograph, *The death of the Big Men and the rise of the Big Shots*, published by Berghahn in 2013, and a number of published articles covering issues of contested transactions, social movements, land tenure, tourism, and possessive individualism. *Department of Anthropology, University of Oslo, PO Box 1091, Blindern, NO-0317 Oslo, Norway. k.j.c.martin@sai.uio.no*

Marit Melhuus is Professor of Social Anthropology at the University of Oslo. She has conducted research in Argentina, Mexico, and Norway, focusing on economics, gender, morality, and biotechnologies. She is the author of *Problems of conception:*

issues of law, biotechnology, individuals and kinship (Berghahn Books, 2012); and has co-edited (with Kristi Anne Stolen) *Machos, mistresses, madonnas: contesting the power of Latin American gender imagery* (Verso, 1996) and (with Marianne Elisabeth Lien) *Holding worlds together: ethnographies of knowing and belonging* (Berghahn Books, 2007). *Department of Anthropology, University of Oslo, PO Box 1091, Blindern, NO-0317 Oslo, Norway. marit.melhuus@sai.uio.no*

Susana Narotzky is Professor of Social Anthropology at the University of Barcelona. She has been awarded a European Research Council Advanced Grant to study the effects of austerity on Southern European livelihoods (*Grassroots Economics* [GRECO]). Her work is inspired by theories of critical political economy, moral economies, and feminist economics. Her recent writing addresses the themes of political mobilization, class, and making a living in futures without employment. She is the co-editor (with Victoria Goddard) of *Work and livelihoods: history, ethnography and models in times of crisis* (Routledge, 2017; winner of the Society for the Anthropology of Work book prize 2017) and has recently published articles in *Anthropological Theory, Annual Review of Anthropology, History and Anthropology,* and (with Niko Besnier) *Current Anthropology. Departament d'Antropologia Social, Universitat de Barcelona, C/Montealegre 6-8, 08001 Barcelona, Spain. narotzky@ub.edu*

Elisabeth Schober is Associate Professor in Social Anthropology at the University of Oslo. Previously, she has investigated responses to US bases in South Korea. Recently, she has focused on the challenges emerging from the relocation of manufacturing from South Korea to the Philippines. She is the author of *Base encounters* (Pluto Press, 2016) and has co-edited (with Thomas Hylland Eriksen) a special issue of *Ethnos* entitled 'Economies of growth or ecologies of survival?' *Department of Social Anthropology, University of Oslo, PO Box 1091, Blindern, NO-0317 Oslo, Norway. elisabeth.schober@sai.uio.no*

Sylvia Yanagisako is the Edward Clark Crossett Professor of Humanistic Studies and Professor and Chair of Anthropology at Stanford University. She is the author of *Producing culture and capital: family firms in Italy* (Princeton University Press, 2002). Her book (with Lisa Rofel) *Made in translation: a collaborative ethnography of Italian-Chinese global fashion* is being published by Duke University Press. *Department of Anthropology, Stanford University, 450 Serra Mall, Building 50, Stanford, CA 94305-2034, USA. syanag@stanford.edu*

Introduction. Dislocating labour: anthropological reconfigurations

PENNY HARVEY *University of Manchester*

CHRISTIAN KROHN-HANSEN *University of Oslo*

In the introduction to this volume on 'dislocating labour' we seek to lay the ground for an anthropology of labour that extends beyond the industrial heartlands from which the concept emerged. Remaining aware of the analytical purchase of the focus on the labour/capital relation, we argue that the ethnographic exploration of this relation allows us to extend the reach of the labour concept. It also allows us to explore the diverse ways in which labour relations are experienced beyond the confines of the economic, bringing kinship, personhood, affect, politics, and sociality firmly back into the frame of capitalist value creation. We draw on the notion of dislocation to extend the repertoire of labour analysis beyond that of dispossession and/or disorganization. By dislocation we refer to the unevenness of transnational capitalism's unfolding and the ways in which both places and persons are reconfigured by the movements of capital. Dislocation thus refers to the spatial movements of refugees and migrant workers, but also to other senses of disruption, such as the sentiment of feeling out of place, or of losing your bearings as things move and change around you.

Dislocating labour

The essays collected here attend to how labour practices register processes of dislocation in which both places and persons are reconfigured by the movements of capital. Our analyses are grounded in the anthropological awareness that capital does not circulate as an abstract force, but has to accommodate to the specific social and cultural formations that both facilitate and limit the possibilities for accumulation. Our ethnographic accounts draw on a range of examples, primarily from the Global South, and attend to how the historical particularities of place are integral to the relations between labour and capital. The essays also show how the dynamic and emergent qualities of these relations in turn shape people's social and material worlds. Our contributors explore a wide range of issues through the interrogation of the labour/capital relation: the ways in which industrial outsourcing and subcontracting change the conditions, possibilities, and politics of work; the effects of economic deregulation on agricultural economies and on local markets; the manner in which migration reconfigures understandings of productive power in places that once depended on the physical and social energies of

Journal of the Royal Anthropological Institute (N.S.), 10-28
© Royal Anthropological Institute 2018

people who now labour elsewhere; how cash economies begin to take hold in places where wage-labour has had limited significance; and how, in turn, the appearance and/or disappearance of waged work reconfigures foundational understandings not only of the relationship between productive and reproductive labour, but also of personhood, citizenship, and place.

Our focus on labour emerged from a shared ethnographic interest in processes of social change that were overtly dislocating (disturbing, disorienting, displacing) previous practices and assumptions. Talking and working together over several years,[1] we critically explored the potential of labour as an analytic that could be used to develop new insights on the contemporary effects of capital's perpetual mobility, and the many new and emerging forms of connectivity and disconnection that this mobility provokes. At the same time, we also addressed the concept of labour itself. We were increasingly convinced that this concept, which had become so firmly associated with a particular approach to political economy, could fruitfully be mobilized to address a far wider field of anthropological concerns. Investigating, rather than assuming, the relation between labour and capital (as Sylvia Yanagisako puts it – this volume) encouraged us to bring together a range of ethnographic explorations that might, at first glance, seem to lead us to incommensurable social worlds: the shipyards of Hanjin in South Korea, the craft workshops of Oaxaca in Mexico, the furniture markets of Santo Domingo, the new state administrative offices on the Tokelau atolls in the South Pacific, or a small rural roadside town in the Himalayan mountains – to name but a few.

Theoretically, we were also drawn to explore how labour, as an established but not necessarily widely used analytic, might offer new possibilities for the shaping of our ethnographic accounts of dislocation. Marx's insight that labour is not simply an economic relation but an economic relation that makes a difference to people's lives, their sense of identity, their relationship to places, to things, and to other people, invites attention to the intersections of analytical abstraction and empirical description. Anthropology has a strong tradition of using the concept of labour to explore the structuring conditions of economic life, to which we turn shortly. Nevertheless, there are also good reasons why many anthropologists became wary of a concept that is so closely tied to a specific historical moment, and which has often been deployed unreflexively as a universally relevant analytic. We also discuss these concerns as we outline our broader theoretical aim for this collection. However, the articles collected here suggest that the complex and intersecting forms of capital accumulation, and the distributed effects of these formations, *can* usefully be approached through the concept of labour. In what follows, we argue that a focus on labour, in this second decade of the twenty-first century, configures a field of ethnographic concern that conjures both the systemic force of capital, and the historical specificity of how these ever-shifting capital relations play out in practice across the world. How so?

In 2007 Michael Jackson wrote a moving essay about a visit to the copper mine at Falun in Sweden. The site had been worked since Viking times, and in the seventeenth century it produced 70 per cent of the world's copper. Closed since 1992, the mine is now a tourist attraction and a World Heritage site. The mine invoked in Jackson a sense of the 'thankless labor' that can build the fortunes of a national economy but without any parallel sense of gain for those who toiled underground, and who are now all but forgotten. His account seeks to recover something of what was at stake in such labour, both the pain and the small pleasures that shaped the experience of the miners and of the mining community. Jackson favours a phenomenological approach, and his discussion of labour thus hinges on the definitive transformation in human experience that the closure of the pit would have involved – the dislocation not simply of the labour force, but also of the place once configured by their working lives and all that it took to sustain them. As the mine became a heritage site, so the sensory connections between the miners and the site of their labour were also transformed, kept alive in memory, in narrative, or in the physical traces of former times … or perhaps simply forgotten. Such closures are of course not limited to workplaces in Western Europe. Capital is always looking for sites where labour is cheaper and where regulations are less onerous, where sites of production are nearer to growing markets and/or more technologized. These are not unidirectional processes, and the feedback loops between movement and stasis are well captured by the term 'dislocation' in English. Dislocation implies spatial movement, but it also refers to other senses of disruption or disorientation, such as the sentiment of feeling out of place, or of losing your bearings or sense of self as things move and change around you. The term allows us to encompass previous discussions of dispossession and of disorganization (Harvey 2003; Kasmir & Carbonella 2008; 2014), but also extends these concerns to the more phenomenological concerns that Jackson brings to the fore: the structures of feeling and the affective forces that colour contemporary experiences of labour.

Ongoing debate over the Apple iPhone indicates some of the issues in question. In September 2013, the *Guardian* reported that the new cheaper iPhone that Apple would soon unveil to a global audience was being produced under illegal and abusive conditions in Chinese factories by one of America's largest manufacturing businesses. The plant was owned by Florida-based Jabil Circuit, a US company with plants in over thirty countries. Jabil was founded in 1966 in a garage in Detroit. As American companies such as Apple outsourced their manufacturing to countries with lower wages, Jabil followed, opening its first plant outside the United States in Scotland in 1993. Operations subsequently expanded to China, Brazil, India, and Vietnam (Garside & Arthur 2013). Subsequently, further discussion emerged on the supply chains and labour processes involved in producing the mobile phones, including 'coltan extraction in eastern Congo, trade pacts and shipping lanes, the 55 kilograms of carbon emissions it [the iPhone] produces over its lifetimes, as well as the Foxconn factory and high street shop' (Toscano & Kinkle 2015: 194), raising questions about the systematic erasure of consumer awareness of the wider geopolitical contexts that support the production process across many otherwise dispersed sites. Taken from this perspective, the labour processes involved in producing the iPhone have implications for an ever-widening field, and ever more differentiated labour processes. We are interested in exploring the tension between the ways that global capitalism might connect the experience of labour on the assembly lines of the Chinese factory to the experiences of those engaged in the mining of coltan or working in the container shipping industry – while at the same time not connecting them at all, not simply fragmenting but also necessarily responding to hugely varied histories and fields of expectation. There are many ways to make a living and many ways to accumulate capital along the extensive routes of contemporary supply chains, and there are also diverse modes of exclusion, expropriation, and dispossession enacted along the way. The essays by Sylvia Yanagisako, by Elisabeth Schober, and by Marit Melhuus in this volume take sites of capitalist production as their starting-point, but the resonant effects of these global systems of production are also tangible forces in the potential or actual migratory journeys referred to by Penny Harvey, Ben Campbell,

Journal of the Royal Anthropological Institute (N.S.), 10-28
© Royal Anthropological Institute 2018

Ingjerd Hoëm, and Jan Grill, and in the specific labour markets that Keir Martin, Alanna Cant, and Christian Krohn-Hansen describe.

During the last four decades or so a significant number of nations, both within and beyond the OECD, have been experiencing growth in GDP with scant, stagnant, or even falling employment – characterized as the paradoxical phenomenon of 'jobless growth'. As Tania Li (2010: 67) put it a few years ago in an Asian context, the exclusion of so many today from the wage-labour economy is 'a sign of their very limited relevance to capital at any scale' (see also Denning 2010). The formation of nation-states and the relation of states to wider processes of capital accumulation are also in flux. Nation-states are in some ways increasingly marginal to capital growth. While the first 'export processing zone' or 'free trade zone' was established in Puerto Rico in 1947, by 2007 there were 3,500 such zones worldwide, employing more than 60 million people in over 130 countries. Today these special zones (in which states abstain from fundamental sovereign rights such as taxation and the collection of customs duties in order to attract investment) are the central locations for the world's light-industrial manufacturing (Cross 2010; Fernández-Kelly 1983; Neveling 2015; Ong 2006). Transnational companies in the oil industry and other extractive industries use forms of 'modularity' – mobile personnel, technologies, and legal structures – in their continual efforts to remove themselves from local social entanglements (Appel 2012). Offshore banking helps conceal assets and undermine states' power to tax (Maurer 2008; Maurer & Martin 2012).

The dismantling of full-time, stable, not to say life-long, employment in many places where Fordism was strong from the mid-1940s to the 1970s has eroded many people's sense of security and faith in a predictable future. It has also undermined the ways in which labour mediates relationships between citizens and the state both through the payment of taxes, and through the commitment of state authorities to ensuring livelihoods by protecting the right to work. This growing sense of destabilization led commentators concerned with the post-industrial societies of Europe, North America, Japan, and elsewhere to think more directly about new forms of precarious work and precarious life, new types of institutionalization and the normalization of temporary and irregular employment, zero-hour contracts, and the unpaid labour of interns and volunteers (Allison 2012; Neilson & Rossiter 2005; Standing 2014). The privatization of state welfare and social services has also led to new levels of reliance on unpaid, voluntary, and care work, which in turn has given rise to discussion of the specific burdens of affective labour (e.g. Muehleback 2011).

The transformations in the former Soviet Union and Eastern Europe have rendered these processes even more conspicuous. In the wake of the collapse of the Soviet Union, huge territories with large populations have seen a radical shift from state provisioning to 'free-market' or neoliberal policies. The outcomes are diverse. But all these areas have registered profound changes in the relationship between capital and labour, in prevailing labour regimes and labour practices, and in the citizens' rights and obligations linked to labour (Humphrey 2002; Pine 2014; Reeves 2012; Yurchak 2003; see also Grill, this volume).

These contexts of radical social change have implications for the lived realities that anthropologists are currently attempting to comprehend. They are also the subject of much discussion across the social sciences in rich literatures on neoliberalism, precarity, post-Fordism, post-socialism, and post-industrialism.[2] Anthropological work on labour has much to offer these discussions, not least a deeper and more textured understanding of the multiple contemporary manifestations of capitalism than short-hand concepts such as 'post-Fordism' or 'neoliberalism' allow.[3] Contemporary changes also disrupt otherwise settled categories. Marit Melhuus (this volume) argues that supposedly self-sufficient peasant production never was as autonomous as the concept of 'autarky' suggested. Ben Campbell's ethnographic account of the multiple threats to rural agricultural livelihoods in contemporary Nepal (this volume) is another stark empirical demonstration of the inadequacy of the concept.

Technological changes, the rise of finance capital (Ho 2009a; Maurer 2005), and shifts in the global organization of supply chains (Bellante & Nabhan 2016; Tsing 2009; 2015) have undoubtedly changed experiences and understandings of labour, and by extension the emergent experiences and understandings of place. In both non-industrialized and de-industrialized contexts, millions are not just unemployed but surplus to the requirements of capital accumulation.[4] In rural and urban landscapes where there is little or no possibility of productive labour, people increasingly look for ways of making legitimate distributive claims (Ferguson 2015). For many people, livelihoods depend on accessing state benefits, aid money, or other forms of charitable funding. New moral and political agendas of responsibility, fairness, and dignity are emerging alongside practices of care and modes of struggle that have for many become central to the everyday problems of livelihood (Smith 2012). In these settings the focus on 'labour', as both a social category and a social practice, offers a window through which to grasp key contemporary material, affective, moral, social, and political processes. We also suggest that 'labour' offers us an analytical hinge – a point of connection between the phenomenal encounters and sensory engagements that labour entails, and the wider social and political structures that shape and are in turn shaped by such encounters. In this respect the abstract category of 'labour' remains extremely useful as an analytic that signals the relevance of ethnographic work to this broad field of social research.[5] However, in what follows, we subject the concept to some conceptual dislocation, seeking to draw attention to the particular histories from which this term emerged, and to the ways in which it has been subject to critique in more recent times.

Dislocating the labour concept: wage-labour and surplus value

Marx's analysis of labour remains a vital point of departure from which to understand capital's ability to harness living labour to the production of surplus value (Marx 1990 [1867]). Marx sought to reveal the source of capitalist profit-making by shifting the key focus of analysis to the social organization of production based on wage-labour. The wage that a capitalist employer pays a worker enacts a formal separation of the worker from the product of his or her work in an act of alienation. In this way, labour is systematically exploited in capitalist relations that focus on the extraction of 'suplus value', that is, the economic value created by the worker over and above that which the employer pays for the work. Marx's focus on exploitation, the commodification of labour, and the extraction of surplus value revealed the political dimensions of the organization of labour, and thereby reworked the ways in which capitalism was understood as a particular form of 'political economy'. Marx thus showed that labour practices under capitalism are about much more than the economy. For him, work is a total phenomenon. It forms part of economic, social, cultural, and political processes, and is inextricably tied to fundamental issues concerning the scope and the possibility of human sovereignty and freedom. To seek to explore the organization of labour is thus to seek to understand forms of inequality and domination (Cohen 2001; Donham 1990; Roseberry 1997).

Journal of the Royal Anthropological Institute (N.S.), 10-28
© Royal Anthropological Institute 2018

While most early ethnographies in the structural functionalist tradition mentioned the kinds of *work* done by the people studied, the foundational capitalist *labour* relation did not receive much theoretical or analytical attention in anthropology until the latter half of the twentieth century – as discussed by Marit Melhuus (this volume) in her analysis of *how* surpluses were produced by, and appropriated from, the tobacco-growing sharecroppers whom she studied in Argentina in the mid-1970s. A notable exception was the pioneering research conducted under the auspices of the Rhodes-Livingstone Institute from the late 1930s and 1940s in what is now Zambia. This research was concerned with understanding the mass migrations from rural areas to the towns and burgeoning mines of Central Africa. Godfrey Wilson, the Institute's first director, viewed the transformations affecting Central Africa as an industrial revolution closely linked to the dynamics of the global economy. Subsequently, and in a dramatic expansion of the field of anthropological concern under the leadership of Max Gluckman, who succeeded Wilson at the Institute before taking up the Chair of Social Anthropology in Manchester, the anthropologists of the 'Manchester School' examined the implications of the penetration of capital in the shape of the mining industry and of new labour forms, including wage work (Epstein 1958; Gluckman 1949; 1958; C.J. Mitchell 1956; Wilson 1941). They did so by systematically treating rural areas, mining centres, and towns not as separate social units, but, instead, as interrelated locations belonging to one social field, one structure of power.[6]

During the 1960s, 1970s, and early 1980s, anthropology saw rapidly growing interest in Marxist-orientated perspectives, world-systems theory, and history. The discipline developed an increased awareness of the need to understand the historical process of Western global domination. A vitalized, globally oriented economic anthropology resulted in an outpouring of historical-ethnographic studies in capitalist change and the organization of production and labour. Many of the most influential works from these years were focused on social change as encountered in agrarian and mining economies, and in the dramatic global rise in migration and urbanization (e.g. Bloch 1983; Godelier 1977; Hart 1982; Meillassoux 1981; Mintz 1960; 1974; Nash 1979; Scott 1985; Taussig 1980; Wolf 1966; 1982). There were many different ideas among these authors as to how to combine ethnography and history. But there was also a more general interest in approaching 'economy' as the site of production, distribution, and consumption, embedded in particular institutions and social systems.

Several of the perspectives on global capitalism and labour regimes generated in this period have now become part of the discipline's standard tool-kit – and in this collection we put them to use. In particular, we assume that capitalism has always been transnational, and that the traversing of political borders is immanent in its historical trajectory. We thus stress that it is imperative to approach specific labour regimes in relation to global configurations. Capitalist restructurings or dislocations of labour in one (historically and socially generated) place are intimately connected to capitalist processes and changes in other corners of world society.[7]

However, substantivist approaches to economic anthropology that stress the embeddedness of economic processes in specific social and cultural relations are equally important. What matters is how these two perspectives on global circulations and local specificities are brought together in the analysis of labour dislocations. Keir Martin (this volume) discusses the porous boundaries of wage-labour, reminding us that the coexistence of the two perspectives is not simply an analytical problem, but a more direct existential dilemma for the people he was working with in Papua New Guinea.

Journal of the Royal Anthropological Institute (N.S.), 10-28
© Royal Anthropological Institute 2018

They were uncertain whether payment of a wage would effectively trump kinship and curtail claims that could be made on moral (rather than economic) grounds. Martin describes how such concerns were also common in the capitalist heartland of mid-nineteenth-century London, referring to Charles Dickens' novel *Dombey and Son*, and Dombey's concerns over whether payment to a wet-nurse fully achieves the separation of her person from the child whom she has suckled.

These arguments resonate with Susana Narotzky's reminder (this volume and 2015) that Marx was not only concerned with the abstraction of labour – that is, the ways in which labour power became a commodity to be bought and sold. He was also attentive to how capitalism understands and captures the embedded value in that labour. The focus on embedded value brings the substantivist position back into view. Indeed, Narotzky is critical of the way in which Polanyi set up an opposition between formal economic logics and embedded substantivist relations (the realm of cultural values and moral concerns). She argues that Marx had claimed not that embedded value was abandoned by capital in the formation of modern market economies, but rather that embedded value is always *used* by capital to generate and increase profit. This particular point about value was also central to the global feminist movement 'wages for housework' that began in Italy in the 1970s. The campaign was based on the demand for recognition of the fact that unpaid domestic labour was appropriated by capital for the reproduction of a (largely male) workforce (Malos 1995; Weeks 2011: 113-50). The feminists argued that labour politics that focused solely on wage-labour was blind to how exploitation worked in practice – although the unpaid labour of the peasant farmer was more likely to be recognized than the unpaid domestic labour of women (see also Melhuus, this volume).

Insights from feminist scholarship continue to complicate some of the more theory-driven Marxist analyses in the ongoing effort to think beyond the limits of an abstracted, economic perspective. Most recently, Laura Bear, Karen Ho, Anna Tsing, and Sylvia Yanagisako (2015) have called for a broader understanding of capitalist relations than offered by the fixed structures and models of established Marxist analysis. Ethnographic methods highlight the ambiguities and nuances of lived experience, and allow us to look more broadly at the multiple relations of power and differentiation through which inequality is enacted and reproduced – bringing 'kinship, personhood, the household, and social reproduction' firmly back into the frame of capitalist value creation. Similar to Narotzky, Bear *et al.*'s Gens manifesto posits 'the foundational argument that forms and senses of self, family, ethnicity, race, and community are always "inside" and mutually constitutive of capitalist social relations and vice versa'. 'Real' labour, unlike the abstract labour of economic models, is 'concrete', and concrete labour is always performed with and through relationships with others, and in terms of cultural understandings and experiences of gender, age, race, class, religion, nationality, citizenship, and so on. Capitalism seeks to realize the potentialities of labour (among other things) and does so through the ways in which distinctions are drawn – distinctions such as formal/informal, public/private, market/non-market, and so forth. These distinctions come to shape what counts as proper work, and affect the value of the work, not least in terms of what is and what is not legible and/or recognized by the state.

There are, of course, continuities between feminist concerns with structures of inequality and the Marxist approaches to global systems. Keith Hart's early discussions of informal labour (1973; see also 2006) are a case in point. Key to this discussion was the question of 'form' and of 'recognition' (as discussed subsequently by Povinelli

1995, and see also Harvey, this volume). The labour that entered the ledgers of formal economic accounting was work rendered legible to the modern state, as opposed to all the unaccounted, and unofficial, work (including domestic work) on which the formal economy depended. Debates around legal and illegal labour follow a similar line, but are now more clearly articulated to structures of state power. Seasonal fluctuations of non-documented (illegal) Mexican agricultural labour to the United States, for example, keep wages and prices down while also leaving workers vulnerable and unable to protest or to organize for better working conditions (Holmes 2013). Ambiguities around the classification of legal and illegal labour characterize the working conditions for many people in post-Soviet states, where seemingly arbitrary classifications undermine the possibilities for workers to have any certainty with respect to their official status, always unsure as to whether their documents will be taken as genuine or as fakes (Reeves 2013).

The essays that comprise this collection address diverse forms of labour: unionized labour; managerial and self-employed workers; agricultural labour; family firms for craft production and for the manufacture of high-end Italian clothing; small-scale furniture makers; wage-labour within kin groups; co-operative labour; migrant labour; state labour; and unemployment. The wide range of labour practices to which we attend in this volume do not simply serve as a reminder that the labour of production and reproduction takes place with and without the payment of a wage. We are also concerned to underline that these diverse labour forms register processes of dislocation and change that are integral to the capitalist process.

Labour and work

In 1979, Sandra Wallman edited the ASA conference volume *Social anthropology of work*. Rereading this volume, we were struck by the continued relevance of most of its central questions, despite the fact that the global social landscape has changed so profoundly in the intervening years. The volume did not directly engage industrial labour (a criticism voiced at the time), but the backdrop of labour questions would have been self-evident to readers. This was the year that Margaret Thatcher came to power in the United Kingdom with a mandate that was explicitly about labour and particularly about unemployment, then running at a post-war high. It was a time of explicit concern over state welfare and the role of trade unions, following the 'Winter of Discontent', when widespread strikes by public sector workers severely disrupted transport services, hospitals, refuse collection, and even grave-digging. The volume did, however, pose the question of how *anthropology* might contribute to discussions around 'work'. Taking a broadly comparative approach, and attending ethnographically to diverse classifications of work, contributors explored the complexities of context, the contradictions of values, and the anomalies of ordinary life. The tensions between 'making a living' and 'making a life worth living' were highly visible in concerns over the relations between resources, values, and identity structures, and the effort to understand work as transaction as much as material production.

These issues of value open another strand of thought that might explain a certain reluctance on the part of anthropology to move too rapidly between the categories of work and labour. While capitalist relations are, as we have argued, highly pervasive, they certainly do not apply to all the many ways in which human beings engage the everyday problems of livelihood. Marilyn Strathern's hugely influential work *The gender of the gift* (1988) questioned whether labour was an appropriate category to apply to the 'economic' relations that she observed in Mt Hagen, Papua New Guinea. She asked what exactly was implied by the argument that men control the labour of their wives. Exploitation was the issue. Were the men of Mt Hagen exploiting their wives? Strathern notes that the question is relevant in relation to deeply embedded Western notions that 'freedom' relates to the individual's control of his or her own labour and that exploitation occurs when another appropriates the value of that labour, value that should (in this argument) accrue to the person who has done the work. Alienation, in the Marxist understanding of labour, as previously discussed, refers to the separation of a person from the fruits of his or her work.

But Strathern was interested in two quite separate spheres of value, spheres of value that her Melanesian informants kept firmly differentiated in terms of their understandings of labour. The domestic labour most pertinent to this argument involved raising pigs for food. The argument is that this labour is not alienated. The relations involved in the production of food are acknowledged and labour is not abstracted. But in the sphere of exchange, where pigs circulate as prestige items, not as food items, and where men accrue renown for their capacity to put pigs into circulation, the labour of raising the pigs is concealed. However, Strathern argues that it is both men's and women's labour that is concealed in the circuits of exchange that focus not on the raising of pigs but on the capacity to offer pigs to another. She concludes that there is concealment, but not of the economic in non-economic form. There is domination but not through the exploitation of labour. The acknowledgement of the joint production of economic use value of domestic sociality is transformed, in the context of ceremonial exchange, to a demonstration of wealth and prestige, manifest as the capacity to give to another. In both cases there is acknowledgement of multiple authorship. The pigs are never fully separated from the relations that produced them. It is just that in the two realms (of food production and of ceremonial exchange) different relations are brought into view. It is in this context that Strathern suggests 'perhaps one should abandon the term labor altogether' (1988: 160).

Strathern's argument is tightly woven into ongoing debates on exchange and prestige in Melanesia, but it resonated far more widely, not least because it called on ethnographers to pay more systematic attention to the cultural assumptions that were foundational to their own analytical categories. Talk of labour required attention to the particular system in play, and thus the question was raised: is it appropriate to talk in terms of labour at all? Or does labour always imply culturally specific understandings of property, autonomy, and freedom? These understandings, as Strathern indicates, refer back to Lockean concepts of labour and property, and the notion that property is created through the addition of labour to 'nature' (Locke 1986 [1689]). The issue for anthropological analysis concerns how awareness of a concept such as labour is engaged reflexively.

Keir Martin's contribution to this volume does just that as he explores the partibility of labour in more detail both in the history of Western political thought and in his ethnography from contemporary Papua New Guinea. Drawing out the contrasts between Locke's and Marx's theory of the person, he disputes the grounds on which the analytical distinction between Melanesian and Western ontologies of personhood have so frequently been drawn from readings of Strathern's work.[8] His argument is central to our attempt to re-purpose labour for contemporary anthropological analysis. He reminds us that the combination of comparative anthropology and ethnographic methods always puts concepts in question. However, as Martin's work exemplifies, discussion of the applicability of Marx's concept of labour beyond the specific historical condition from which it arose (e.g. Tsing 2009: 153-4), is not a call to abandon the concept. It implies rather that we need to remain aware of the specificity of our concepts.[9]

Both Marx and Strathern were engaged in creating analytical models rather than accounts of an 'objective reality'. David Graeber (2011) notes that one of the problems with models, particularly models that are analytically very productive, is that they get treated as objective realities – and much effort is then put into arguing that the world was never really like that, a fate that has fuelled debate on both Marx's and Strathern's works! The question at stake for us here concerns the effects of using one model (of capitalist relations) to capture another (the Melanesian exchange system). We need to be clear about the particularities of the system in question, and be aware of how people experiment with the models that shape the spaces of everyday encounters.

This brings us back to our core interest in the expansiveness of contemporary capital: the technological possibilities and the physical mobility that draw systems together that, while they were never as discrete as the models portray, are now quite clearly in a far more intense and frequent articulation than ever before (Mezzadra & Neilson 2015). An anthropology of labour thus has to engage the oscillation between the abstractions of analytical models (or ideal systems), on the one hand, and the complexity of real-life articulations, on the other. We return here to questions of how capital, work, and labour articulate with place and processes of dislocation. In their Gens manifesto, Bear *et al.* (2015) call for more ethnographic attentiveness to how the social relations of capitalism are generated out of divergent life projects. Their suggestion is to approach capitalism as unstable and contingent networks, disaggregated practices of human and nonhuman relations, generated from heterogeneity and difference, from the varied ways of being and becoming of particular kinds of people, families, communities – and presumably also firms, corporations, state systems, and so on. Others, notably Susana Narotzky and Niko Besnier (2014), have made similar arguments in an attempt to show that capitalism is more fragile and more intimate than discussions of structural contradictions or determining logics allow.

These are not naïve or optimistic calls. The fact that capitalism is not a singular system but harbours inherent multiplicity and heterogeneity does not offer a simple message of hope. On the contrary, the inherent instability is also productive of contingent violence and destruction. Michael Taussig's (1986; 1992) description of the violence of the Amazonian rubber boom is an excellent example, as is Timothy Mitchell's (2002) account of the emergence of Egypt's modern economy. In both these cases these authors show that the levels of violence and destruction they document are not necessarily either planned or logical, but might simply register the destructive force of contingent encounters.

Here again, labour comes into the story with considerable force, serving as a hinge or point of connection between the fragility and the strength of capitalism, and between those approaches that focus on instability and contingent outcomes and those that track capitalism as a mode of power that has great success in realizing the potentialities of resources, money, labour, and investment, as the Gens group discuss (Bear *et al.* 2015). All the essays in this collection confront the multidimensionality of social process, and explore the ways in which 'labour' provides a bridging concept between the settling and the unsettling of capital. Labour is thus the concept used to refer to a particular manifestation of the power of capital. It also constitutes the site of its fragility, as Marx taught us. Feminist approaches have widened the scope of this generative tension. No longer confined to industrial capital and wage-labour, the concept of labour itself expands to all those forms of productive engagement that capital itself extends to.

Anthropological reconfigurations

Susana Narotzky's essay takes up many of the issues raised in this general introduction. Her contribution brings a specific focus to the question of 'labour' as the articulation of 'human energy expenditure' (work) and capital, emphasizing the analytical importance of maintaining the distinction between concrete labour practices and the abstract value of labour in processes of capital accumulation. By tracing the genealogy of the labour concept, she articulates its historical specificity. At the same time, she notes how contemporary processes of globalization have extended capital's reach, thereby opening the concept of labour to more complex social dynamics than traditionally incorporated in political economic analyses. Despite anthropological reservations over the use of such an abstract (and thus implicitly universalizing) category, her argument supports the core proposition of this special issue that 'labour' offers an important and relevant analytic perspective for contemporary anthropology. Narotzky's contribution ends with a programmatic statement on how the labour concept might usefully be deployed as an analytic. She emphasizes that while the theoretical abstraction is integral to the strength of the labour concept, it is the immediacy of ethnographic experience that will open the way to theoretical breakthroughs and practical avenues for transforming society.

It is the ethnographic exploration of this dynamic tension between concrete and abstract labour which the contributors to this volume offer. We have grouped the essays into three thematic sections: (1) labour and capital; (2) disorganization, precarity, and affect; and (3) shifting relations between state, capital, and place. However, the reader is also encouraged to read across the sections. Ethnographic accounts resist categorization and our three core topics resonate across all the contributions, and collectively demonstrate the relevance of the labour concept for contemporary anthropological thought. Anthropological understandings of the specific relational dynamics between capital and local forms of labour can greatly enrich our understandings of the diverse ways in which contemporary capitalism operates and inflects the lived realities of many, if not all, of the sites of contemporary ethnographic research. The essays collected here demonstrate how the labour concept (for all its cultural and historical specificity) can provide the ground for comparisons and the possibility for new conversations.

Labour and capital

The four essays in this section focus squarely on labour as an economic relation, but also show that we cannot take the distinction between labour and capital for granted. They all demonstrate the importance of interrogating the labour/capital relation by thinking with the specificities that ethnographic studies bring to light. They also provoke reflection on the entanglements of economic and affective relationships, extending understandings of how economic relations are, or are not, separated from other relational dynamics. The tension between the values of concrete and abstract labour, and the ambiguities that inhere in these categories, take different forms in each case, but each study clearly demonstrates how concrete and abstract labour *together* shape the social worlds to which they pertain.

The issue is at the core of Sylvia Yanagisako's essay on the outsourcing of Italian luxury textile and garment production to China, as traditional family-owned firms were attracted by a cheaper and non-unionized workforce. Yanagisako's research shows how the boundary between labour and capital is dynamic, specific, and historically and culturally constituted. Her ethnography also shows how global supply chains dislocate both people and labour processes. It is the managers, not the owners, of the Italian firms who move to China. These managers embody the value of Italian taste and design and play a key role in the promotion and protection of the brand, commanding far higher salaries than would be open to them in Italy. However, the move to China precludes the conversion of their labour into capital. In Italy, managers would expect to build their own businesses, opening new subcontracting firms and combining their experience and their local networks with the ability to draw on unpaid family labour to establish new enterprises. In China, with neither family nor local networks to draw on, this possibility is not available to them.

Alanna Cant's work on Mexican artisanal woodcarvers offers a very different example of the relationship between property, ownership, labour, and capital. Her ethnography is also concerned with family firms whose brand is closely associated with a specific place: not Italy, but the small Oaxacan village of San Martín Tilcajete, where artisan producers are also precluded from converting their labour into capital. In this case the labour/capital relation does not rest on access to the means of production as the materials, skills, and technologies are available to most, if not all, local families. However, Cant argues that the value of the carvings in international art markets relies on the limited attribution of authorship. Only the owners of the workshops sign the carvings. The labour of the workers who actually make the carvings is erased. The inequalities of this process emerge from the intermingling of two crucial factors: the global art market's ideology of individual authorship; and the social intimacy inherent in the affective and moral relations, primarily of kinship, through which labour is recruited. Kinship gives access to work, and in this way helps to 'make' both labour and capital in a context of extreme insecurity and massive out-migration.

The labour/capital relation was also the central focus of Marit Melhuus's research on landless tobacco growers in the Corrientes region of Argentina in the mid-1970s. In the essay presented here, Melhuus reappraises the value of household analysis, and proposes that the household concept has much to offer a contemporary anthropology of labour. Her former analysis of household economies clearly demonstrated how the labour costs of the tobacco industry were effectively erased. The self-employed sharecroppers of Corrientes carried all the risk of changing market prices, of state intervention, and of the weather, which could ruin a crop in any given year. Household analysis showed exactly how economic value was created and circulated, and in the process revealed the ways in which working lives and family lives came together for the reproduction of capital. The analysis also showed how the precarity of these workers was directly connected to the structural conditions of economic exclusion, as the landowners, the tobacco industry, and the state controlled and curtailed the terms on which these workers could make a living.

The porous relationship between 'wage-labour' and other labour forms takes a different turn in the contribution by Keir Martin. Martin focuses on the performative dimensions of labour/capital transactions, arguing that the categorization of wage-labour shapes its economic and social effects as much as it describes them. He bases his argument on fieldwork conducted with the Matupit people in Papua New Guinea's East New Britain province. An increase in cash cropping has given increased importance to the control of land as private property, and wage-labour relations have become more common. In this context, the payment of a 'wage' to a relative appears as a means of

Journal of the Royal Anthropological Institute (N.S.), 10-28
© Royal Anthropological Institute 2018

limiting claims or rights to land or land use based on kinship. Martin emphasizes the real and lasting force of wage-labour's effects. At the same time, the ambiguities inherent in the distinctions between wage-labour and kin-based support draw attention to the unstable boundaries between labour categories. Martin shows that it takes a lot of hard work to effectively convert ongoing reciprocal obligations to a one-off transaction of wage-labour.

Disorganization, precarity, and affect

The vulnerability of labour to capital is experienced in different ways, in different parts of the world, and in quite divergent labour settings. Each of the three essays in this section traces the specific historical circumstances through which capital flows systematically dislocate (disrupt and dislodge) the possibilities for organized labour and for building strong social collectives able to produce and maintain a degree of autonomy from the demands of capital. At the same time, all the essays attend to the concrete nature of labour relations, and the ethnographies demonstrate the effort to preserve affective and moral relations as the basis of ongoing, if fragile, collective formations.

The dislocation of wage-labour in the wake of the collapse of the Soviet Union and the imposition of neoliberal economic policies in Eastern Europe is the setting of Jan Grill's study of Roma/Gypsies in Slovakia. Once employed in factories, construction companies, and agricultural co-operatives, many Roma/Gypsies are now facing life without work. In a context where public welfare has been dramatically reduced, these former workers are required to participate in state-sponsored 'Activation Works' programmes. The work they have to do to receive the token payments that supplement their meagre unemployment benefits is understood by all involved as 'fake work'. There is virtually no material product, only the pretense that the 'activation' programme will help people back to proper waged work in the future. Everybody knows that there are no jobs to be had, and that labour futures involve migration. Understandings of place, personhood, and citizenship are dislocated, and precarity becomes a long-term prospect in these ambiguous zones of not quite 'productive work', not quite 'informal labour'.

The growing sense of disconnection, and the tensions between formal and informal labour, resonate with the case that Penny Harvey presents from rural Peru. Her essay highlights the structural precarity of rural labour collectives (both peasant communities and agricultural co-operatives) whose formal status and economic viability have been systematically undermined by the effects of a liberalizing economy and a decentralizing state. In Peru as in Slovakia, the state seeks to elicit evidence of active citizenship in the widespread use of corvée labour in exchange for support for basic infrastructural provision. Rural communities, in turn, deploy the idiom of reciprocal labour exchanges that have long structured the affective ties of community in the Andes, as they attempt to engage state officials and ensure their collaboration and support for specific local ventures. Harvey argues that the structural ambiguities around formality and informality fundamentally undermine the possibilities for securing autonomous collectives through which to build more hopeful futures.

Elisabeth Schober's essay describes how the industrial labour force of the Hanjin shipyard in South Korea was decimated through massive industrial restructuring in the wake of the Asian financial crisis. The traditionally militant workers were disorganized and fragmented. Their despair was registered in a series of tragic workplace suicides. These suicides were subsequently mobilized by union activists as highly affective and effective modes of protest. These powerful forms of protest also mobilized the 'Hope-Bus' movement in South Korea, temporarily bringing the issue of worker precarity on to the national agenda. As the workforce was reduced in South Korea, the company relocated to Subic Bay in the Philippines. Here they have built an enormous production site where unionized labour and the related possibilities for collective action have been systematically prevented.

Shifting relations between state, capital, and place

The three case studies in this final section all explore the transformations and disruptions in spaces of everyday living that result from the diverse ways in which national or local economies are restructured by changing engagements with transnational capital flows. The contributions powerfully describe the specific processes of dislocation that result from the spatial unevenness of transnational capitalism's unfolding. They also focus on the state as a decisive generating and mediating force.

The collapse of established agrarian household regimes in Northern Nepal is the subject of Ben Campbell's essay. The Nepalese state's new-found environmentalism in support of the tourism industry and in response to global agreements on environmental sustainability led to a shift in the possibilities for the agricultural livelihoods of the Tamang-speaking communities who are the subject of Campbell's work. Key provisioning possibilities became illegal and hard to circumvent in the militarized arenas of a protracted guerrilla war that shaped opportunities in that region. Labour migration, particularly of young men, to other parts of Asia and increasingly to the Gulf States heralded a transition to a remittance economy. This dislocation of a core sector of the productive labour force has challenged the viability of the Tamang subsistence economy. It affects not only the kinds of crops that can be grown, and the foods that can be eaten, but also the social relationships that can be made in and through a particular place. Campbell provides a multi-faceted account of how these histories of engagement with the state are fundamental to local experiences of dislocation.

Similar forces appear in a very different guise in the essay by Ingjerd Hoëm. While a large part of the world has seen a clear turn towards neoliberalism, deregulation, and withdrawal of the state from many areas of social provision since the 1970s and 1980s, some places, like Tokelau, have not. Tokelau is a semi-dependent territory of New Zealand in the South Pacific that consists of three atolls with a population of some 1,400. This small society is currently developing its own state, funded by large amounts of aid money directed to the territory in response to 'underdevelopment' and high levels of 'unemployment'. Tokelauans increasingly prefer to work for salaries in the newly founded state system, as teachers, health workers, and office employees. Meanwhile, many of the traditional labour forms such as fishing and weaving are no longer valued as skilled work, and are not recognized as formal modes of employment. Furthermore, non-monetary circulations are increasingly read as 'corruption'. Hoëm maintains that it remains to be seen whether waged labour and the accompanying imperative of capitalist development can be successfully combined with the entrenched values of an 'egalitarian' society.

Christian Krohn-Hansen's essay also carries forward our discussions of the ways in which the state shapes the relations between capital and labour, often in terms of disruptive and disordering interventions. His ethnography follows how Dominican furniture makers are constantly adapting to the changing dynamics of state/capital relations, and to the complex rhythms of capital circulations. Capitalism for these producers is not synonymous with speed. On the contrary, the nation's small workshops and firms experience constant delays, exacerbated by an unreliable electricity supply. They are made to wait, as they find themselves shut out from lucrative markets, and marginalized from arenas of national productivity, which are monopolized by those with effective (often family) links to state power. In the early 1990s, the Dominican economy was conspicuously liberalized, under IMF stabilization programmes. Furniture makers now face increasingly tough competition from cheaper imports. Krohn-Hansen argues that a focus on labour practices reveals the temporal discrepancies that people are required to navigate in the course of their everyday working lives.

Our hope for this collection is that it will rekindle a general interest in the complex relations between capital and labour among anthropologists, many of whom might not necessarily see themselves as working primarily on economic relations. Ethnographers, wherever they are based, will confront the lived realities of dislocation that affect the ways in which people attempt to secure livelihoods, and to sustain 'lives worth living' in the face of what are often extreme conditions of uncertainty and instability. Detailed ethnography and a comparative approach to 'labour' that extends beyond the industrial heartlands from which the concept emerged offer a means of extending thought as we attempt to find ways to respond to the challenges of our contemporary world.

NOTES

We are grateful to two anonymous readers and to the guidance of Cathrine Degnen in bringing this manuscript to press. We would like to thank the Research Council of Norway for the funding of the project 'Anthropos and the Material: Challenges to Anthropology', which supported our initial group discussions on 'labour'. We also acknowledge the wider intellectual and financial support of the Institute of Social Anthropology at the University of Oslo, and the Department of Social Anthropology at the University of Manchester.

[1] The collection emerges from an extended conversation on labour that began in a reading group at the University of Oslo in 2013. One of the excitements of this conversation was that it did not arise from a sense of prior specialization. Our agenda was more exploratory and ethnographically driven as we read and discussed how a return to the concept of labour might inform our ethnographic analyses in new ways. Different people came in and out of the group – as visitors to Oslo, and as participants in panels and conferences that we organized in Manchester, and at the Edinburgh ASA conference in 2014. In addition to those whose work is collected here, Susanne Brandtstädter, Massimiliano Mollona, Knut Nustad, Ruth Prince, and Astrid Stensrud made significant contributions to our conversations.

[2] See, for example, Chari & Verdery (2009); Hardt (1999); Hardt & Negri (2000); Harvey (2005); Meagher (2016); Weeks (2011); Yanagisako (2012).

[3] Our anthropological work on labour ought to include detailed analysis of concrete, specific history. As many have underscored, labour relations in many places were highly insecure and precarious well before recent forms of precaritization, and Fordism did not pertain across much of the world – or at least it was enacted or experienced in different ways (see, e.g., Ferguson 2013; Millar 2014; Munck 2013).

[4] Changes in various non-industrialized contexts are analysed in this volume by, respectively, Campbell, Harvey, Hoëm, and Martin. Grill's essay examines a set of processes in a de-industrialized social landscape.

[5] Some thought-provoking anthropological-ethnographic works from the last ten or fifteen years that, in dissimilar ways, demonstrate the extent to which 'labour' remains enormously productive as an analytic are: Bear (2007; 2014); Campoamor (2016); Dunn (2004); Ferguson (2013); Gregory (2015); Ho (2009b); Lazar (2012; 2017); Li (2014); Millar (2014); Molé (2010); Mollona (2009; 2015); Prentice (2012); Rodkey (2016); Shever (2013).

[6] Let us underscore that a central contribution of the Manchester School was not just to treat rural and industrial areas as interconnected, but to take industrial social formations on their own terms rather than as hang-overs from 'traditional' rural life. The major shortfall of this research was its failure to take sufficient account of the imperial history and the colonial structures that had shaped, and continued to shape, the processes it sought to analyse (Asad 1991; Ferguson 1999: 24-37).

[7] For two important works on the possibility of a profoundly global anthropology of labour, see Kasmir & Carbonella (2008; 2014).

[8] Strathern herself acknowledged that the contrast drawn between Melanesian and Western notions of personhood was deployed as a heuristic device, orientated as much to the questioning of normative Euro-American understandings as it was to the ethnographic description of Melanesian ones. Her primary interest was to expand anthropological awareness of distinct modes of relationality. The elaboration of such ideal types (Gell 1999) was not intended to preclude grounded ethnographic description – either in Papua New Guinea or in Western Europe.

[9] Edwards, Evans, and Smith (2012) have explored similar concerns around the concept of 'class'. They argue that

> ethnographic examples make possible a critique of those accounts that assume class to be always and everywhere paramount no matter what, and at the same time they allow for an interrogation of those analyses in which class is deemed to be irrelevant just because research subjects do not 'talk class' or use it as a primary frame of reference (2012: 4).

Their approach is thus not to decide once and for all on the usefulness or otherwise of 'class' as an analytical concept, but rather to trace the effects of bringing 'class and capital's ordering and reordering effects in and out of focus' (2012: 4).

REFERENCES

ALLISON, A. 2012. Ordinary refugees: social precarity and soul in 21st century Japan. *Anthropological Quarterly* **85**, 345-70.

APPEL, H. 2012. Offshore work: oil, modularity, and the how of capitalism in Equatorial Guinea. *American Ethnologist* **39**, 692-709.

ASAD, T. 1991. From the history of colonial anthropology to the anthropology of Western hegemony. In *History of anthropology, vol. 7: Colonial situations* (ed.) G. Stocking, 314-24. Madison: University of Wisconsin Press.

BEAR, L. 2007. *Lines of the nation: Indian railway workers, bureaucracy, and the intimate historical self.* New York: Columbia University Press.

——— 2014. For labour: Ajeet's accident and the ethics of technological fixes in time. *Journal of the Royal Anthropological Institute* (N.S.) Special Issue: Doubt, conflict, mediation: the anthropology of modern time (ed.) L. Bear, 71-88.

———, K. HO, A. TSING & S. YANAGISAKO 2015. Gens: A feminist manifesto for the study of capitalism. Fieldsights – Theorizing the Contemporary. *Cultural Anthropology* (available on-line: *http://www.culanth.org/fieldsights/652-gens-a-feminist-manifesto-for-the-study-of-capitalism*, accessed 4 January 2018).

BELLANTE, L. & G.P. NABHAN 2016. Borders out of register: edge effects in the US-Mexico foodshed. *Culture, Agriculture, Food and Environment* **38**, 104-12.

BLOCH, M. 1983. *Marxism and anthropology.* Oxford: Clarendon Press.

CAMPOAMOR, L. 2016. Who are you calling exploitative? Defensive motherhood, child labor, and urban poverty in Lima, Peru. *Journal of Latin American and Caribbean Anthropology* **21**, 151-72.

CHARI, S. & K. VERDERY 2009. Thinking between the posts: postcolonialism, postsocialism, and ethnography after the Cold War. *Comparative Studies in Society and History* **51**, 6-34.

COHEN, G.A. 2001. *Karl Marx's theory of history: a defence* (Expanded edition). Princeton: University Press.

CROSS, J. 2010. Neoliberalism as unexceptional: economic zones and the everyday precariousness of working life in South India. *Critique of Anthropology* **30**, 355-73.

DENNING, M. 2010. Wageless life. *New Left Review* **66**, 79-97.

DONHAM, D. 1990. *History, power, ideology: central issues in Marxism and Anthropology.* Cambridge: University Press.

DUNN, E. 2004. *Privatizing Poland: baby food, big business, and the remaking of labor.* Ithaca, N.Y.: Cornell University Press.

EDWARDS, J., G. EVANS & K. SMITH 2012. Introduction: the middle class-ification of Britain. In *Class, community and crisis in post-industrial Britain.* Theme Section for *Focaal – Journal of Global and Historical Anthropology* (eds) J. Edwards, G. Evans & K. Smith, **62**, 3-16.

EPSTEIN, A.L. 1958. *Politics in an urban African community.* Manchester: University Press.

FERGUSON, J. 1999. *Expectations of modernity: myths and meanings of urban life on the Zambian Copperbelt.* Berkeley: University of California Press.

——— 2013. Declarations of dependence: labour, personhood, and welfare in Southern Africa. *Journal of the Royal Anthropological Institute* (N.S.) **19**, 223-42.

——— 2015. *Give a man a fish.* Durham, N.C.: Duke University Press.

Journal of the Royal Anthropological Institute (N.S.), 10-28
© Royal Anthropological Institute 2018

Fernández-Kelly, M.P. 1983. *For we are sold, I and my people*. Albany: State University of New York Press.

Garside, J. & C. Arthur 2013. Workers' rights 'flouted' at Apple iPhone factory in China. *Guardian*, 5 September (available on-line: *https://www.theguardian.com/technology/2013/sep/05/workers-rights-flouted-apple-iphone-plant*, accessed 4 January 2018).

Gell, A. 1999. Strathernograms, or, The semiotics of mixed metaphors. In *The art of anthropology: essays and diagrams* (ed.) E. Hirsch, 29-75. London: The Athlone Press.

Gluckman, M. 1949. *Malinowski's sociological theories* (Rhodes-Livingstone Paper 16). Livingstone, Northern Rhodesia: Rhodes-Livingstone Institute.

——— 1958. *Analysis of a social situation in modern Zululand* (Rhodes-Livingstone Paper 28). Manchester: University Press.

Godelier, M. 1977. *Perspectives in Marxist anthropology*. Cambridge: University Press.

Graeber, D. 2011. *Debt: the first 5,000 years*. New York: Melville House.

Gregory, S. 2015. *The devil behind the mirror: globalization and politics in the Dominican Republic*. Berkeley: University of California Press.

Hardt, M. 1999. Affective labor. *boundary 2* 26: 2, 89-100.

——— & A. Negri 2000. *Empire*. Cambridge, Mass.: Harvard University Press.

Hart, K. 1973. Informal income opportunities and urban employment in Ghana. *Journal of Modern African Studies* 11: 3, 61-89.

——— 1982. *The political economy of West African agriculture*. Cambridge: University Press.

——— 2006. Bureaucratic form and the informal economy. In *Linking the formal and informal economy: concepts and policies* (eds) B. Guha-Khasnobis, R. Kanbur & E. Ostrom, 21-35. Oxford: University Press.

Harvey, D. 2003. *The new imperialism*. Oxford: University Press.

——— 2005. *A brief history of neoliberalism*. Oxford: University Press.

Ho, K. 2009a. Disciplining investment bankers, disciplining the economy: Wall Street's institutional culture of crisis and the downsizing of 'corporate America'. *American Anthropologist* 111, 177-89.

——— 2009b. *Liquidated: an ethnography of Wall Street*. Durham, N.C.: Duke University Press.

Holmes, S. 2013. *Fresh fruit, broken bodies: migrant farmworkers in the United States*. Berkeley: University of California Press.

Humphrey, C. 2002. *The unmaking of Soviet life*. Ithaca, N.Y.: Cornell University Press.

Jackson, M. 2007. On the work of human hands. In *Excursions*, 61-79. Durham, N.C.: Duke University Press.

Kasmir, S. & A. Carbonella 2008. Dispossession and the anthropology of labor. *Critique of Anthropology* 28, 5-25.

——— (eds) 2014. *Blood and fire: toward a global anthropology of labor*. Oxford: Berghahn Books.

Lazar, S. 2012. A desire to formalize work? Comparing trade union strategies in Bolivia and Argentina. *Anthropology of Work Review* 33, 15-24.

——— 2017. *The social life of politics: ethics, kinship, and union activism in Argentina*. Stanford: University Press.

Li, T.M. 2010. To make live or let die? Rural dispossession and the protection of surplus populations. *Antipode* 41: S1, 66-93.

——— 2014. *Land's end: capitalist relations on an indigenous frontier*. Durham, N.C.: Duke University Press.

Locke, J. 1986 [1689]. *The second treatise on civil government*. Amherst, Mass: Prometheus.

Malos, E. (ed.) 1995. *The politics of housework* (New edition). Cheltenham: New Clarion.

Marx, K. 1990 [1867]. *Capital*, vol. 1 (trans. B. Fowkes). London: Penguin.

Maurer, B. 2005. Due diligence and 'reasonable man', offshore. *Cultural Anthropology* 20, 474-505.

——— 2008. Re-regulating offshore finance? *Geography Compass* 2, 155-75.

——— & S.J. Martin 2012. Accidents of equity and the aesthetics of Chinese offshore incorporation. *American Ethnologist* 39, 527-44.

Meagher, K. 2016. The scramble for Africans: demography, globalisation and Africa's informal labour markets. *Journal of Development Studies* 52, 483-97.

Meillassoux, C. 1981. *Maidens, meals, and money: capitalism and the domestic community*. Cambridge: University Press.

Mezzadra, S. & B. Neilson 2015. Operations of capital. *The South Atlantic Quarterly* 114, 1-9.

Millar, K.M. 2014. The precarious present: wageless labor and disrupted life in Rio de Janeiro, Brazil. *Cultural Anthropology* 29, 32-53.

Mintz, S.W. 1960. *Worker in the cane: a Puerto Rican life history*. New Haven: Yale University Press.

——— 1974. *Caribbean transformations*. Chicago: Aldine.

MITCHELL, C.J. 1956. *The kalela dance: aspects of social relationships among urban Africans in Northern Rhodesia* (Rhodes-Livingstone Paper **27**). Manchester: University Press.

MITCHELL, T. 2002. *Rule of experts: Egypt, techno-politics, modernity.* Berkeley: University of California Press.

MOLÉ, N.J. 2010. Precarious subjects: anticipating neoliberalism in Northern Italy's workplace. *American Anthropologist* **112**, 38-53.

MOLLONA, M. 2009. *Made in Sheffield: an ethnography of industrial work and politics.* Oxford: Berghahn Books.

——— 2015. Working-class politics in a Brazilian steel-town. In *Anthropologies of class: power, practice, and inequality* (eds) J. Carrier & D. Kalb, 149-63. Cambridge: University Press.

MUEHLEBACK, A. 2011. On affective labor in post-Fordist Italy. *Cultural Anthropology* **26**, 59-82.

MUNCK, R. 2013. The precariat: a view from the South. *Third World Quarterly* **34**, 747-62.

NAROTZKY, S. 2015. The payoff of love and the traffic of favours: reciprocity, social capital and the blurring of value realms in flexible capitalism. In *Flexible capitalism: exchange and ambiguity at work* (ed.) J. Kjaerulff, 268-310. Oxford: Berghahn Books.

——— & N. BESNIER 2014. Crisis, value, and hope: rethinking the economy: an introduction to Supplement 9. *Current Anthropology* **55: S9**, 4-16.

NASH, J. 1979. *We eat the mines and the mines eat us: dependency and exploitation in Bolivian tin mines.* New York: Columbia University Press.

NEILSON, B. & N. ROSSITER 2005. From precarity to precariousness and back again: labour, life and unstable networks. *The Fibreculture Journal* **5**, FCJ-022.

NEVELING, P. 2015. Export processing zones and global class formation. In *Anthropologies of class* (eds) J.G. Carrier & D. Kalb, 164-82. Cambridge: University Press.

ONG, A. 2006. *Neoliberalism as exception: mutations in citizenship and sovereignty.* Durham, N.C.: Duke University Press.

PINE, F. 2014. Migration as hope: space, time, and imagining the future. *Current Anthropology* **55: S9**, 95-104.

POVINELLI, E. 1995. Do rocks listen? The cultural politics of apprehending Australian Aboriginal labor. *American Anthropologist* **97**, 505-18.

PRENTICE, R. 2012. 'No one ever showed me nothing': skill and self-making among Trinidadian garment workers. *Anthropology & Education Quarterly* **43**, 400-14.

REEVES, M. 2012. Black work, green money: remittances, ritual, and domestic economies in Southern Kyrgyzstan. *Slavic Review* **71**, 108-34.

——— 2013. Clean fake: authenticating documents and persons in migrant Moscow. *American Ethnologist* **40**, 508-24.

RODKEY, E. 2016. Disposable labor, repurposed: outsourcing deportees in the call center industry. *Anthropology of Work Review* **37**, 34-43.

ROSEBERRY, W. 1997. Marx and anthropology. *Annual Review of Anthropology* **26**, 25-46.

SCOTT, J.C. 1985. *Weapons of the weak.* New Haven: Yale University Press.

SHEVER, E. 2013. 'I am a petroleum product': making kinship work on the Patagonian frontier. In *Vital relations: modernity and the persistent life of kinship* (eds) S. McKinnon & F. Cannell, 85-107. Santa Fe, N.M.: School for Advanced Research Press.

SMITH, K. 2012. *Fairness, class and belonging in contemporary England.* Basingstoke: Palgrave Macmillan.

STANDING, G. 2014. *The precariat: the new dangerous class* (Revised edition). London: Bloomsbury Academic.

STRATHERN, M. 1988. *The gender of the gift: problems with women and problems with society in Melanesia.* Berkeley: University of California Press.

TAUSSIG, M. 1980. *The devil and commodity fetishism in South America.* Chapel Hill: University of North Carolina Press.

——— 1986. *Shamanism, colonialism, and the wild man.* Chicago: University Press.

——— 1992. *The nervous system.* London: Routledge.

TOSCANO, A. & J. KINKLE 2015. *Cartographies of the absolute.* London: Zero Books.

TSING, A.L. 2009. Supply chains and the human condition. *Rethinking Marxism: A Journal of Economics, Culture & Society* **21**, 148-76.

——— 2015. *The mushroom at the end of the world: on the possibility of life in capitalist ruins.* Princeton: University Press.

WALLMAN, S. (ed.) 1979. *Social anthropology of work* (ASA Monograph **19**). London: Academic Press.

WEEKS, K. 2011. *The problem with work: feminism, Marxism, antiwork politics, and postwork imaginaries.* Durham, N.C.: Duke University Press.

WILSON, G. 1941. *An essay on the economics of detribalization in Northern Rhodesia (part I)* (Rhodes Livingstone Paper 5). Livingstone, Northern Rhodesia: Rhodes-Livingstone Institute.

WOLF, E.R. 1966. *Peasants*. Englewoods Cliffs, N.J.: Prentice-Hall.

——— 1982. *Europe and the people without history*. Berkeley: University of California Press.

YANAGISAKO, S. 2012. Immaterial and industrial labor: on false binaries in Hardt and Negri's trilogy. *Focaal – Journal of Global and Historical Anthropology* **64**, 16-23.

YURCHAK, A. 2003. Russian neoliberal: the entrepreneurial ethic and the spirit of 'true careerism'. *The Russian Review* **62**, 72-90.

Introduction : le travail disloqué : reconfigurations anthropologiques

Résumé

Dans l'introduction au présent dossier consacré au « travail disloqué », les auteurs tentent de jeter les bases d'une anthropologie du travail dépassant le noyau industriel qui a donné naissance au concept. Demeurant conscients de l'avantage analytique qu'offre une focale placée sur la relation capital-travail, l'exploration ethnographique de celle-ci leur permet d'étendre la portée du concept de travail. Elle leur permet également d'explorer les diverses manières dont les relations de travail sont vécues, au-delà des confins de l'économie, en replaçant délibérément la parenté, la personne, l'affect, la politique et la vie sociale dans le cadre de la création de valeur capitaliste. Ils profitent de la notion de dislocation pour étendre le répertoire des analyses du travail au-delà de la dépossession ou de la désorganisation. Par dislocation, ils envisagent les disparités du déploiement du capitalisme transnational et les manières dont les mouvements des capitaux reconfigurent lieux et personnes. La dislocation évoque donc les mouvements dans l'espace des réfugiés et des travailleurs migrants, mais aussi d'autres ruptures vécues telles que le sentiment de ne pas être à sa place ou de perdre ses repères tandis que les choses bougent et changent autour de nous.

1

Rethinking the concept of labour

Susana Narotzky *University of Barcelona*

Is labour a useful concept for anthropology today? This essay attempts to respond theoretically to the challenge that the contributions to this special issue empirically pose. The essay rethinks the concept of labour by addressing three questions that deal with the relation of human work effort and capital accumulation: the first refers to alienation; the second to the difference between abstract and concrete labour; and the third to ambiguity. Over the years, these issues have addressed particular aspects of social reproduction, helping define labour as a concept, albeit a heterogeneous one, that is relationally linked to capital. Dislocation, together with the parallel concepts of dispossession, disorganization, disconnection, and differentiation, emerges prominently in the analyses of contemporary labour transformations and specificities. Finally, the essay engages with seemingly disappearing labour futures and what this means for the concept of labour. What is the value of work for capital and, conversely, the value of labouring for people today?

Introduction: a problem of method

This special issue on labour raises important questions that we will probably not be able to resolve but which should not be hastily dismissed. First, there is the epistemological question of the value of concepts cross-culturally and cross-historically, in this case the value of the concept of 'labour'. Anthropologists (but also historians) have been struggling with this thorny issue from the outset. How useful is an extraneous concept to understand the processes, conflicts, settlements, tensions, and harmonies that take place in a historically and culturally different environment where our present-day Western categorizations may not exist, or may be embedded in a very different reality? As many have argued, the nature/culture divide or the self-contained individual may not be significant, whereas other unknown forms of categorization may be present that we cannot fathom or imagine. In sum, this epistemological question determines our method and the internal tension that makes its value. If we abandon the quest for universally applicable concepts, we are at pains to justify the worth of our discipline for we cannot compare, and the terrifying 'so what?' dilemma emerges as we become cornered into being mere consumers of native theory. If we do not acknowledge the concreteness of living experience and its eventual incommensurability, on the other hand, we may fail the quest for ethnographic understanding. Understanding the world and its diverse inhabitants in their own terms, their specific connections and disconnections, dissolves distance. Yet modernist epistemology requires a separation between subject and object and the creation of some fictional building blocks (concepts) which are thinking tools: that is, they do not *describe* reality; they attempt to *explain* it by producing abstract paths, logics, articulations (cf. Lakoff & Johnson 1980 on the Western building metaphor of scientific arguments). Hence, do we need a concept at all if every cultural understanding of life-sustaining practices is not only different but also part of a way of being in the world and becoming a concrete and unique entity? Can a concept such as labour bridge the gap between the inescapable concreteness of lived experience and the diverse abstractions used to make sense of it? Can it be useful as a tool for explaining what goes on in different parts of the world regarding the forms in which energy is expended, co-ordinated, and organized in order to sustain life and make it worth living? If we think of the world as connected, it makes methodological sense; if we think of the world as an aggregate of multiple worlds, it may make little sense.

So there is a preliminary decision that refers to method. Anthropologists have been stressing the connection between the world's inhabitants (human and nonhuman) in the era of colonial expansion and later globalization. Therefore, movements and logics are also historically connected, dependent phenomena rather than independent materializations (manifestations). Moreover, capitalism, or the 'self-expansion of the money form of value' (Elson 1979: 165), has been deployed in most places, although with its particular forms of embeddedness, translation, and interpretation which are tied to historically uneven and combined developments, and sociocultural imperatives (Allinson & Anievas 2009; Rosenberg 2006). As feminist economists, anthropologists, and critical social scientists in general have pointed out frequently, this form of value and the relations it entails do not saturate the social space. What is probably even more significant, they are not separated from other forms of value and relationships, nor do they function in another realm. In fact, it would seem that the way in which these other relations and values appear is central to how capitalist relations develop and enable the 'self-expansion of the money form of value' to take hold. Capitalist relations are always parasitical on ongoing relational connections that guide worthy life-sustaining practices.

Harvey and Krohn-Hansen in the introduction to this issue define their aim as

> exploring the tension between the ways that global capitalism might *connect* the experience of labour on the assembly lines of the Chinese factory to the experiences of those engaged in the mining of coltan or working in the container shipping industry – while at the same time *not connecting them at all*, not simply fragmenting but also necessarily responding to hugely varied histories and fields of expectation (p. 12, emphasis added).

At the same time, the issue attempts to investigate 'dislocation in which both places and persons are reconfigured by the movements of capital' (p. 10). It remains to be seen if the connected-disconnected-dislocation triad the authors of this issue are exploring rests on labour *as a concept* rather than labour as a description of local experiences in a world dominated by global capitalism. The introduction, in a clear support of labour's conceptual strength, points out that 'a focus on labour, in this second decade of the twenty-first century, configures a field of ethnographic concern that conjures both the systemic force of capital, and the historical specificity of how these ever-shifting capital relations play out in practice across the world' (p. 11). Theoretically exploring this assertion is the objective of this essay.

Journal of the Royal Anthropological Institute (N.S.), 29-43
© Royal Anthropological Institute 2018

Historicizing labour

The history of the concept of labour in Western thought shows how its development was tied to productive tasks (in particular agriculture) and drudgery. In late medieval times, an idea of a 'common good' objective in the motivation of work transforms the originally servile substance of the concept into a vocational one which refers to the divinely preordained tasks of one of the three orders of society (*oratores, bellatores, laboratores*). It describes status adscription rather than a property of the individual (Duby 1980; Le Goff 1980). In its development as a concept, three processes become salient: (1) the shift of productive effort from a derogatory to a positive status in the late Middle Ages; (2) the idea that it expresses the participation in a collective (social) process aiming at the common good; and finally (3), with the coming of modernity, the individualization of the human productive relation to nature (Castel 2013; Locke 1986 [1689]). These three aspects – productivist, social, and individual – become entangled in the concept that political economists inherit and that in turn Marx will develop as the cornerstone of his theoretical construct. As a consequence, the dominant concept of labour rests on an idea of society or a collective good, an idea of individually self-contained creative energy, and an idea of the objectification of energy in material production. These elements are present in the labour theory of value and in the triad of aspects that support it, namely the concrete, social, and abstract forms of labour.

In addition, as a social science concept, labour is generally paired with capital and referred to historical contexts where work is somehow connected with the process of capital accumulation. Beyond the understanding of labour as a wage relationship with the owners of the means of production that enables workers to make a living, many forms of relations have been explored that connect unwaged work (communal, unpaid, volunteer, affective, unregulated tasks) and even non-work (unemployment, leisure, idleness) with capitalist accumulation processes. This extension of the concept of labour still preserves as its core meaning the multiple forms of its relation to capital.

In the last fifty years at least, the concept has suffered extremely pertinent and creative critiques, mostly by feminist scholars who have introduced reproductive work into the conceptual realm of labour, pointing to the centrality of its particularities (e.g. emotional and relational value) for the social reproduction of a labour force (Dalla Costa & James 1972; Hochschild 2003 [1983]; Lawson 2007; Nelson 2006). Anthropologists as well have provided important critical perspectives that show the cultural and historical embeddedness of life-sustaining practices and question the universal applicability of the Western concept of labour to make sense of the diversity of human livelihood practices (Escobar 2008; Gudeman & Rivera 1990; Malinowski 1978 [1935]; Strathern 1988).

So where does this leave us? We are confronted with a need to rethink the concept of labour or else abandon it, not least because the actual practices that supported the original development of the Western concept have been transformed while the connectivity of life-sustaining practices has expanded globally. This is the task that this special issue provocatively proposes. Is a concept of labour useful? How is it useful? And what concept should that be?

Work and labour

English-speaking scholars have often been using a distinction between 'work' and 'labour', where labour is defined as human effort which pertains to capitalist relations of production, and work describes the rest of human energy expenditure in relation to non-capitalist realms, whether these be reproductive tasks (which eventually became subsumed by the 'care' concept) or socially relevant, non-market-orientated tasks (generally but not solely productive) in the margins and interstices of the capitalist market system or in non-capitalist historical or present-day societies. However, this distinction cannot be drawn in other languages (e.g. Spanish or French), where there is a common word for work and labour, and, conversely, other languages have various significant categories to describe creative effort (Frayssé 2014). While this might be taken as a hindrance to the development of a clear concept of labour, it also points at what anthropologists confront in the field: scientific conceptual distinctions cannot rest on a nominalist basis, although naming the world is a form of engaging with it that has practical consequences and hence must be acknowledged by those seeking to explain it.

The main problem with the work/labour conceptual distinction, in my opinion, is that it makes two presuppositions: first, that there is something inherently different between one form of effort expenditure and the other, namely the kind of value that is created; and, second, that they cannot be simultaneously present in the human experience of energy expenditure. This brings up three questions that need to be addressed in order to rethink the concept of labour: the first refers to alienation; the second to the difference between abstract and concrete labour; and the third to ambiguity.

Alienation: the objectification and exploitation of labour

The idea of alienation as defined in Marxist literature describes, on the one hand, the separation of the product of labour from the person who has produced it (this is the process of objectification) and, on the other hand, the appropriation of a person's labour and hence its product by someone not involved in its production (exploitation) (Axelos 1976; Marx 1959 [1844]). Moreover, alienation has also been understood as the separation of labour in capitalism from its concrete conditions of reproduction (what makes a life worth living), a process that Karl Polanyi (1957; 1971 [1944]) described as the disembedding of social relations and the production of labour as a fictitious commodity. Yet it is because productive activity is understood as the concrete self-realization of the individual worker that its estrangement through the double form of alienation becomes the critical aspect of capitalist relations.

Objectification of concrete labour has often been accepted as a universal phenomenon inasmuch as the framework of individuation and material autonomy of the product are taken for granted. Exploitation, on the other hand, has been strongly circumscribed to particular historical periods and often limited to capitalist relations, where wage-labour and commoditization of social reproduction prevail. This neat conceptual separation is difficult to sustain with the ethnographic record, not only for non-capitalist-dominated realms of social interaction and non-Western cultural environments, but even for commodity chains in contemporary capitalist production. Indeed, the conceptual attachment of creative energy to the human individual as a power producing life and providing rights through its expenditure is itself an ideological creation of particular historical interactions which are not restricted to the liberal enlightenment, as Aron Gurevich (1985) shows for medieval Iceland. Creative energy can be understood as distributed in networks that bring together human and nonhuman entities – as Actor Network Theory proposes in present-day Western scholarship – or the individual can be but a volatile form of social interaction (Strathern 1988), and objectification may occur partially, if at all (as with artisan artistic branding of oeuvres: Cant, this volume). The more general critique is that even in a context dominated by capitalist relations, human labour is never fully disembedded. In fact, by following supply commodity chains, we can observe that the alienable aspect of labour, what makes it exploitable in a particular way, always depends on its inalienable ties to the social environment. Hence when we observe the concrete life projects of people as they unfold in different parts of the world, and how they are woven into particular forms of surplus extraction or appropriation, we immediately realize how important relations such as kinship obligations and claims are to the setting of localized forms of capitalism. I would argue, nevertheless, that there is a logic to the way surplus extraction operates at different scales, and that it is not mere contingency of emergent and unpredictable forms. Two complementary processes are always at work in capitalist accumulation: rent extraction (through land rent, financial fees, patent rights, etc.) and surplus value extraction (through exchange relations, contractual agreements, or predatory domination). The first rests on privileged rights of access, the second on reduction of the cost of labour by competitive means, crude domination, or otherwise. And both rely on the entanglement of values pertaining to different realms of moral obligation (personal, intimate, social, market, contract, etc.) and on the tensions and overlaps between the concrete and abstract value of labour.

Concrete and abstract labour: a reassessment

Much of the anthropological unease with the Marxian labour theory of value stems from its development of a dual aspect of labour, namely the distinction between the concrete and abstract labour embodied in the commodity. Concrete labour has been defined as the energy, embodied skills, cultural beliefs, and forms of co-operation expended to create a specific product (or service). Abstract labour has usually been understood as related to the existence of a developed market exchange system that would theoretically pool all socially necessary labour (i.e. the labour needed to reproduce a society) and hence enable the evaluation of the proportional quantity of social labour embodied in a particular item. Following this, concrete labour could become a universally applicable concept, whereas abstract labour was circumscribed to societies (and sectors of production) where capitalism was hegemonic. This questioned the core of the labour theory of value and became one of the major challenges among Marxist feminists when trying to think about the value of domestic labour and its possible exploitation in relation to systemic capital accumulation processes. The same problem assailed anthropologists studying small family production and subsistence work in agriculture all over the world, and sociologists looking at self-provisioning practices (Pahl 1985). Those studying societies (or activities) hypothetically isolated from capitalist forms of market exchange had no direct use for the theoretical duality in Marxian value theory. However, Diane Elson (1979: 144, also 148), in a clarification of Marx's 'value theory of labour', proposes that the four aspects (concrete/abstract and private/social) of labour are present in *all* societies, and, according to Marx, what differs is the social form in which they appear: 'What is specific to a particular kind of society is the relation of these aspects to one another and the way they are represented in the precipitate forms' (1979: 149). In particular, abstract labour is not limited to societies where market exchange prevails in social reproduction. The abstraction refers to a quantitative proportion of the human energy and time necessary to reproduce the social totality as a meaningful whole, and this whole encompasses any collective effort in whatever form it is co-ordinated (i.e. not necessarily through market co-ordination). Elson adds that 'the objectification of the concrete aspect of labour is universal [in the concrete object or service], but

Journal of the Royal Anthropological Institute (N.S.), 29-43
© Royal Anthropological Institute 2018

the objectification of the abstract aspect of labour [in money] is not: it is specific to capitalist social relations' (1979: 150). What is elusive in non-capitalist societies is the representation of this abstraction in a particular physical form (i.e. a unique universal equivalent, money) (1979: 164-5). That is, in the labour concept, the aspect of abstract labour exists in all historical societies but its objectification, its materialization in an object, does not. This, then, would be the main specificity of societies where capitalism is dominant: the fact that in the value of commodities the objectified abstract aspect of labour (money) reflects value which 'produces the illusory appearance that value in its money form *is* an independent entity' (1979: 165, original emphasis). Abstract labour in its objectified form, then, subsumes (but does not obliterate) the other aspects of labour and becomes the hegemonic driver of production. Making money instead of making useful objects.

This reading of Marx's theory renders his multidimensional concept of labour more useful to anthropologists because, on the one hand, it opens the field of possible forms of objectification of the abstract value of labour to whatever is the dominant universal value equivalent present in a particular society (e.g. kinship, prestige, etc.). The concept can also be extended to include the entanglement of dominant and non-dominant value realms of society, and of activities that are sustained by ambiguous claims to labour, as when unwaged kin working in a family farm produce food within a global commodity chain (Martin, this volume; Melhuus, this volume; Narotzky 2016). On the other hand, it refocuses the Marxist question on labour instead of value. Indeed, the 'value theory of labour' is not the 'labour theory of value'. Labour – that is, human life expenditure in order to reproduce life – is at the centre of Marx's theory, a preoccupation that began as an inquiry placing 'real life' and 'practice' as the starting-point (Marx 1969 [1845]). From this perspective, labour and life are two sides of the same coin and their entanglement is universal (see Collins 2016 for a reassessment of the labour theory of value taking these issues into account). Of course, some conceptual problems remain, in particular the individualization of human energy and its creative power, although it is always presented as attached to the collective and relational objective of social reproduction, which constitutes, in fact, the argument for the existence of abstract labour.

Hence, the concrete and abstract aspects of labour cannot be separated. They are intimately co-dependent and transform each other simultaneously. In addition both, even in Marx's original theory, are social and relational processes whose form is contingent on historical and spatial unfolding. In sum, we should ask ourselves what *kinds* of labour are mobilized to reproduce a society and, in a context of dominance of the capitalist form of value expansion, what aspects of concrete historical and sociocultural contexts are encroached upon, co-opted, or transformed by capitalist relations in the process of global accumulation. This volume's contributions present enlightening cases of how these developments can occur.

Ambiguities of labour and capital
The essays in this volume underline the different ways in which labour is connected with capital. Very central to this is the stress on the concrete aspect of labour with the embodied experience that it supposes and the placeness of the relationships in which this experience can occur. In each place, difference becomes the paramount value that capital puts to work. Yet we must beware of considering capital as a homogeneous and a-temporal force that impacts or transforms some traditional labour relations. Conceptually, capital and labour are forces co-emergent at different scales,

simultaneously local and global and constrained by other forces and their agents, such as those making the state or driving the actions of various power-holders. As the concrete aspect of labour gives form to the manner in which abstract labour is configured, the reverse also holds: there is a concrete aspect of capital, of the way in which concrete agents create capital as a particular relation with labour in one or multiple locations (Bourdieu's social, symbolic, and cultural capitals attempt to capture this diversity for the French context). Perhaps Sylvia Yanagisako's essay in this volume is an extremely clear example of this, but it is present in all the pieces, because labour and capital, as concepts, exist only as a relationship, which is concrete and place-bound (i.e. different) while it simultaneously is abstract and hence distributed across the globe in its objective of expanding the money form of value (i.e. equivalent). As a result, the relational forms of these historical precipitates of concrete and abstract aspects are dynamic, even if, conceptually, what defines that relationship is the self-expansion of the money form of value and the subsumption of other forms of value to this objective.

As anthropologists, we are driven to the concrete expressions of the labour/capital relation out of necessity, as this is the experience that the ethnographic method provides us with and becomes the basis on which theory is developed. Indeed, when we observe labour forms, we tend to set off from their embedded character: the way that kinship, cultural understandings, and historical factors are central to the way people engage productively with local and global forms of capital. Keir Martin, in this volume, illustrates this embeddedness in an apparently paradoxical manner when he points at how the local use of the labour category (here defined as wage-labour) defines a particular relationship to land and labour that is not tied to 'custom' ('*kastom*'). Instead, it attempts to assert private property over land, turning it into a small commodity production factor in the wider context of agricultural contract farming (see also Li 2014 and Moberg 2014 for similar examples). What seems to emerge in this ethnographic account is the scope for interpretation that kin-related persons' work on a piece of land may hold. We are presented with the struggles around the attempt by different actors to circumscribe the work's worth and the value realm to which it pertains either in capitalist exchange or in custom. Conflicting processes of distinction and of blurring of the categories describing activities as wage-work, or help, or respect become instruments for defining land ownership and access rights. Beyond the instrumental use that various categories enable, ambiguity emerges in these conceptual struggles as an expression of the fact that people try to negotiate ambivalent value domains in everyday practice (also Harvey, this volume; Hoëm, this volume). The tensions between concrete and abstract aspects of labour are always present together with the simultaneous experiencing of different domains of social interaction where worth and value are not the same or even congruent. Particular forms of agency, of exploitation, of governmentality, of resistance, of struggle, result from the way in which local value realms overlap in the space of global capitalism. As a result, sites of labour/capital conflict shift, are blurred, and become dislocated in global capitalism.

Dislocation: place and time

In the present volume, the idea of dislocation emerges as key to the understanding of a renewed concept of labour. Dislocation refers to the spatial unevenness of capitalism's global unfolding as well as to recent upheavals in the livelihood experience of people in places. It relates to structures of feeling that are both temporally and spatially volatile, inconsistent, or violently transformed. One may argue that dislocation is not

Journal of the Royal Anthropological Institute (N.S.), 29-43
© Royal Anthropological Institute 2018

new in the process of capitalist expansion, nor in past historical forms of predatory conquest (Gill & Kasmir 2016). At various moments in various places, life (human, nonhuman, environmental, and symbolic aspects of it) has appeared as dislocated by the forceful expansion of the money form of value in the case of capitalism, in a process of commodification akin to that described by Polanyi (1971 [1944]) for 'fictitious commodities' (see also Burawoy 2010). Indeed, this aspect should be included in the concept of labour for it is a core defining dimension of the experience of the emergent relation between capital and labour. Dislocation, however, complements two other key aspects of the process of uneven development of capitalism as it affects labour, namely dispossession (Harvey 2003; Kasmir & Carbonella 2008; Palmer 2014) and political disorganization of labour (Kasmir & Carbonella 2008: 12). These three aspects together point to the relational unfolding of social relations in global capitalism: culturally embedded forms of organization are disorganized; place-bound paths of dispossession are continuously generated; and waged and unwaged forms of making a living change repeatedly and pull people apart or together at different conjunctures through space and time. All contribute to the historical dynamics of remaking differences that reconfigure labour/capital power geometries.

David Harvey (1990) theorized the process of time/space compression that linked technologies with the acceleration of the circulation of capital and, hence, accumulation (this is particularly salient in financial capitalism). In parallel, the injunction of productivity has accelerated work rhythms while compressing leisure, rest, and work time in many new forms of labour. Christian Krohn-Hansen, in this volume, presents the opposite dislocation of temporal work rhythms as the national brokerage networks, deficient infrastructures, and global competition provide an erratic base for the deployment of productive labour in the Dominican Republic. Elsewhere, the distinction between labour and personal time or productive and reproductive time (and spaces) disappears for an increasing sector of the world's population as income-generating labour invades home and leisure spaces and timeframes. The way the dislocation of time emerges is linked to local conditions of opportunity and to how people attempt to make a living in places. Displacement may appear as forced mobility, as when local populations are displaced by the opening of a mine that destroys their town but where they might have preferential job opportunities. It is often a simultaneous process of dispossession of land, of sacred sites, of ways of living. Conversely, mobility may become the only remaining form of autonomy, as when hope for the future gets tied to migration projects (Cole 2014; Glick Schiller & Çağlar 2009; Pine 2014). Yet movement always tends to disorganize some institutional frameworks while it opens the way to new forms of organization by reconfiguring meaningful connections between people.

The processes of dislocation in capitalism interweave individual, household, and social networks of working lives with past histories of labour/capital relations as they have unfolded both locally and globally, at once limiting, opening, and defining the available opportunities to make a living and the kinds of social recognition they entail. James Ferguson has pointed our attention towards the relevance of 'structures and processes of disconnection' (2009: 316) that produce

> abjected, 'redlined' spaces of decline and disinvestment in the contemporary global economy [which] are as much a part of the geography of capitalism as the booming zones of enterprise and prosperity ... They refer to processes through which global capitalism constitutes its categories of social and geographical membership and privilege by constructing and maintaining a category of absolute non-membership (2009: 317).

Journal of the Royal Anthropological Institute (N.S.), 29-43
© Royal Anthropological Institute 2018

Indeed, geographical membership and the privileges attached to it seem to be emerging as crucial sites of conflict among labour as they express the reorganization of spaces of capital and its spatial fixes and the dislocation of the livelihood systems attached to them.

Place is formed and transformed by the articulated forces of capital, labour, and the state in the *longue durée*, as Huw Beynon, Ray Hudson, and David Sadler (1994) pointed out over twenty years ago, but also by the forces of local responsibilities, meanings, and expectations that are part of the historical entanglements of the place (see Escobar 2008; Harvey, this volume). Place is the domain of concrete, existing people while space often appears as an abstraction. But space, in an analogy with the abstract aspect of labour, stresses the relational value of places for social reproduction, and appears as an inseparable aspect of the concrete place. Space, on the one hand, engages with capital as an emergent abstraction of relationally located, connected, and disconnected social relations, while capital can only be realized in places, through places and their concrete social differentiations. Space expresses the power of the state (and capital) as an *abstract* relation of domination, although this power can only be realized in places through the concrete production and (often violent) enforcement of difference or, on the contrary, through the enforcement of homogenizing norms. Place, on the other hand, grows from the meaningful relationships that people build with each other in the long term and from their engagement and creative production of institutions in particular locations. Place is multidimensional and the primary referent of people's lives, of the everyday practice of located sociability. Often described as a local affair, however, place is also multiscalar, as social, economic, and power relationships that produce place occur at various scales (local, regional, national, global) and simultaneously transform the operational scale of political-economic processes in space (Peck 2002; see in particular the essays by Cant, Campell, Hoëm, and Schober in this volume). Concrete agents' understandings inform practices occurring at multiple scales that take into consideration the values (or value) most dear to each actor and use them to make differences. Hence differences are created as a resource to take advantage of, resist, exploit, or capitalize. Some people (within households, regions, firms, or institutions) will have a great capacity to define, impose, and benefit from particular differences between and within places (and people) while others will have a limited one. Geometries of power result from the capacity of some agents to define, enforce, and take advantage of difference both within and between places (and people) in their interest. Making difference between places is also often making difference between the past of these places and an alleged better (or worse) present or future there or elsewhere.

Much in both the concrete and abstract aspects of labour depends on the historical processes of making differences and on how they combine with each other globally at particular junctures. Spatial differentiation, then, produces topographies of value where life and work are not worth the same; it materializes and induces a process of dislocation through movement that complements other dislocations linked to the life rhythms and time/effort ratios for earning a livelihood.

A labour concept for 'no labour' futures?
Recently, anthropologists (Ferguson 2013; Li 2009; Smith 2011) have been pointing to a reality that was already debated in the 1960s and 1970s by Latin American scholars (Nun 1969; Quijano Obregón 1974 and the surplus population debate). The capitalist system seems to have no use for an increasing number of people, either as labour, consumers, or rent providers. This has been publicly acknowledged by policy makers,

mainstream economists, and the media admitting that 'full employment' is impossible and that structural unemployment rates will grow as a consequence of technological innovation, robotization, and globalization.

Does this mark the end of a concept of labour? A look into the former debate surrounding development policies and the place of the so-called 'informal sector' in them brings some useful insights. In the 1970s and 1980s, the distinction between stable, contractual, protected, waged labour relations and insecure, precarious, often personalized work relations or self-employment ventures became the basis for describing the economy as a dichotomous structure of mutually excluding and hierarchically ordered arenas of production: the formal and the informal sectors (a distinction that development agencies such as the International Labor Organization supported and extended; see Peattie 1987). Additional observation of the endless variations of possible relations of production/reproduction that exist in global capitalism, including at its margins and in its interstices, led to an early critique of this dichotomous opposition, while the connection between formal and informal 'ways of doing' and making a living was stressed (Mingione 1991; Peattie 1980; 1987; Portes & Sassen-Koob 1987). John Weeks (1971) pointed out that 'unemployment' rarely describes a permanent out-of-work situation and is often premised on a particular administrative definition of employment as contractual wage-work in the formal sector. Jan Breman's classical critique of the formal/informal sector duality in the 'third world' (1976a; 1976b; 1976c) observed that the dichotomy lost 'sight of the unity and totality of the productive system' and he emphasized instead 'the fragmented nature of the entire labour market' (1976a: 1871). In this view, the labour market is fragmented but continuous, and the social relations that constitute it in everyday practice are multiple, entangled, and result from their historical interaction.

Anthropologists, in particular, paid attention to household resources, micro-power relations, mobilities, and temporalities that structured differential access and reciprocal relations within and between households (Melhuus, this volume). This perspective highlighted the diversity of jobs that household members undertook and the fluidity between stable, protected, waged work (formal), self-employment, peasant farming or small workshop ownership (partially regulated), casual jobs and unregulated self-employment (informal), and unemployment. The ingenuity of poor households to pool and distribute all kinds of resources to 'make ends meet' was acknowledged by the 'livelihood means' and the 'resources of poverty' development literature, where this diversity was rebranded as an asset for household reproduction (Scoones 1998). Mercedes González de la Rocha (2001), however, has pointed out that, following structural adjustment policies in Mexico that eroded labour market opportunities, households were at pains to survive because waged and non-waged income resources were complementary rather than a substitute for each other. 'A new type of labor market segmentation seems to be emerging, not along formal/informal lines but between a very privileged group of workers and the vast majority who struggle to survive with very limited resources' (González de la Rocha 2001: 90).

One of the findings of this initial assessment of the complexities of labour relations in 'third world' regions may prove particularly useful to present-day analysis of precarity in 'post-industrial' economies. This is the observation that scarcity of income-generating opportunities often results in 'the necessity to fence off one's own domain', looking for 'protection along vertical lines, the contracting of obligations in patronage and brokerage relationships with privileged kin or social superiors' (Breman 1976c: 1942;

also 1976*b*: 1908). However, when (and if) the situation of generalized precariousness becomes extreme, even vertical loyalties and particularistic obligations disintegrate and personalized claims are interpreted as predatory (Breman 1976*c*: 1942). Thus, extreme labour market fragmentation is also a process of dispossession that generates particularistic forms of protection, even as it disorganizes collective ones (see also Kasmir & Carbonella 2008: 14-15). The loss of wage-labour is experienced as an end to life, the ultimate dispossession, as when the Korean Metal Workers' Union leader says in 2013: 'There is no future!', or when a representative during a South Korean parliamentary hearing in 2011 argues that the Hanjin Heavy Industries and Construction shipyard's chairman had 'murdered his employees with massive lay-offs' (Schober, this volume, pp. 134 and 142). Death is both a metaphor of an industrial past where labour was relevant for social reproduction and an embodied materiality in increased morbidity and suicide.

In the post-industrial era of 'mature' capitalist regions such as Europe or North America, the demise of waged work dominance recalls forms of labour differentiation, insecurity, and precariousness that were imagined as more suitable to other times or other countries. Working lives are pushed outside of the relatively secure income-generating environments of stable wage employment, which appear as a short-lived historical exception. They now resemble the fragmented experiences that have been ubiquitous in the so-called 'third world/global South' for a long time and recall the thwarted 'expectations of modernity' of development ideologies (Breman & van der Linden 2014; Ferguson 1999). On the one hand, supply-side models of the economy have guided policy towards the degradation of waged labour protection, resulting in an expansion in temporary and part-time jobs and in flexible work. On the other hand, self-employment and petty entrepreneurialism as recourses against the failing of secure wage employment opportunities have been actively promoted as a way to enhance individual autonomy and escape the shame of depending on state benefits. The expansion of precarious labour (including self-employment and petty entrepreneurship) has political consequences for the forms of vertical or horizontal solidarity that are more likely to develop and for what the objectives of a labour struggle would be. It revisits the issue of whether different experiences of work invalidate the commonality of labour (both as a concept *and* as a position in practice) in its relation to capital, as Guy Standing's (2014) concept of the 'precariat' would have it (for a critique, see Breman 2013; Palmer 2014).

If labour has been understood in the social sciences as directly or indirectly involved in capital accumulation, then what happens to labour as a conceptual tool when increasing numbers of people are described as functionally unnecessary, absolute surplus labour: that is, useless in any form to capital? The question is whether their disconnection from capital is absolute and permanent or rather a concrete expression of labour's relational aspect to the dynamics of capital accumulation in time and space as a response to the spatial, technological, product, and financial 'fixes' that define the strategies of capital in its engagement with labour (Silver 2003; 2014). If, indeed, people's diverse strategies to survive, to earn a livelihood by pooling or, on the contrary, by excluding others from encroaching on scarce resources, are entirely disconnected from the social reproduction of a capitalist system, then how are these toils to be conceptually addressed?

Michael Burawoy (2010) has proposed a renewed Polanyian perspective that attempts to bridge conceptual fragmentation by tying labour to the other fictitious commodities, money and nature. Here, what become relevant are the situated processes of (re-/de-)commodification of labour relationally. A move from emphasizing labour/capital relations in production to stressing the commodity aspect would enable people to forge linkages beyond labour but within capitalist relations. Burawoy's model 'centers on the commodification of labor, money and nature and their inter-relations. The argument is premised on commodification being the key experience in our world today, and that exploitation, while essential to any *analysis* of capitalism, is not *experienced* as such' (2010: 307, original emphasis). Commodification, then, would bring together the myriad experiences of dispossession and could eventually produce commonality.

Conclusion

For most people in the world, what we witness is the entanglement of many forms of work, multiple kinds of social relations, institutional involvement in regulation and deregulation, the mobilization of vertical and horizontal solidarities to access resources, and the encroachment of commodification in everyday life. There is nothing inevitable about these circumstances, which are the result of political economic decisions. Indeed, after a period of extreme free-trade policy models (with their obvious caveats of monopoly protection in practice), we may be witnessing the dawn of a protectionist trend that will transform global markets. The predatory nature of unbridled neoliberal capitalism has also generated a return to forms of stewardship of or integration with nature that are curtailing extractive capitalism and supporting alternative subsistence practices (Edelman 2005; Escobar 2008). These processes are complex, and often conservation policies can have negative consequences for local people, depriving them of their access to protected resources they relied on for subsistence (Campbell, this volume; Fairhead, Leach & Scoones 2012; West 2005). Ethnographies, in any case, point to the end of secure gainful labour as an expectation of a developed economy, and to the anxieties and strategies that this unforeseen reality produces. In a world with a shrinking labour market, work takes on a meaning increasingly removed from a material productivist aspect and linked instead to the self-realization and recognition value aspects (Fraser 2001). For many people living in a state of permanent or cyclical unemployment, the value of work is very centrally its social aspect: being someone is tied to doing something that is recognized in some way as part of what society values (Joshi 2009; Narotzky & Besnier 2014). Many 'Activation Works' organized by the state, such as that described by Jan Grill in this volume, or volunteer work framed by religious, union, or community associations, such as what Andrea Muehlebach (2012) describes for Northern Italy, become work substitutes that provide a form of worth that remains tied to labour identities.

In this conjuncture of alleged surplus population (i.e. surplus in relation to the ability or willingness of capital to put it to use in the valorization process), how should we reconceptualize labour? Robert Castel (2013) argues that in France non-labour (*hors-travail*) situations remain inscribed in identities that refer to labour, to the paradigm of Fordist, stable, gainful, and socially dignifying experience. Even when absent, labour would maintain the position of core signifier of social value, marking individual self-reliance, productivism, the moral critique of idleness, and free co-operation as the ideological backbone of society. But is this true everywhere? Experiments with alternative forms of provisioning and new value frameworks are transforming the field of possibilities open to populations (including youth in Western Europe, indigenous groups, outcasts, etc.) pushed to the zones of abandonment by the relation between capital and the state. Depending on the remaining connections between these practices and the process of self-expansion of the money form of value, I would argue, some of these activities may still provide for the reproduction of labour and hence be related to capital, even when fully embedded in anti- or non-capitalist value domains.

Is a concept of labour useful or even possible as an analytical tool for anthropologists? While capitalism remains hegemonic, I suggest that we do not abandon the concept of labour, as it addresses the connection of people and places in a process that overpowers their will to make a life worth living and abducts them into the aim of the expansion of money value. Even when unpaid and hidden forms of labour may be on the rise, such as neo-bondage, contract farming, or self-employment, these unwaged workers are crucial to capitalist social reproduction. Moreover, the ways in which they become valuable for capital accumulation include their configuration as consumers of commodities, rent, and interest providers.

What minimal content, then, should an anthropologically useful concept of labour propose? First, I suggest that labour as a concept should be restricted to work effort (human energy expenditure) in its relation to capital, taking into account, however, that this relation has many forms, including many non-commodified and unwaged forms which can be dominant in certain historical conjunctures (Narotzky 2016). Second, the concrete/abstract distinction should be maintained as the key to understanding what makes difference valuable as an asset for the valorization of life and of capital. Third, within the concrete aspect of labour (and capital), ambiguity needs to be present. And finally, dislocation, the process of permanently disrupting and reorganizing the spatial-temporal dimensions of everyday life, is a crucial element in the determination of power geometries between labour and capital. Anthropologists have the capacity to interrogate the concept of labour from their immediate ethnographic experience, a situation which opens the way to innumerable theoretical breakthroughs and practical avenues for transforming society. But this must be realized through the tension between concrete experience and theoretical abstraction.

ACKNOWLEDGEMENTS
Research and writing were funded by the European Research Council Advanced Grant 'Grassroots Economics: Meaning, Project and Practice in the Pursuit of Livelihood' [GRECO], IDEAS-ERC FP7, Project Number 323743. I am grateful to Penny Harvey and to Christian Krohn-Hansen for inviting me to participate in this special issue, and to the anonymous reviewers, whose comments helped me clarify some points.

REFFRENCES
ALLINSON, J.C. & A. ANIEVAS 2009. The uses and misuses of uneven and combined development: an anatomy of a concept. *Cambridge Review of International Affairs* **22**, 47-67.
AXELOS, K. 1976. *Alienation, praxis, and techne in the thought of Karl Marx*. Austin: University of Texas Press.
BEYNON, H., R. HUDSON & D. SADLER 1994. *A place called Teesside: a locality in a global economy*. Edinburgh: University Press.
BREMAN, J. 1976a. A dualistic labour system? A critique of the 'informal sector' concept: I: the informal sector. *Economic and Political Weekly* **11**, 1870-6.
———— 1976b. A dualistic labour system? A critique of the 'informal sector' concept: II: a fragmented labour market. *Economic and Political Weekly* **11**, 1905-8.
———— 1976c. A dualistic labour system? A critique of the 'informal sector' concept: III: labour force and class formation. *Economic and Political Weekly* **11**, 1939-44.
———— 2013. A bogus concept? *New Left Review* **84**, 130-8.
———— & M. VAN DER LINDEN 2014. Informalizing the economy: the return of the social question at a global level. *Development and Change* **45**, 920-40.
BURAWOY, M. 2010. From Polanyi to Pollyanna: the false optimism of global labor studies. *Global Labour Journal* **1**, 301-13.

CASTEL, R. 2013. *La montée des incertitudes: travail, protections, statut de l'individu*. Paris: Seuil.

COLE, J. 2014. Producing value among Malagasy marriage migrants in France: managing horizons of expectation. *Current Anthropology* **55: S9**, S85-94.

COLLINS, J.L. 2016. Expanding the labor theory of value. *Dialectical Anthropology* **40**, 103-23.

DALLA COSTA, M. & S. JAMES 1972. *The power of women and the subversion of the community*. Frome, Somerset: Falling Wall Press.

DUBY, G. 1980. *The three orders: feudal society imagined* (trans. A. Goldhammer). Chicago: University Press.

EDELMAN, M. 2005. Bringing the moral economy back in … to the study of 21st-century transnational peasant movements. *American Anthropologist* **107**, 331-45.

ELSON, D. 1979. *Value: the representation of labour in capitalism*. London: CSE Books Humanities Press.

ESCOBAR, A. 2008. *Territories of difference: place, movements, life, redes*. Durham, N.C.: Duke University Press.

FAIRHEAD, J., M. LEACH & I. SCOONES 2012. Green grabbing: a new appropriation of nature? *Journal of Peasant Studies* **39**, 237-61.

FERGUSON, J. 1999. *Expectations of modernity: myths and meanings of urban life on the Zambian Copperbelt*. Berkeley: University of California Press.

——— 2009. Global disconnect: abjection and the aftermath of modernism. In *Industrial works and life: an anthropological reader* (eds) M. Mollona, G. de Neve & J. Parry, 311-29. Oxford: Berg.

——— 2013. Declarations of dependence: labour, personhood, and welfare in southern Africa. *Journal of the Royal Anthropological Institute* (N.S.) **19**, 223-42.

FRASER, N. 2001. Recognition without ethics? *Theory, Culture & Society* **18: 2-3**, 21-42.

FRAYSSÉ, O. 2014. Work and labour as metonymy and metaphor. *tripleC* **12: 2**, 468-85 (available on-line: http://www.triple-c.at/index.php/tripleC/article/view/546, accessed 8 January 2018).

GILL, L. & S. KASMIR 2016. History, politics, space, labor: on unevenness as an anthropological concept. *Dialectical Anthropology* **40: 2**, 87-102.

GLICK SCHILLER, N. & A. ÇAĞLAR 2009. Towards a comparative theory of locality in migration studies: migrant incorporation and city scale. *Journal of Ethic and Migration Studies* **35**, 177-202.

GONZÁLEZ DE LA ROCHA, M. 2001. From the resources of poverty to the poverty of resources? The erosion of a survival model. *Latin American Perspectives* **28: 4**, 72-100.

GUDEMAN, S. & A. RIVERA 1990. *Conversations in Colombia: the domestic economy in life and text*. Cambridge: University Press.

GUREVICH, A.J. 1985. *Categories of medieval culture*. London: Routledge & Kegan Paul.

HARVEY, D. 1990. *The condition of postmodernity*. Oxford: Blackwell.

——— 2003. *The new imperialism*. Oxford: University Press.

HOCHSCHILD, A.R. 2003 [1983]. *The managed heart: commercialization of human feeling*. Berkeley: University of California Press.

JOSHI, C. 2009. Despair: the decline of the Kanpur textile mills. In *Industrial works and life: an anthropological reader* (eds) M. Mollona, G. de Neve & J. Parry, 331-9. Oxford: Berg.

KASMIR, S. & A. CARBONELLA 2008. Dispossession and the anthropology of labor. *Critique of Anthropology* **28: 1**, 5-25.

LAKOFF, G. & M. JOHNSON 1980. *Metaphors we live by*. Chicago: University Press.

LAWSON, V. 2007. Geographies of care and responsibility. *Annals of the Association of American Geographers* **97**, 1-11.

LE GOFF, J. 1980. *Time, work, and culture in the Middle Ages* (trans. A. Goldhammer). Chicago: University Press.

LI, T.M. 2009. To make live or let die? Rural dispossession and the protection of surplus populations. *Antipode* **41: S1**, 66-93.

——— 2014. *Land's end: capitalist relations on an indigenous frontier*. Durham, N.C.: Duke University Press.

LOCKE, J. 1986 [1689]. *The second treatise on civil government*. Amherst, Mass.: Prometheus.

MALINOWSKI, B. 1978 [1935]. *Coral gardens and their magic: a study of the methods of tilling the soil and of agricultural rites in the Trobriand Islands*. New York: Dover.

MARX, K. 1959 [1844]. *Economic and philosophic manuscripts of 1844*. Moscow: Progress Publishers (available on-line: https://www.marxists.org/archive/marx/works/download/pdf/Economic-Philosophic-Manuscripts-1844.pdf, accessed 8 January 2018).

——— 1969 [1845]. Theses on Feuerbach. In *Marx/Engels selected works*, vol. **1**, 13–15. Moscow: Progress Publishers (available on-line: https://www.marxists.org/archive/marx/works/1845/theses/theses.htm, accessed 8 January 2018).

MINGIONE, E. 1991. *Fragmented societies: a sociology of economic life beyond the market paradigm.* Oxford: Blackwell.

MOBERG, M. 2014. Certification and neoliberal governance: moral economies of Fair Trade in the eastern Caribbean. *American Anthropologist* **116**, 8-22.

MUEHLEBACH, A. 2012. *The moral neoliberal: welfare and citizenship in Italy.* Chicago: University Press.

NAROTZKY, S. 2016. Where have all the peasants gone? *Annual Review of Anthropology* **45**, 301-18.

——— & N. BESNIER 2014. Crisis, value, hope: rethinking the economy. *Current Anthropology* **55: S9**, 4-16.

NELSON, J.A. 2006. *Economics for humans.* Chicago: University Press.

NUN, J. 1969. Superpoblación relativa, ejército industrial de reserva y masa marginal. *Revista Latinoamericana de Sociología* **5**, 178-236.

PAHL, R.E. 1985. *Divisions of labour.* Oxford: Blackwell.

PALMER, B.D. 2014. Reconsiderations of class: precariousness as proletarianization. *Socialist Register* **50**, 40-62.

PEATTIE, L.R. 1980. Anthropological perspectives on the concepts of dualism, the informal sector, and marginality in developing urban economies. *International Regional Science Review* **5**, 1-31.

——— 1987. An idea in good currency and how it grew: the informal sector. *World Development* **15**, 851-60.

PECK, J. 2002. Political economies of scale: fast policy, interscalar relations, and neoliberal workfare. *Economic Geography* **78**, 331-60.

PINE, F. 2014. Migration as hope: space, time, and imagining the future. *Current Anthropology* **55: S9**, S95-104.

POLANYI, K. 1957. The economy as instituted process. In *Trade and market in the early empires: economies in history and theory* (eds) K. Polanyi, C. Arensberg & H. Pearson, 243-69. New York: Free Press.

——— 1971 [1944]. *The great transformation.* Boston: Beacon.

PORTES, A. & S. SASSEN-KOOB 1987. Making it underground: comparative material on the informal sector in Western market economies. *American Journal of Sociology* **93**, 30-61.

QUIJANO OBREGÓN, A. 1974. The marginal pole of the economy and the marginalized labour force. *Economy and Society* **3**, 393-428.

ROSENBERG, J. 2006. Why is there no international historical sociology? *European Journal of International Relations* **12**, 307-40.

SCOONES, I. 1998. Sustainable rural livelihoods: a framework for analysis. IDS Working Paper **72**.

SILVER, B. 2003. *Forces of labor: workers' movements and globalization since 1870.* Cambridge: University Press.

——— 2014. Theorizing the working class in twenty-first-century capitalism. In *Workers and labour in a globalised capitalism: contemporary themes and theoretical issues* (ed.) M. Atzeni, 46-69. London: Palgrave Macmillan.

SMITH, G. 2011. Selective hegemony and beyond – populations with 'no productive function': a framework for enquiry. *Identities* **18**, 2-38.

STANDING, G. 2014. *The precariat: the new dangerous class* (Revised edition). London: Bloomsbury Academic.

STRATHERN, M. 1988. *The gender of the gift: problems with women and problems with society in Melanesia.* Berkeley: University of California Press.

WEEKS, J. 1971. Does employment matter? *Manpower and Unemployment Research in Africa* **4: 1**, 67-70.

WEST, P. 2005. Translation, value, and space: theorizing an ethnographic and engaged environmental anthropology. *American Anthropologist* **107**, 632-42.

Repenser le concept de travail

Résumé

Le travail est-il aujourd'hui un concept utile en anthropologie ? Le présent essai tente de résoudre du point de vue théorique la difficulté empirique que posent les contributions à ce numéro spécial. Il repense le concept de travail par le biais de trois questions, en lien avec la relation entre l'effort humain et l'accumulation de capital : la première est celle de l'aliénation, la deuxième de la différence entre travail abstrait et concret et la troisième celle de l'ambiguïté. Au fil des années, ces questions se sont posées par rapport à certains aspects de la reproduction sociale et ont aidé à définir le travail comme un concept qui, bien qu'hétérogène, était en relation avec le capital. La dislocation et les concepts parallèles de dépossession, de désorganisation, de déconnexion et de différenciation émergent de façon saillante des analyses des transformations et particularités contemporaines du travail. Enfin, le présent essai s'intéresse à la disparition apparemment imminente du travail et à ce qu'elle implique pour le concept de travail. Quelle est la valeur du travail pour le capital et, à l'inverse, la valeur de l'acte de travailler pour les humains d'aujourd'hui ?

Journal of the Royal Anthropological Institute (N.S.), 29-43
© Royal Anthropological Institute 2018

Labour and capital

2

Reconfiguring labour value and the capital/labour relation in Italian global fashion

SYLVIA YANAGISAKO *Stanford University*

This essay draws on ethnographic research conducted from 2004 to 2012 among Italian firms involved in the manufacture and distribution of textiles and clothing in China to argue that the boundary between labour and capital cannot be assumed as fixed and stable, but rather is continually remade through particular, situated historical processes. I show how the Italian national legacy of capital/labour relations both set the stage for the outsourcing of manufacturing to China and shaped Italian firms' investment and labour management strategies. As Chinese consumers became increasingly crucial to the European fashion industry, Italian firms reorganized their production and distribution processes to live up to the prestige value of 'Made in Italy'. This brought about an ironic twist in the fetishism of commodities in which the proclaimed immaterial value of Italian commodities was appropriated by Italian managers, enhancing their labour value. At the same time, however, the dislocation of Italian managers impeded the process through which labour had been converted into capital in Italian industrial districts, hardening the boundary between capital and labour and altering the dynamic structure of capital/labour relations.

The increasing reliance of capital on global supply chains over the past three decades has dislocated both people and labour processes, drawing attention to the ways in which these chains function to discipline labour, devalue it, and undercut organized labour resistance. Considerably less attention has been paid to the ways in which conversion processes between labour and capital have been affected by these dislocations and, along with them, the boundary between labour and capital. In this essay, I draw on ethnographic research that Lisa Rofel and I conducted from 2004 to 2012 among Italian firms involved in the manufacture and distribution of textiles and clothing in China to argue that the boundary between labour and capital cannot be assumed as fixed and stable, but rather is continually remade through particular, situated historical processes.[1]

Since the 1990s, Italian textile and garment-producing firms – like those from many other countries – have outsourced a large part of their manufacturing to China. While an analysis of the transnational relations of production among the Italian and Chinese firm owners, managers, and workers in these capitalist ventures must be situated in the contemporary structure and dynamics of global supply chains, it is equally crucial to

Journal of the Royal Anthropological Institute (N.S.), 47-60
© Royal Anthropological Institute 2018

locate them in the historical trajectories that led the parties to these ventures. I begin by showing how the Italian national legacy of capital/labour relations set the stage for their transnational capitalist projects in China.

At the core of the relations among firms in Italian industrial districts was a fluid process whereby labour could be converted into capital through the upward mobility of family firms. Unpaid and underpaid labour of family and relatives made possible the accumulation of profits that could be converted into capital and reinvested in productive resources (land, buildings, manufacturing equipment, hiring wage-labour) in order to expand the firm. Those firms that were more successful in this expansion process could, in turn, buy the manufacturing services of smaller, less-capitalized family firms that aspired to follow the same path to upward mobility. In short, the conversion of family labour into capital was central to the dynamic structure of Italian industrial manufacturing districts.

When the larger Italian firms in this sector began outsourcing phases of the manufacturing process to China in the 1990s, they were primarily interested in China as a source of cheap labour. As Chinese consumers became increasingly crucial to the European fashion industry, however, Italian firms reorganized their production and distribution processes to live up to the prestige value of 'Made in Italy'. This produced an ironic twist in the fetishism of commodities in which Italian managers appropriated the immaterial value of *Italian* commodities to constitute their own labour power and affirm the hierarchy of labour in production and distribution. The dislocation of Italian managers to China, however, significantly reduced opportunities for them to open new subcontracting firms in their home industrial districts. The Italian managers employed abroad in these transnational ventures enjoyed higher incomes and the benefits of a cosmopolitan life-style, but they lacked both family labour on which they could draw to survive the early lean years of a business and local production networks into which they could insert themselves. This has greatly impeded the processes through which Italians have been able to convert labour into capital in both Italy and China, hardening the boundary between capital and labour.[2]

Legacies of capital and labour in Italian industrial districts

Industrial districts specializing in the manufacture of particular commodities are a well-documented and much-discussed feature of Italian industrial history (Frey 1975; Locke 1995; Piore & Sabel 1984). They have been widely described by economic historians and sociologists as composed of dense networks of small to medium-sized firms, which provided the organizational structure for Italian manufacturers specializing in products ranging from wine and food to ceramics, machine tools, textiles, and electrical appliances. These networks, moreover, existed side-by-side with larger vertically integrated firms and mass production assembly lines; indeed, the two were dependent on each other. This was especially true of the manufacture of textiles, which was at the forefront of industrialization in Italy, as it has been in many countries.

From the beginning of Italian industrialization around the time of Italian unification (1866), cotton, linen, wool, and silk production were each located in specific districts in the 'industrial triangle' of Milan, Turin, and Genoa. In each of these industrial districts, small, specialized firms that engaged in one or two phases of the manufacturing process were linked in what has been variously referred to as a 'decentralized', 'dispersed', or 'fragmented' system of production. The vast majority of firms engaged in only one or, at most, two phases of the production process – including the spinning, twisting, and texturization of thread, the dyeing, weaving, and printing of fabric, the preparation of screens for printing, and packaging and marketing. The production chain was co-ordinated by a 'converter' (called an '*impannatore*' in Prato) firm, which took orders from textile wholesalers and clothing manufacturers and then set the production process in motion through a series of subcontracting arrangements (Yanagisako 2002: 29). Converters were the industrial age equivalent of merchant capitalists, who, in the previous period, had organized a system of cottage production by providing households with the raw materials and equipment to produce thread and fabric. As we shall see shortly, just as the organization of the industrial production of textiles bore the legacy of the prior period of merchant capitalism, so the current era of transnational production bears the legacy of the prior period of industrial manufacture.

Even in the period between the two world wars, when the Italian Fascist state protected and supported large-scale industrialization in sectors such as the chemical industry, small and medium-sized firms accounted for the bulk of Italian manufacturing. This continued throughout the 'Italian miracle' – the period from the end of the Second World War to 1973, when state-owned and -controlled industries, focused on steel, iron, and energy, took off at the same time that large private companies such as Fiat employed a Fordist mass production model in the manufacture of durable consumer goods. Despite the increase in the number of workers employed in heavy industry and the mean number of workers per firm, Italian manufacturing remained rooted in small firms and light industry. Firms like this would also be the basis of the 'Third Italy', the new industrial districts that emerged in the central and northeastern regions of the country in the 1970s.[3]

The clusters of small and medium-sized firms in these industrial districts commonly arose out of rural households that had pursued a mix of agriculture and commerce. The emergence of these spatially concentrated industries has been attributed to a number of factors, among them the low cost of property in rural or urban peripheries, the high levels of trust and co-operation among firms, which enabled the rapid diffusion of technological innovation, and favourable tax and labour regulations. Whatever the historical reasons for their origin, the vast majority of the small and medium-sized firms in these industrial districts have been owned and managed by families. At the beginning of the twenty-first century, family firms constituted between 75 and 95 per cent of all registered companies in Italy, and nearly 50 per cent of the top 100 Italian corporations were family-controlled (Colli 2003: 16). The result was the formation of networks of highly specialized but flexible firms that were rooted in kinship, friendship, and local community relationships.[4]

Although some northern industrial districts, such as Como's silk industry, had existed since the nineteenth century, it was only in the 1980s that they attracted significant international attention from scholars. The economic success in the 1970s of the 'Third Italy' – the central and northeastern areas of the country – led to a period in which they were lionized as a new form of industrial capitalism.[5] The flexible specialization and innovation of these firms, it was claimed, enabled them to better weather the economic challenges of the 1970s and 1980s. Indeed, scholars such as Piore and Sabel (1984) went so far as to claim that these Italian districts were ushering in a new period of industrialization which offered a viable alternative to Fordist mass production. Yet, as I have argued elsewhere (Yanagisako 2002), the rise of the 'Third Italy' in the mid-1970s was hardly the first time that small and medium-sized firms linked in local production networks had predominated in Italy. Even in those periods when the average firm size grew and when large companies like Fiat employed Fordist mass production to manufacture goods, or when large state-owned companies controlled steel, iron, and energy production, small and medium-sized firms were responsible for the bulk of Italian manufacturing.

In most of the small firms, but also in medium-sized ones, the owner and his or her family and relatives commonly worked alongside other employees – in many cases, on the factory floor. Among these were a wide range of kin, including siblings, siblings' spouses, uncles and aunts, affinal kin, and their children. Whether they worked on the factory floor or in the office, whether as production line workers, technicians, factory supervisors, bookkeepers, or sales managers, the work of the owner and his or her family members alongside non-family employees blurred the distinction between labour and capital. This integration of labour and capital, moreover, was not merely a discourse spun by firm owners to motivate workers and legitimate profits; it also reflected and affirmed strongly felt sentiments and experiences of work, family, and personhood – especially among the members of the proprietary family, for whom capital was deeply entangled with their labour.[6]

While the histories, business strategies, and practices of family firms in textile districts like Como varied and were shaped by a multiplicity of factors – including the phase of manufacturing in which they engaged and the extent of their capital investment – the families who owned and managed these firms shared kinship and gender ideologies and sentiments that operated as forces of production of both firm and family. The goals of family firm owners, who were usually men, were rooted in ideas about the masculine self and men's desires to retain authority in their families. A father's goal of handing the firm on to his adult sons (and, to a much lesser extent, his adult daughters) was motivated by his desire to provide his sons with the means to remain independent of other men (employers) and, at same time, to provide himself with the means of maintaining his authority and centrality in the family. Italian family firms were generally organized according to a patriarchal structure in which the head of the firm (usually the father) made decisions in consultation with adult children (usually sons, but increasingly daughters) who managed divisions of the firm. By the time the second generation had taken over, brothers or siblings jointly managed the firm according to a managerial division of labour that commonly placed one in charge of production and others in charge of sales or client relations. Most family firms did not survive to the third generation, but those that were successful enough in accumulating capital and investing in the expansion of the firm were commonly directed by an executive committee composed of siblings or cousins, each of which managed a section or branch of the firm.

Whether they survived beyond the first, second, or third generation, family firms were the breeding grounds for managers and technicians who commonly left to start up their own firms. This was a crucial dynamic of the 'flexible specialization' of the innovative small firms in industrial districts of northern and central Italy which tended to be overlooked by scholars, who identified them as offering a promising alternative to Fordist mass production (Piore & Sabel 1984). Many of the owners of subcontracting firms began their careers working as technical directors or managers in other firms, often with the clear intention of learning their employers' techniques and acquiring the practical training and clients that would enable them to open their own firms. Some of these were relatives of the firm owners, including cousins and in-laws.

The transformation of technical directors, factory supervisors, and managers into the owners of subcontracting firms was a well-established pattern of upward mobility in industrial districts such as Como and an integral part of the process of the reproduction of the network of firms. It also meant that a firm's managers could become its competitors. The thin line between on-the-job training and industrial espionage reinforced owners' disinclination to place non-family members in upper-level management positions, creating a 'kinship glass ceiling' beyond which those who were not members of the immediate family did not rise (Yanagisako 2002: 138). This cap on advancement, in turn, fuelled the frustrations of ambitious managers who would then leave to start their own firms. Combined with the desire of men to be their own boss, the above process generated a constant supply of new subcontracting firms. Indeed, the dynamism of Italy's industrial districts depended in good part on what was experienced by Como firm owners as forms of betrayal.

My research on family firms in the silk industry of Como revealed that in the period from the end of the Second World War until the 1980s, the continual creation of new firms by managers and technical directors in the same sector in which they had been employed was responsible for a good deal of the dynamic character of the industrial district. The existence of small, specialized firms alongside larger, more vertically integrated firms enabled ambitious employees who found themselves being blocked from promotion by the kinship glass ceiling to start up their own firms, sometimes by taking some of their former employers' clients with them. Ten of the fifteen founders of subcontracting firms in my sample had worked for a firm in the same sector before opening their own firms, and three more had been employees of firms in an allied sector of the industry (Yanagisako 2002: 123). Other studies have likewise discovered a high degree of upward mobility in localized industrial districts, particularly in central and southern Italy, but also in the north (Martinelli & Chiesi 1989).

The capital required to open a small subcontracting firm was limited and came mostly from the founder's own savings and small loans from relatives and business associates. What was crucial in the early years of these firms was the labour of family and relatives, who commonly made up a significant part of their workforce. The employment of relatives increased the labour flexibility of these firms because they could be asked to work extra hours when needed. Relatives were also viewed as more trustworthy and so were assigned managerial and administrative tasks; they were treated as a more flexible workforce that could move between shop floor and office depending on the need.

Once they opened their own firms and even as they worked as subcontractors for larger firms, the more ambitious owners of these subcontracting firms hoped to move up the manufacturing chain to the later and greater profit-making stages of production – in other words, closer to the distribution and sales end of the supply chain. The most successful of these were able to evolve from being providers of manufacturing services for larger firms to offering their own product directly to clients. Over time they were able to move from being salaried managers who provided labour for larger firms to being entrepreneurs who could reap profits and accumulate and reinvest capital. In short, they were able to convert their labour into capital.

Transnational expansion and conversion strategies

China was already becoming known as the workshop of the world when Italian textile and clothing firms began moving production there in the 1990s. Like firms in other countries, Italian manufacturers were initially lured to China by the low cost of labour and subsequently by its huge domestic market. By the late 1990s, the increasingly favourable environment for foreign investment and trade created by various levels of the Chinese government made China the preferred nation for the outsourcing of some or all the phases of production of Italian textiles and clothing. After 2000, these shifts in policy, along with the growth of the Chinese domestic market and the end of the import quotas established by the Multi-Fibre Agreement, led to a further increase in Italian textile and clothing firms engaged in manufacturing in China through a variety of forms of collaboration with Chinese partners. The Italian firms involved in these collaborations are all family firms that are both owned and managed at the upper levels by family members. Their presence in China parallels the predominance of family firms in Italian capitalism recounted above. Some of these firms produce clothing priced for the middle level of the fashion market, others for the luxury market. Yet others produce silk and other high fashion textiles.

As these Italian firms continued to expand production in China in the first decade of the 2000s, it also became the fastest-growing market for Italian luxury fashion. As a result, some luxury fashion brands decided to forge joint ventures with Chinese firms. The aim of these joint ventures was four-fold: first, to manufacture in China a less expensive version of the luxury brand for Chinese customers; second, to gain entry into a market sector that the Chinese manufacturer had already successfully penetrated, by drawing on the latter's expertise and social ties to navigate complex state bureaucracies and distribution networks; third, to develop a network of factories that would be prepared to produce the Italian luxury brand itself – if and when customers (both Chinese and European) were ready to buy Italian luxury brands made in China; and, fourth, to produce accessories (e.g. wallets, shoes, ties, bags) for the luxury brand which customers would be willing to purchase even though they were made in China.

One consequence of the expansion of Italian family firms into China has been the alteration in the relations between proprietary families and the managers they hire (Yanagisako 2013). The establishment of overseas manufacturing divisions, joint ventures, and distribution offices has created managerial positions that family members are unwilling to fill. As lucrative as China has become for these firms – both as a site of cheap labour and as a growing market for their products – the members of Italian bourgeois families still consider it a cultural hinterland and an undesirable place to live. Whether they are members of the senior generation of the family, who hold the highest-level positions in the firm, or members of the rising generation, who manage departments or regions, family members generally limit their stays in China to short visits of up to two weeks. During these trips, they commonly visit the firm's headquarters in Shanghai or Beijing, meet with its Chinese partners or the entrepreneurs who outsource production to Chinese factories, inspect factories, and grace the opening ceremonies of new ventures and retail outlets. With one exception,[7] however, we did not find any member of a proprietary family who lives in China. As a consequence, Italian family firms expanding their activities to China have been forced to rely on non-family managers.

Overseas expansion of production and sales has thus increased the opportunities for non-family managers, who can now rise to higher levels of management, such as director of production in China, director of a joint venture with a Chinese partner, or director of the company's operations in Asia. Non-family managers working in China occupy a range of positions – from setting up the management structure of a new joint venture, to directing production in a joint venture's manufacturing plants, marketing franchises to sell an Italian designer brand, and finding and recruiting

Journal of the Royal Anthropological Institute (N.S.), 47-60
© Royal Anthropological Institute 2018

Chinese manufacturers to collaborate in joint ventures with an Italian firm that produces several middle-market brands. Managers on the production side work closely with Chinese factory managers, shift supervisors, accountants, technicians, and office staff, but they rarely supervise Chinese factory workers. Those involved in distribution and sales, on the other hand, work with Chinese franchise managers, retail clerks, warehouse managers, and office staff.

As family firms began outsourcing production to China in the 1980s, and when they began forming transnational joint ventures in the 1990s, the shortage of Italian managers in China strengthened managers' ability to negotiate with firm owners for salaries and benefits. Until 2004, industry and commercial consultants in Shanghai agreed that the greatest obstacle facing Italian firms in China was the shortage of 'human resources'. What they meant by this was the shortage of managers in whom firm owners felt comfortable placing their trust, with whom they could communicate, and who shared their cultural sensibilities. These firms not only lacked the recruitment resources of large companies, but they were less attractive because they offered more limited opportunities for job advancement.

In the first few years of the millennium, the shortage of managers was so acute that some companies even resorted to hiring academics who originally came to China to study Chinese language and literature. After 2004, the shortage decreased as a growing number of university graduates sought work in China rather than face unemployment in Italy. Despite this increase in Italians willing to work in China, the pool of Italian managers with experience and knowledge of the country remained small. By early 2010, in the midst of the economic downturn in the United States and Europe, moreover, Italian and other European luxury brands were expanding their distribution in China. The combination of the downturn of sales in Europe and the United States and the stimulus incentives offered by the Chinese government had further increased the importance of the growing Chinese market in these firms' global business plans. Italian firms, especially luxury brands, accordingly began shifting more resources and energy to the Chinese domestic market, actively wooing experienced managers from other companies in the same and allied sectors. Thus, even with the decline in the shortage of 'human resources', Italian managers with experience in China gained bargaining power in relation to firm owners.

Most of these Italian managers are men, but there are some women managers, especially in distribution and retail.[8] Two-thirds are married or have a steady partner, and they are, on the whole, young – all but a couple are between the ages of 26 and 40. Most have the Italian equivalent of a bachelor's or master's degree in business, although a minority have degrees ranging from psychology to chemical engineering and Chinese language and literature. About half of the managers had worked for their employer in Italy before being transferred to China either to initiate operations or to join an already established office.

Most managers consider living and working in China to be a daunting experience. Even Shanghai, with its international restaurants, large European expatriate community (including an Italian community estimated at around 1,000 people), glittering shopping malls, international schools, and Italian restaurants, is considered to be a formidable challenge. In spite of this, Italian managers view the career opportunities offered there to be far superior to what is available to them in Italy. They acknowledge that, had they remained in Italy, they would never have obtained positions or salaries as good as their present ones. They point to the 10 per cent growth rate in China's gross

Journal of the Royal Anthropological Institute (N.S.), 47-60
© Royal Anthropological Institute 2018

domestic product – in contrast to the slow rate of economic growth in Europe and the United States – and to the commensurate growth of their firms' business in China.

Italian managers pride themselves in providing these transnational collaborations with crucial knowledge and skills that are beyond the capabilities of both their employers and the Chinese with whom they work. They generally express strong praise for the technical skills and abilities of Chinese workers, whom they describe as very good at adapting Italian machinery to meet local production needs and quick to learn computing tasks.[9] Praise for the technical skills and work ethic of Chinese workers by Italian managers, as well as by firm owners, was often paired with criticisms of Italian workers, who were characterized as less industrious and unwilling to engage in hard work. These complaints about the degradation of the Italian workforce must be situated in the post-Second World War history of Italian capital and labour. In the 1990s, I heard similar lamentations by firm owners in the silk industry of Como, many of whom blamed labour unions and the stringent labour regulations that were put in place in the 1970s for causing the decline in the quality of labour in Italy. For Italian firm owners and managers, the industriousness of Chinese workers represents precisely what they view as the deficiencies of Italian labour – which is what they say prompted Italian firms to relocate production to China in the first place.

Italian managers are much less favourably impressed, however, by the entrepreneurial and managerial skills of their Chinese partners. Indeed, they have a bevy of complaints about the latter's shortcomings. Among these are their poor planning skills, their lack of professional training in management systems, their lack of creativity, and their lack of initiative in problem-solving. As one Italian manager put it,

> The Chinese in the production unit often don't understand how what they are doing fits into the larger picture: they just focus on their small part of the process and don't think about how it fits into the rest. They don't really understand what they are making or how it should look as a finished product.

Another manager exclaimed that despite his efforts to be open to cultural difference, he continued to be surprised by the inflexibility and lack of creativity of his Chinese counterparts. Like other Italian managers, he attributed the lack of 'mental elasticity' and 'creativity' of Chinese to communist education and policies.

The oppositions according to which Italian managers characterize the differences between Chinese managers and themselves are hardly unfamiliar to us. Although Italy did not have colonial projects in China or any other areas of Asia, Italians are well steeped in nineteenth- and twentieth-century Orientalist discourse on the Far East. It is hardly surprising, therefore, that oppositions between tradition and modernity, despotism and democracy, collectivity and individualism, authority and creativity, underlie a good deal of what they have to say about their experience of working with Chinese. Simona Segre Reinach, who collaborated with Lisa Rofel and me on our Italy-China research project, has argued that the Orientalist discourse that characterizes the Chinese as behind Italians in their knowledge and appreciation of fashion relies on the suppression of China's long history of textile production and clothing aesthetics (Segre Reinach 2006a; 2010; in press). This discourse is reflected in Italian managers' complaints about their Chinese collaborators' lack of fashion sense. According to Italian managers and firm owners, it will be many years before the Chinese will be able to move beyond copying Western fashion and fully understand its semiotics and sensibilities.

Given the underdeveloped state of Chinese fashion sensibilities, Italian managers view themselves as crucial to guaranteeing quality control, brand management, and effective marketing. Whether they are overseeing a factory in a joint venture, arranging for subcontracting by Chinese factories, or setting up franchise retail outlets, Italian managers feel they must be constantly vigilant in order to maintain the quality and prestige of the brand. The greatest fear of Italian firms – and one that kept some firms from engaging in production and distribution in China for years – is that their brand image will be damaged, whether by shoddy presentation or by having their designs stolen and made into cheap copies. Chinese cannot be trusted, above all, with preserving the brand's 'Italianità' – its Italian-ness. This includes not only the quality of the manufactured product but also the design features that convey the Italianità of the brand.

Because the exchange value of the commodities produced through Italian-Chinese collaborations is inextricably linked to their Italianità, it is hardly surprising that Italians claim that their labour – whether in design, manufacturing, branding, or retailing – is more valuable than the labour of Chinese. These claims must be understood in the context of the post-Second World War success of the Italian fashion industry. Although Italian fashion has a long history, the decade in which 'Made in Italy' brands really took off and became a global success story was the 1980s. This success was due in good part to the 'Made in Italy' marketing campaign launched in that decade by the Italian Trade Commission. This campaign, which has continued into the present, trumpets the 'Italian-ness' captured in a range of Italian commodities from clothing and shoes to furniture and motorcycles, evoking Italian artisanal and craft traditions that can be traced back to the Renaissance – all of which endow these products with a rich cultural heritage, which in turn legitimates their high price. In the spring of 2009, for example, the Italian Trade Commission recruited the actress Isabella Rossellini as a spokesperson for its campaign in the United States. Rossellini is quoted as saying: 'Italian style signifies quality. Quality gained from centuries of work by artists and artisans and combined with Italian charm, humor and warmth'. Along these lines, when the Salvatore Ferragamo company celebrated its eightieth anniversary with an exhibition in Shanghai in April 2008, prominently displayed along with the vintage shoes manufactured by the company was the tableau of a workshop in which two Italian artisans dressed in white lab coats were crafting shoes by hand.

There are a couple of historical ironies in the 'Made in Italy' campaign when it comes to textiles and clothing. First, as Segre Reinach (2006b) has pointed out, 'Made in Italy' fashion was created not by relying on artisanal production but rather by supplanting it with industrial manufacturing. In other words, the 1980s model through which 'Made in Italy' made its name was a form of industrial fashion. Although it was initially Florentine luxury ready-to-wear designers with aristocratic names such as Marchese Emilio Pucci who launched the post-Second World War challenge to French hegemony in high fashion, soon after Italian fashion moved from Florence, the Renaissance city of art, to Milan, the city of commerce and industry. The result was ready-to-wear fashion associated with what some fashion historians call the 'industrial aesthetics' of the 'Fab Four': Armani, Ferré, Missoni, and Krizia. These were the designers/entrepreneurs who created 'Made in Italy' by combining clothing designs with a sizing system that was suitable for industrial production. The second historical irony is that the global expansion of 'Made in Italy' fashion relied on overseas production. The 1980s – the decade in which Italian fashion became a global success – was the same decade in which Italian textile and garment manufacturers began exporting phases of production overseas to countries such as China.

Although the 'Made in Italy' marketing campaign highlights the artisanal craft and skill of Italian workers, in the transnational production and distribution process, Italian managers have become crucial in infusing commodities with Italian charm. In affirming and elaborating the claims of *Italianità* touted by 'Made in Italy', Italian managers appropriate the fetishized powers of the commodity to constitute their own labour power. Whereas in Marx's model of commodity fetishism the social powers of workers are captured in the commodity, in this case the social powers attributed to commodities are recaptured in the labour power of Italian managers. By presenting themselves as the guardians of a legacy of artisanal production and claiming its productive powers for themselves, Italian managers obscure the industrial labour of Chinese workers. Interestingly, their emphasis on the cultural knowledge, information, communication skills, and creativity they bring to the production process echoes popular models of the shift to a post-industrial age in which information and communication have become key to the global economy. Like the discourse of Italian managers, these claims of an epochal shift to a 'knowledge economy' in which 'immaterial labour' is hegemonic (Hardt & Negri 2004) conceal the industrial labour of workers in countries to which manufacturing has been outsourced. While the 'Made in Italy' campaign locates the production process in a pre-industrial age of craft production, discourses of the 'knowledge economy' and 'immaterial labour' locate it in a post-industrial age, thus skipping over the industrial age in which it is, in fact, located.

The appropriation of *Italianità* by managers is, in part, an intended consequence of the collaborative project of firm owners and managers to imbue commodities manufactured in China with Italian character. Although the goals of firm owners and managers differ, they are complementary. By claiming that these commodities meet Italian standards of quality and design, firm owners cast managers as guardians of *Italianità*. Managers, for their part, find the value of their labour enhanced by claims that their managerial skills guarantee 'Italian quality' even when commodities are produced in China. This appropriation of the value of *Italianità* by managers entails an ironic twist on Marx's model of commodity fetishism. Whereas in the Marxist model, the social powers of labour are captured in the commodity, in this case, the social powers of the commodity have been appropriated by managers as their own labour power.

Italian managers arrive in China well versed in both the recent promotional campaign of *Italianità* and the long history of Italian achievements in art, craftsmanship, and design. Their knowledge and skills of fashion production and distribution vary widely given their diverse educational backgrounds and job experiences. Some clearly knew a great deal more than others about textiles, clothing design, distribution, and marketing when they began their jobs in China. Yet, through their managerial practices and experiences in China, they all acquire the cultural powers of *Italianità*.[10] In short, *Italianità* is not what managers bring to their work in China, but what they acquire through their work in China. Rather than a 'skill set' that managers arrive with, *Italianità* is instantiated through the managerial work process and experienced by managers as an integral part of their cultural being and cultural life.

At the same time that they emphasize the crucial value they bring to Italian-Chinese ventures, the Italian managers are not optimistic about their prospects for moving up the managerial hierarchy in the firm. To the contrary, they express little hope of returning to Italy in the near future. There are several reasons for this. First, as has been mentioned above, in the first decade of the twenty-first century, the European and US markets for luxury goods declined. Even before the global recession of 2009, jobs in this sector were shrinking throughout Europe and the United States. Second, a horizontal move to a comparable position in Italy would mean a significant drop in purchasing power, life-style, and social status. Third, the cultural and local knowledge gained by living in China, while viewed as invaluable for producing and marketing the brand in the country, is not seen as useful for manufacturing and distributing the brand in Europe and the United States. Finally, the chances of a manager advancing to a better position in the firm's home office are slim and, in some cases, non-existent. Managers are well aware that their advancement to the highest levels of management in a family firm is limited by the kinship glass ceiling. As a result, the most promising opportunities for career advancement lie in being assigned to lead the firm's expansion in another non-European country (e.g. Turkey, Vietnam, India) – or in being recruited by a firm in a related sector in China.

The limited opportunities for promotion – whether by their current employer or by another firm – are compounded by the fact that these transnational managers are blocked from what had been the main path of social mobility in Italian industrial districts discussed above, namely opening a firm of their own. The outsourcing of manufacturing to China has largely closed off this avenue of career advancement and class mobility to managers. As large, vertically integrated firms sent subcontracting work overseas, the opportunities for opening small, subcontracting firms in industrial districts like Como shrank. Transnational managers are in an especially weak position to embark on this path of class mobility because they lack strong and productive social networks both in their home communities in Italy and in China. They have neither family labour on which to draw nor industrial networks that provide them with the labour and social capital to open a firm. Initiating a business in China without these resources requires a large amount of financial capital – much more than they have. Their expatriate social network, while useful for finding other managerial jobs, does not give them access to either the financial or social capital necessary for opening a new firm. With one exception, the Italian managers I spoke with in China did not consider initiating a new firm a viable option. The exception was quite telling. Riccardo Ferrero, who had learned the local dialect, married a local woman, and developed a local network of male friends in the industrial district where his employer's factory was located, was the only Italian manager who said that he was considering opening his own firm in the event that his employer sold his or shut it down.

In sum, the boundary between Italian firm owners and their managers and technicians, which had been permeable in Como and other Italian industrial districts characterized by decentralized production, has become more rigid and impermeable as a consequence of the outsourcing of manufacturing. So has the distinction between capital and labour.

Conclusion

In this essay I have argued for the analytic benefits of a dynamic approach to the relation between labour and capital that investigates, rather than assumes, how the boundary (whether fragile or robust, stable or unstable) between them is made and remade through historically specific processes. I have approached labour as a form of productive power infused with people's sentiments and ideas about their generative capacities. These capacities may be variously 'employed' in wage-labour, salaried management, and profit-seeking business. In any of these endeavours, however, these productive powers cannot be contained either by the organization of production or by abstract models of labour, even though they are constituted, in part, by people's material and social experiences of work (Bear, Ho, Tsing & Yanagisako 2015).

We have seen how Italian entrepreneurs and managers bring their historical legacies of labour and capital with them. In extending the geographic range of their decentralized production and distribution networks to China, Italian firms have drawn on some of the same strategies that were crucial both to their success and to the ever-shifting sentiments of collectivity and betrayal that pervaded industrial districts in Italy. Operating simultaneously in different phases of the production and distribution chain, sometimes in direct competition with their clients, forging multiple partnerships, some of which are in competition with each other, sloughing off employees who were crucial in an earlier phase of the firm – all are strategies and practices in which these firms engaged in Italy and which they have continued in China. In the latter, however, Italian managers have been blocked from what had been their main path of social mobility in Italian industrial districts, namely opening a firm of their own. The outsourcing of manufacturing to China has largely closed off this avenue of career advancement and class mobility to managers who have neither family labour on which to draw nor business networks that would provide them with sufficient social capital to open a firm. Without these productive social resources, initiating a business in China requires a large amount of financial capital – much more than Italian managers and technicians have access to.

In recounting this shift in the boundary between labour and capital for Italian managers and firm owners, my concern has been with how to study and refine our understanding of transnational capitalism. To understand how people come to produce forms of transnational capitalism, we must approach it not as the enactment of an immanent logic in particular circumstances, but as the product of the continually changing social engagements among people whose encounter is shaped by specific historical legacies of nation, capital, and labour. One way we can do this is to scrutinize closely the ways in which the capital/labour relation, along with various means of converting labour into capital, is constantly being reconfigured in specific historical conjunctures.

NOTES

The research in this essay was gathered in collaboration with Lisa Rofel, with whom I co-authored the book *Made in translation: a collaborative ethnography of Italian-Chinese global fashion* (Duke University Press, in press). It was supported by grants from the National Science Foundation and the Wenner-Gren Foundation for Anthropological Research. An earlier version of this essay was presented as a paper in the workshop on 'The Reconfiguring of Labour: Reflections for Contemporary Anthropology' organized by Christian Krohn-Hansen and Penny Harvey in Oslo, 12-13 June 2015. This version has benefited greatly from the dialogue at that workshop, from the suggestions by Krohn-Hansen and Harvey, who are the editors of this special issue, and the comments of two anonymous *JRAI* reviewers.

[1] Between 2002 and 2012, Lisa Rofel and I conducted ethnographic research on the transnational relations of production among Chinese and Italians in the unique historical context of China's shift to a market economy and the relocation of manufacturing by Italian, as well as US, Japanese, and other European, companies to China. Our research was conducted primarily in two sites: the eastern coast of China around Shanghai, which has served as one of the central locations for foreign investment in China, particularly in labour-intensive industries such as textiles and clothing geared for export; and northern Italy, in particular Milan, which is the centre of the Italian fashion industry.

[2] At the same time, the encouragement of entrepreneurialism by the post-Maoist state fuelled Chinese managers' and workers' desires for social mobility through profit-seeking enterprises. Many became engaged

in the process of converting family labour into capital by creating family businesses. By 2010, Italian and Chinese managers and workers in these transnational ventures held different visions of their productive capacities for converting labour into capital. This essay is limited to the analysis of the reconfiguring of the boundary between labour and capital among the Italians in the joint ventures we studied. For an analysis that includes both the Italians and Chinese, see Rofel & Yanagisako (in press).

[3] A constant throughout these shifts in Italian industrial history has been the country's reliance on external sources of raw material, capital, and energy. This orientated Italian manufacturing towards less capital-intensive production and a focus on the manufacture and export of finished commodities.

[4] At the same time that these firms were embedded in local production networks, they were far from isolated from transnational supply and distribution networks (Yanagisako 2002).

[5] In the 1970s, the period just prior to the outsourcing of Italian manufacturing to China, a combination of international and domestic political and economic forces led to the emergence of new industrial districts in northeastern and central Italy and to the reinvigoration of decentralized production in older industrial districts. Among these forces were the increased cost of oil in the wake of the oil crisis of the early 1970s, which led to a decline in energy-intensive mass production and increased demand for human labour, and the intense struggle between labour and capital in Italy (and other countries), especially from 1969 to 1974, which led firm owners to decentralize production in order to reduce their vulnerability to labour demands and strike action (Yanagisako 2002).

[6] Elsewhere (Yanagisako 2002), I have argued that sentiments operate as crucial productive forces in capitalist projects and practices. In contrast to those (e.g. Hardt & Negri 2000; 2004) who posit the hegemony of affective labour in the recent transformation of capitalism, I show how affect and sentiment are integral to labour and production processes in industrial capitalism. Among the bourgeois families of Como, moreover, sentiment not only incited capitalist investment and accumulation, but it also shaped strategies of accumulation, reinvestment, firm expansion, diversification, and management structures.

[7] The exception is the owner of an Italian textile firm who has opened a factory in China in collaboration with Chinese and Japanese investors. He lives at the factory for several months each year. This firm owner is unusual in several ways. First, he is not from a family with roots in one of the industrial districts in which most of the Italian firms originated; instead, his family has a history of merchant capitalism. Second, he is married to a Japanese woman whose parents owned a textile firm in Japan.

[8] Of sixteen Italian managers, twelve are men and four women. I should note there that there is an obvious bias to my sample (in addition to bias affected by self-selection of firms that were willing to be studied). Our study includes only firms that have been successful in forging joint ventures or other forms of collaboration in China. We do not have good figures on the proportion of textile and clothing firms that have failed in these transnational ventures in China, but one of the directors of the Italian Trade Commission in Shanghai estimated that this is 75 per cent.

[9] This is a dramatic shift from the attitudes towards Chinese workers expressed by Italian managers and firm owners in the 1980s and 1990s when I conducted my research on family firms in the silk industry of Como. At that time, Como's silk manufacturers derided the technical capabilities of Chinese, characterizing them as far inferior to Italian ones. By autumn 2004, however, both managers and firm owners reported that as a result of acquiring state-of-the-art machinery and technical know-how, Chinese productive capacity had improved so rapidly that they could now produce textiles and clothing equal in quality to Italian ones.

[10] Not all managers' notions of *Italianità* are necessarily forged exclusively through their work in China. A few have also worked for their firm in Mexico and Turkey, and hence they integrate their experiences at these sites as well into their concept of *Italianità*. The vast majority of the managers in our study, however, have worked overseas only in China.

REFERENCES

BEAR, L., K. HO, A. TSING & S. YANAGISAKO 2015. Gens: A feminist manifesto for the study of capitalism. Fieldsights – Theorizing the Contemporary. *Cultural Anthropology* (available on-line: *http://www.culanth.org/fieldsights/652-gens-a-feminist-manifesto-for-the-study-of-capitalism*, accessed 4 January 2018).

COLLI, A. 2003. *The history of family business: 1850-2000*. Cambridge: University Press.

FREY, L. (ed.) 1975. *Lavoro a domicilio e decentramento dell'attività produttiva nei settori tessile e dell'abbigliamento in Italia*. Milan: F. Angeli.

HARDT, M. & A. NEGRI 2000. *Empire*. Cambridge, Mass.: Harvard University Press.

——— & ——— 2004. *Multitude: war and democracy in the Age of Empire*. New York: Penguin.

LOCKE, R.M. 1995. *Remaking the Italian economy*. Ithaca, N.Y.: Cornell University Press.

Martinelli, A. & A. Chiesi 1989. Italy. In *The capitalist class: an international study* (ed.) T. Bottomore, 140-76. London: Harvester Wheatsheaf.

Piore, M.J. & C.F. Sabel 1984. *The second industrial divide: possibilities for prosperity*. New York: Basic Books.

Rofel, L. & S. Yanagisako in press. *Made in translation: a collaborative ethnography of Italian-Chinese global fashion*. Durham, N.C.: Duke University Press.

Segre Reinach, S. 2006a. *Orientalismi: la moda nel mercato globale. Manuale di sociologia, comunicazione e cultura della moda*. Rome: Meltemi.

——— 2006b. Milan: the city of *prêt-à-porter* in a world of fast fashion. In *Fashion's world cities* (eds) C. Breward & D. Gilbert, 123-44. New York: Berghahn Books.

——— 2010. Italian and Chinese agendas in the global fashion industry. In *The fashion history reader* (eds) G. Riello & P. McNeil, 533-42. London: Routledge.

——— in press. One fashion, two nations: Italian-Chinese collaborations. In *Made in translation: a collaborative ethnography of Italian-Chinese global fashion*, L. Rofel & S. Yanagisako. Durham, N.C.: Duke University Press.

Yanagisako, S.J. 2002. *Producing culture and capital: family firms in Italy*. Princeton: University Press.

——— 2013. Transnational family capitalism. In *Vital relations: modernity and the persistence of kinship* (eds) S. McKinnon & F. Cannell, 63-84. Santa Fe, N.M.: SAR Press.

Reconfigurer la valeur du travail et sa relation avec le capital dans la mode italienne mondialisée

Résumé

Le présent essai s'appuie sur une recherche ethnographique menée de 2004 à 2012 dans des sociétés italiennes participant à la fabrication et à la distribution de textiles et de vêtements en Chine. Il affirme que la frontière entre travail et capital ne peut pas être envisagée comme fixe et stable mais se recompose sans cesse sous l'action de processus historiques particuliers et localisés. L'auteure montre comment l'héritage national des relations entre capital et travail en Italie a jeté les bases de l'externalisation de la fabrication en Chine, tout en modelant les stratégies d'investissement et de gestion du personnel des sociétés italiennes. À l'heure où l'industrie européenne de la mode dépend de plus en plus des consommateurs chinois, les sociétés italiennes ont réorganisé leurs processus de production et de distribution afin de profiter du prestige du « Made in Italy ». Il en est résulté un tournant ironique dans le fétichisme des marchandises, puisque les managers italiens se sont emparés de la valeur immatérielle proclamée des marchandises italiennes et ont ainsi augmenté leur valeur en termes de main-d'œuvre. Pourtant, dans le même temps, la dislocation de ces managers a freiné le processus par lequel le travail se convertissait en capital dans les régions industrielles italiennes, durci la frontière entre capital et travail et altéré la structure dynamique des relations entre l'un et l'autre.

3

'Making' labour in Mexican artisanal workshops

Alanna Cant *University of Kent*

The anthropology of art and craft has been reinvigorated by new theoretical approaches to materiality, creativity, and skill. While this research has been connected to larger political economic processes such as nationalism, identity, and consumerism, these approaches have not been wholly brought to bear on questions of labour. Based on ethnographic research in San Martín Tilcajete, a woodcarving village in Oaxaca, Mexico, this essay shows how labour is made in artisanal workshops through the social and material relations that take place within them. I argue that rather than ownership of the means of production, in San Martín relations of labour are generated by the intermingling of the art world's ideology of 'authorship' with the intimate relations of kinship. The art market locates the production of value in the work of those who are recognized as authors, eliding the labour of many of the workers who produce the carvings. Labourers who work for family members struggle to establish themselves independently in this market because of the multiple and socially salient relations of obligation and respect that are central to kinship and because their own creative work becomes subsumed into the general style of the workshop where they are employed.

> Through work, people create themselves through their agency and at the same time create others for whom they work, or with whom they share the fruits of their labours.
>
> Harris 2007: 143

In early January, when the cool morning air takes many hours to heat to its height of the day, Amado finally puts down his blade, steps back from his carving block, and admires his handiwork.[1] Over the last weeks he has transformed a rough *copal* branch into the sleek, proud form of a coyote perched on its haunches. Running his palm over the wood, Amado takes a moment to check the horizontal balance of the piece, making a small adjustment to the curvature of its muzzle before giving it a cursory sanding. The coyote will be properly sanded later by someone else in the workshop. With a black permanent marker, he writes 'LIBRE' on masking tape on its flank to indicate that it has not been ordered by a client and is free to sell. Placing it on a shelf where, despite Oaxaca's arid climate, it will take many months to dry out, Amado immediately turns his attention to a new piece of wood, checking the schedule to see what kinds of carvings

Journal of the Royal Anthropological Institute (N.S.), 61-74
© Royal Anthropological Institute 2018

have been ordered by clients this month. Two months later, on a late March afternoon, Alice and Mark Wilson are visiting Mexico from the United States. They want to order a woodcarving and are looking through the unpainted figures on the shelves when they find the coyote. They agree that this is just the kind of carving they would like to have and begin browsing through the sixty or so vinyl picture albums that document the many different combinations of colours and patterns that can be used to produce the distinctive style that has made this particular workshop famous. Selecting a picture of a mountain lion, they tell Perla, who is taking their order, that they would like this style of painting but with 'earthier colours': heavier tones of ochre, sage, and rust. Perla notes these directions down in a notebook and records an order number, which she duplicates on the Wilsons' credit card receipt and the flank of the coyote. Later that year, in September, as the rainy season draws to a close, Citlali reads over Perla's notes on the colour palette requested by the Wilsons. The coyote has recently received a basecoat of light buff-coloured paint from one of the women who do piecework sanding and painting for the workshop in their own homes. Over the next few weeks, Citlali uses her creativity and knowledge of colours, shapes, and forms to cover the coyote with the fine, geometric painting that has become the workshop's signature style, choosing colours that both complement and contrast with the earthy tones requested by the Wilsons. Three weeks later, just before it is readied to be shipped to the Wilsons in the United States, Citlali finally applies the workshop's signature to the bottom of the coyote: 'Miguel and Catalina García'.

In recent years, such close descriptions have become an important technique through which anthropologists illustrate and analyse the complex and often collaborative creative processes that take place around craftwork and material culture more generally. This emphasis on 'making' – as opposed to 'production' – has sensitized the anthropology of art and craft to questions of materiality, affect, skill, learning, and cognition, through investigative practices that Tim Ingold describes as 'knowing from the inside' (2013: 1-15; cf. Marchand 2010; Schneider & Wright 2013). The analytical success of this focus on art producers' affective engagements with their materials and work has inspired a renaissance in the anthropology of art and craft: while in the 1990s it could be described as a marginal subfield (Townsend-Gault 1998: 425), in the past ten years multiple volumes, workshops, and digital networks dedicated to such questions have reinvigorated the ethnographic study of art, craft, and design.[2]

Making has pushed theories of craft beyond step-by-step descriptions of how materials are converted into valued objects by emphasizing the experiential, relational, and indeterminate qualities of production (Venkatesan 2010: S168; Wood 2008: 142). But as analysis has moved towards concerns for the aesthetic and affective, it has increasingly become dislocated from questions of labour. In particular, we have not fully reconciled these theoretical interests with the problems of how hierarchies of labour are produced through artisanal work practices and how these practices are integral to capital accumulation at local and translocal levels (Herzfeld 2004; Mohsini 2016; Wilkinson-Weber & Ory DeNicola 2016). This is a troublesome oversight, given the abundance of recent ethnographic work on such themes in industrial anthropology, another subfield generally concerned with the fabrication of objects (e.g. de Neve 2005: 82-136; Kesküla 2014; Parry 2013; Prentice 2015; Sanchez 2016: 127-44). Indeed, the anthropology of craft has previously paid close attention to these concerns: earlier studies of artisan communities focused heavily on how the production and marketing of craftwork reproduced or transformed existing relations of class, gender, and ethnicity (e.g. Cook 1990; Kondo 1990; Nash 1993; Stephen 2005). While this earlier Marx-inspired research offered important insights into the changing conditions of artisans within contexts of emergent capitalism, observed inequalities were often explained as resulting from unequal control of the means of production. Yet, as Rudi Colloredo-Mansfeld suggests, 'too often capital comes up short as an explanation for the specific patterns of economic differentiation amongst artisans ... [P]eople use words, art, crafted objects and consumer goods to construct competition as an economic and moral field and place themselves within it' (2002: 115, 117).

In this essay, I investigate how capitalism both accommodates and is transformed by the cultural and social formations in which it takes place by considering how two extra-economic factors – social intimacy and art world ideology – are central to the production of labour hierarchies and capital accumulation in the workshops and communities in which craft objects are made (cf. Morisawa 2015; Ory DeNicola 2005). Based on ethnographic research with artisans in the village of San Martín Tilcajete, Oaxaca, I argue that hierarchical relations of labour do not necessarily result from the differential control of the means of production. Rather, I suggest that labour – both as a practice of work and as a category of persons – must be actively 'made' in workshops, alongside the material objects of the woodcarvings. I show that this is achieved through the productive interplay between the art world's ideology of authorship and the intimate relations of kinship in the workplace. By viewing labour as an outcome of 'making', the contingent and performative nature of labour relations can be tethered to the actualities of history and place. Accounting for both the emergent and the enduring in experiences of labour is important because, as Harvey and Krohn-Hansen argue in the introduction to this volume, labour mediates between the seemingly malleable and overwhelmingly intractable qualities of capitalism in the contemporary world.

Oaxacan woodcarving in San Martín Tilcajete

Oaxacan woodcarvings, also known as *alebrijes*, provide a particularly good lens through which to investigate the ways that emergent labour regimes are made in contemporary capitalism, since unlike many other forms of craftwork consumed through globalized art markets, the woodcarvings cannot readily be connected to 'traditional' cultural practices. Their recent origins in San Martín Tilcajete are remembered by all but the youngest artisans, and villagers are acutely aware that their production has introduced dramatic changes to their community over a rather short period. The carvings were first developed in the 1960s in the village of San Antonio Arrazola on the outskirts of Oaxaca City, and have always been commercially produced for non-local consumption. It was not until the 1970s that Oaxacan woodcarvings began to be made in San Martín, becoming consolidated as an important source of income for many families in the 1990s (Chibnik 2003: 19-35).[3] Of the three main villages in Oaxaca's Central Valleys region where the carvings are made, San Martín is arguably now the most successful, yet only very few families have been able to translate their work into financial stability. Many villagers must supplement their income from woodcarving with other economic activities, such as operating small corner shops, driving *colectivo* taxis, and working in the tourism and service sectors. While higher-end producers are able to dedicate themselves exclusively to woodcarving, only one family, the Garcías, have become truly economically secure through this work. The Garcías' woodcarvings command very high prices in global art markets that value the aesthetic and technical capacities of the people who produce them. Since they work with the same materials and basic techniques as

Journal of the Royal Anthropological Institute (N.S.), 61-74
© Royal Anthropological Institute 2018

everyone else, to their neighbours their incredible success seems mysterious and difficult, if not impossible, to replicate (Cant 2016a).

While woodcarving does not provide economic security for most Tileños (residents of San Martín), 60 per cent of the village's households are involved in this activity.[4] This is not surprising given the lack of alternative opportunities, a consequence of larger conditions of economic precarity in the region. The state of Oaxaca is characterized by high levels of poverty: the 2010 national census found that 67 per cent of Oaxacans live in either 'moderate' or 'extreme' poverty and a further 24 per cent are 'economically vulnerable' (CONEVAL 2012: 11-12). This is compounded by Oaxaca's generally weak economy: although the state represents 3 per cent of the nation's population, it contributes only 1.5 percent to Mexico's gross national product (Waterbury 2007: 8). While the municipality of San Martín Tilcajete is certainly not among the poorest in Oaxaca, it is nonetheless characterized by 'moderate poverty', that is to say, a majority of Tileños have 'at least one social disadvantage and do not have enough income to meet their basic needs' (SEDESOL 2013). In this context, economic choices for Tileños are limited, and particularly so for young people. Although earlier generations could depend to some degree on peasant agricultural production, the removal of tariffs on imported maize to Mexico in 2008 has made it almost impossible to support a family on agriculture alone (Cohen 2015: 58-9).[5] Higher education has also been difficult to translate into salaried work. Some Tileños in their forties with college degrees in engineering and computer science cannot find work in these fields, although a few women who have trained in law, office management, and accountancy have had more success in Oaxaca City's government and service sectors. Given these conditions, many young men and women view migration to the United States as the only viable means to economic security. Since the 1940s, adult men have travelled to the United States for temporary or seasonal agricultural work. More recently, local men and women have begun to permanently migrate to California and Chicago, where they work in manufacturing, service, and domestic labour, almost always without visas.

To the young women and men who wish to stay in Oaxaca, woodcarving appears to be one of the few options available that might offer them the resources with which to marry and establish their own households. The decision to begin woodcarving is made easier by the fact that there are few barriers of entry to woodcarving work. A small workshop can be set up in any family home, usually in the open courtyard where other household activities take place. The basic costs of tools and materials are generally low; machetes and knives are common implements in most rural Oaxacan homes, and the necessary wood, insecticides, and paint are readily available, costing only a few pesos per figure. As such, it is not ownership of the basic means of production that allows control of the market, since all villagers can access them with ease. The skill required to make the most basic woodcarvings also does not constitute a barrier to entering the work, since there are no formal apprenticeship structures and almost every Tileño has an established artisan in their immediate or extended family who can teach them to carve and paint. In addition, all Tileños, by virtue of being from a recognized craft community, can be officially certified as artisans by the Oaxacan Craft Institute, which provides some marketing, financial, and logistical support and offers an air of legitimacy in the eyes of buyers. The ease of entry to the market has meant that many Tileños now see 'commercial' woodcarving production – low-priced work intended for tourists and wholesalers – as a commonplace activity that shores up incomes from other work. As a result, the lower end of the market has been saturated since the late 1990s (Chibnik 2003: 239-42).

Given these conditions, it might be surprising that 'superstar' artisans like the Garcías have been able to emerge from this market at all, especially considering the struggles faced by Mexico's tourism economy in recent years (cf. Colloredo-Mansfeld 2002).[6] Miguel and Catalina García's continuing success is due to their unique level of exposure to the North American indigenous art market, which has allowed them to carve out a new aesthetic niche within the genre of Oaxacan woodcarving (Cant 2016a). They have also benefited from ongoing relationships with key individuals in the art world of Oaxacan folk art and craft, which is made up of overlapping networks of actors that connect Oaxacan villages with the state capital, Mexico City, and the United States.[7] In Mexico, official promotion of craftwork takes place through public and semi-public institutions like the Oaxacan Craft Institute, the National Fund for the Development of Craftwork, and museums of popular culture. Private dealers and gallery owners based in Mexico and the United States also work to promote those artisans whose work they carry, while looking for new producers whose work might prove marketable. Less directly, journalists, collectors, tour guides, and even tourists participate in the economy of recognition that drives artisanal production in contemporary Oaxaca (Chibnik 2003; Wood 2008). The Garcías have successfully positioned themselves within these networks as both clients and patrons. They cultivate personal relationships with important government officials and dealers of popular art; their close relationship with one American dealer was instrumental to their development in their early years, as he facilitated invitations to exhibitions and sales in the United States, through which they gained exposure to collectors and galleries based there. As their renown has grown, they have increasingly become *de facto* ambassadors of Oaxacan woodcarving, and often represent Oaxacan artisans in general at Oaxacan and federal cultural events and photo opportunities. At the same time, they have become patrons to other artisans as they mediate between their powerful connections and the local market of producers, from whom they also purchase work to sell in their own galleries.

At the time of my research, other Tileños were unable to replicate the aesthetic and performative techniques and social connections that contributed to the exceeding desirability of the Garcías and their work. As I will show, this desirability is underpinned by the ideology of 'authorship' that governs the art and craft markets in which Oaxacan woodcarvings circulate. But it is also reinforced by the social and affective ties of kinship that connect the Garcías to their workers, and their workers to one another. In village-based artisanal production, where the frameworks of intellectual property law are ineffective or irrelevant, maintaining authorship largely depends on individuals' informal willingness to respect the recognized artist's rights to his or her own work. In San Martín, bonds of kinship within and between workshops facilitate this recognition, while also producing and reinforcing hierarchical relationships between those who are recognized as authors and those who are not. Thus, the intermingling of art world concepts of authorship and local experiences of kinship within workshop spaces produces the particular hierarchies of labour that characterize this kind of household-based artisanal commodity production. It is worth emphasizing that however exceptional the Garcías' workshop is, these features are present to some degree in all of San Martín's workshops because Oaxacan woodcarving as a genre is fundamentally organized through relations of kinship and the recognition of authorship. By focusing on the larger and perhaps more inventive workshop of the

Journal of the Royal Anthropological Institute (N.S.), 61-74
© Royal Anthropological Institute 2018

Garcías, however, the details of these processes emerge more distinctly than they might in the small workshops of their neighbours.[8]

In San Martín Tilcajete, the social and affective effects of personal relations, especially amongst kin, transform the rights, obligations, and exemptions that normally exist within relations of employment. To put this another way, while workers in the Garcías' workshop are indeed engaged in waged employment, their employer-employee relationship is mediated by their meaningful personal relationships with the Garcías and with one another. These relationships are always more socially meaningful than employment, even while at work. The effect of these relationships in the workplace is that the workshop is never just a place of labour, and labour at the Garcías is never just about work. In the next section, I show how the intermingling of the intimacy fostered by kinship and the art market's logics of authorship within the space of the workshop creates particular forms and relations of labour which are bound to San Martín Tilcajete as a cultural and social place, but which are also profoundly shaped by the character of the transnational markets for which they work.

Kinship, authorship, and the making of labour

One afternoon in San Martín, I met with Victor Cabrera, a trained computer technician who worked at a motorcycle dealership on the outskirts of Oaxaca City. Although not an artisan himself, in his spare time Victor often helped the municipal artisan association with their event planning. I wanted to discuss the group's relationship with the various government departments that they depended upon. However, Victor wanted to tell me about his son, whose recent withdrawal from his high school course was causing arguments at home. He explained in his typically dramatic manner that his son 'was stuck between a sword, a wall, and Catalina [García]'. He might finish his education, which seemed to offer very little opportunity in Oaxaca's stagnant climate; follow his friends to the United States to work 'without papers' (i.e. illegally); or work in one of the few large woodcarving workshops in the village. Given the physical and financial risks involved in crossing the US border to work without a visa, I was surprised to discover that this option could be preferable to employment in a workshop at home, especially since the Garcías were members of Victor's extended family. As our conversation developed, I realized that for Victor employment by a relative carried the potential for coercion. As he put it, 'once you are in, you cannot get out'.

Most Tileño workshops are centred on a married couple, with the husband and older sons carving the figures, and the husband, wife, and older children of both sexes sanding, priming, and painting. Profits and expenses from carving and other small businesses are directly integrated into the household economy, and many of the artisans I worked with found it difficult to separate their workshop's finances from those of their family. As sons approach adulthood, some may work to establish themselves as recognized artisans in their own right, although many continue to produce their work in their parents' homes, even if they no longer live there. After marriage, daughters may continue painting, especially if their husbands or in-laws are also artisans.[9] Other members of the extended family, especially nieces, nephews, and godchildren, may be included in family workshops on an informal basis, and are usually paid at piece or daily rates. Since they began making carvings in the 1990s, the Garcías have expanded their workshop from this basic arrangement into a more complex venture, with some employees paid hourly wages and others working on piece rates in their own homes.[10] As their business expanded, Miguel and Catalina initially hired close family members before exploiting more distant links of kinship. In addition to sentiments of affection and belonging, in rural Oaxaca relations of kin are ideally grounded in performances of co-operation and mutual aid, which in turn generate *respeto* (respect), an important feature that governs social interactions on a daily basis (Cohen 1999; Hunt 1971; Stephen 2005: 265-7). The Garcías were obligated, in no small way, to allow close family members into their business as they became more successful. As their workshop grew and more distant relatives came to work for them, these relations of respect and obligation expanded to their workers' parents, grandparents, and siblings. Because of this, the Garcías slowly became important local patrons, giving them an air of authority in the community in addition to their importance in the woodcarvings' art market.[11] Most of the Garcías' employees are young people, between 15 and 25 years of age, and the workshop also became a space for courtship. As romantic relationships between workers developed into marriages, the connections of kinship within the workshop intensified, further fortifying the relations of obligation and respect between workers and the Garcías, as these young couples depended on them entirely for their livelihoods.

The familial relations that were nurtured by employment in the workshop were overlaid by yet another form of kinship that carries more formalized obligations than those with relatives or in-laws: *compadrazgo* or ritual co-parenthood. Like elsewhere in Latin America, in San Martín *compadrazgo* is an extremely potent social relationship that demands reciprocal respect and support between a child's parents and his or her godparents, who become *compadres* ('co-parents') with one another. The importance of respect between *compadres* is underscored linguistically: where close friends or relatives may speak in Spanish to one another in the familiar '*tu*' register, once they become *compadres* they must shift to the formal '*usted*'. In rural Mexico, *compadrazgo* is very socially complex, as in addition to the celebration of the Catholic sacraments, including baptism and marriage, it can also be established at secular events, such as the purchase of school supplies or clothing. Although the relationship established at the baptism of a child is paramount, 'lesser *compadres*' also expect mutual co-operation (Cohen 1999: 93-102; Nutini 1984; Stephen 2005: 265-7). As *compadrazgo* establishes an expectation of respect and assistance, it can serve to create or reinforce bonds between unequal parties; for obvious reasons, wealthy or powerful families are generally considered desirable *compadres*. The Garcías have become *compadres* with many of their employees, and have also reciprocated by asking close employee-relatives to become the godparents of their own two children.

Since San Martín is a small community of only about 1,800 people, the multiple layers of kinship and *compadrazgo* that have developed in the Garcías' workshop recast the hierarchal relations normally found between employers and employees as intimate relationships that exist within a larger and particularly dense network of social relations (cf. Yanagisako 2002; this volume). Miguel and Catalina may be the employers of Amado, Perla, and Citlali, but they are also very likely to be their cousins, their parents' or grandparents' *compadres*, or potentially their own *compadres* or in-laws in the future. This means that employees' good relations with the Garcías are important not just for their work, but also for themselves and their families in other arenas of social life in San Martín. A breakdown of employment relations would not just mean being fired, it could also strain relations between many families in the community, all of whom live and work in very close proximity to one another. This is what Victor means when he says 'once you are in, you cannot get out': to remove oneself from employment could undermine the fabric of kinship and *compadrazgo* that binds Tileños tightly to one another. While this intertwining of work and social relationships underpins the hierarchical relations of the workshop, most employees do not view this situation negatively, but rather see it as the natural progression of already-existing intimate relationships between themselves, their families, and the Garcías, who have assisted and engaged with one another in accordance with the expectations of local social norms over generations.

The Garcías' workers, neighbours, and clients also view their authority within the workshop as naturally deriving from their presumed relationship to the objects that are produced there – not because they are the owners of the workshop *per se*, but because they are recognized as the authors of the woodcarvings. Since Oaxacan woodcarving did not emerge organically, so to speak, from established cultural practices, artisans initially did not have concrete expectations about the mores and rationales of commercial artisanal work. However, as greater numbers of Tileños began to produce and sell carvings in the 1990s, they simultaneously adapted their perspectives to the logics and expectations of the art markets into which their work flowed. Markets for craftwork and ethnic art attach meaning and value to objects, people, and forms of production that are characterized as 'traditional' and 'authentic' (Errington 1998; Wood 2008). At the same time, however, they reward individuals who manage to develop a 'name for themselves': in Oaxaca, buyers often seek out already-known artisans whose work has been documented in exhibition catalogues, magazines, and books, and artisans require certificates from state-run institutes and competitions in order to secure visas and invitations to show their work abroad (Chibnik 2003: 174-234).

In order to establish their name within this saturated economy of recognition, artisans need to strike a fine balance between these two opposing principles: they must cultivate an individual style or aesthetic which is sufficiently distinct from other artisans' work, while not diverging substantially from the recognized genre or 'tradition'. This tension has generated a large amount of ambiguity amongst artisans about what buyers really want when they purchase Oaxacan woodcarvings, and about the relationship between authorship and ownership, which crystallizes into intense concerns about copying and competition (Cant 2015). In many ways, 'names' within this market work along similar logics to brands; it is not only the object that is desired by collectors and connoisseurs, but also the combination of the object and the evidence that distinguishes the work of a particular individual or family from similar work made by others, usually in the form of a signature.

Almost all of the woodcarvings produced in San Martín are at least partially made by people who are not recognized as their authors; in small, family workshops where husbands, wives, and children work together, the husband's name almost always serves as the workshop's signature.[12] Since Oaxacan woodcarvings are generally understood as cultural objects, recognized authors must repeatedly emphasize their personal connection to their work, while obscuring the connections created by the work of others who belong to the same culture and place. Thus, while authorship may be abstractly perceived as an inalienable attachment between objects and their makers, the authorial connection is not a certainty and must be continually reproduced and reasserted (Cant 2016b). These processes are most dramatically visible in large workshops like the Garcías' where only a small proportion of the carvings actually pass through Miguel or Catalina's hands. Their 'house style' of carving was initially developed by Miguel over a period of approximately three years in the early 2000s as he and Catalina worked to develop their name. Today, Miguel very rarely carves pieces himself, and yet the creative work of authorship is still considered to have been done by him, even when employees produce forms that he has never made himself. Likewise, it is Catalina who is understood to have authored the painting repertoire of the workshop, including the colour combinations and specific patterns and designs, even when the painters produce new designs or motifs.

It is not just the objects that the workshop produces which are understood as belonging to Miguel and Catalina, but the style itself. Davíd, one of Catalina's relatives who works in their painting workshop, also helps his own parents paint their carvings in the evenings after he has finished work. He explained to me that he would never paint his father's carvings in the style that he worked in at the Garcías', even though they might sell for higher prices. He said that this would not be fair, because it would be like stealing. Citlali, a painter who has worked for the Garcías for over two years, also did not question why they should get credit for her work. On one occasion, when some American tourists were visiting the workshop, a young woman hung back as the group progressed towards the carvers. Although she seemed interested in the details of the piece Citlali was working on, she quietly asked in Spanish whether she ever got to sign her own work, or was 'it always signed by the *jefes* [bosses]?' Citlali's smile flickered for a moment, and then she answered, 'We are all people of this workshop, and this is the name of the workshop, so that is our signature'.

These examples are not meant to suggest that workers are entirely alienated from the objects that their labour produces: employees' creativity and talents are frequently praised and rewarded by the Garcías, and other Tileños recognize many of the workers as some of the best artisans in the village. However, their *authorship* is not recognized as such and is never publicized; tourists and collectors are never told which painter or carver has made the work they have chosen, although workers themselves often remember. In this way, the artisans who work for the Garcías are made into employees, as they cannot build a career upon their own work. Since they are never recognized as the authors of the carvings that they make, they do not develop a name for themselves or recognition within the Oaxacan art world and market, and subsequently they would find it very difficult – at least in the short term – if they left the workshop to make carvings on their own. This situation is compounded by the fact that when workers do contribute their intellectual and creative capacities to the carvings they make, their innovations are subsumed into the general style of the Garcías' workshop, as they are never fully free to abandon the Garcías' house style altogether. Labouring in San Martín's workshops thus differs greatly from the traditional European craft guild structures of apprenticeship in which a trainee worked under the watchful eye of the master until such time as he was deemed qualified enough to practise his craft under his own name. Unlike San Martín, hierarchy in such guilds was by definition temporary – once the apprentice earned his title as a journeyman, he was free, even obliged, to use all of his skills and knowledge to make his own name for himself (Carrier 1992: 545-6; cf. Herzfeld 2004: 14-27). In Oaxaca, the political consequences of the art-world ideology of authorship intermingle within workshop spaces with the affective relationships of kin and *compadrazgo* to produce and maintain over time hierarchical relations between owners and workers, who are in reality *not* apprentices. The durability of these relations is reinforced by the employment of relatives, *compadres*, or godchildren, who are believed to be less likely than non-kin to break the norms of the woodcarvings' art world, which insist that only the recognized author of a style has the right to benefit from its production. This is not only because they would risk a loss of very secure employment within precarious economic conditions, but also because they would also risk creating social frictions that would have consequences for all other aspects of their lives.

Journal of the Royal Anthropological Institute (N.S.), 61-74
© Royal Anthropological Institute 2018

In addition to producing labour as an emergent category of persons, this intermingling of kinship and authorship has important consequences for how performing such labour is experienced in San Martín Tilcajete. Kinship and *compadrazgo* carry heavy social obligations that require kin and *compadres* to support one another through money, goods, and work. While usually reserved for expensive *fiesta* and sacramental life-cycle events, such obligations may be called upon at any time, creating a general condition of interdependence at any given moment. In other such socially dense contexts, wage-labour may be viewed as a technology through which people attempt to curtail expectations of entitlement between kin, as the exchange of money for services may sever future claims upon the social relations created by labouring together (Martin, this volume). For Oaxacan artisans, however, wage-labour itself is sustained by actors' complex relations of kinship, as they are deliberately built on a form of respect that is considered substantially stronger than simple relations of employment. Relations of *respeto* between employers and workers are crucial within the Oaxacan woodcarving economy of recognition, as workshop owners like Miguel and Catalina must be able to have confidence that their employees are not going to steal their styles and undermine their own authorship and name. Without this assurance, making woodcarvings would become nearly impossible as they would be unwilling to allow their workers to learn how to produce their particular styles of carving and painting. As it is, the Garcías take what seems the reasonable risk of teaching the workers their detailed and highly valuable aesthetic, expanding the workshop's output. At the same time, this relation of respect means that the Garcías are generally keen to develop the workers' own skills and to delegate basic aesthetic decision-making to them; so long as the authorship remains firmly attached to the Garcías' name, carvers and painters who have a certain level of skill are generally encouraged to experiment with forms and colours that complement the Garcías' house style. As such, employees are not under pressure to 'steal skills' from their employers as workers may be in other contexts (Herzfeld 2004: 113-38).

The tension, of course, is that this seemingly balanced system of kinship and respect underwriting relations of wage-labour within workshops is simultaneously undermined by the economy of recognition that has contributed to producing it in the first place. In a difficult economic situation where one of the few ways to get ahead is to establish a name for oneself in Oaxacan woodcarving, the pressure to leave employment to begin developing one's own name may be too great in the longer term. Indeed, in the nine years since my fieldwork began, a number of Tileños have begun producing carvings that approximate, with more or less success, the distinctive style of the Garcías' work. By becoming available in the market, these 'imitations', originally made by a few individuals who were not especially close to the Garcías, seem to have rendered aspects of their style up for grabs for use in the repertoire of Oaxacan woodcarving more generally; pieces from the original woodcarving community of San Antonio Arrazola can now be found that are clearly inspired by the Garcías' style (cf. Schneider 2006 on appropriation as artistic practice).[13] A few particularly skilled employees of the Garcías have now decided to strike out on their own in order to establish themselves as artisans in their own right. As these individuals cultivated their skills and developed their own aesthetic sensibilities while working in the Garcías' house style, it is not surprising that their independent work would be influenced by their previous work. Some of these former employees have managed to maintain friendly relations with Miguel and Catalina, while others have not; in any case, the ideology of authorship and the competitive economy of recognition have now profoundly transformed the experience of social intimacy in San Martín Tilcajete.

Conclusion

In the book *Making*, Ingold enjoins us to recognize that form is emergent from the intersections of human and nonhuman processes that act upon materials and the environment. This, he says, will allow us to avoid the conceptual difficulties that arise when we imagine production to be merely the 'projection of cultural form upon raw material supplied by nature' (2013: 44). I have suggested in this essay that labour is likewise processual and emergent from the human and nonhuman conditions in which it is made; however, labour also always emerges from the historical, cultural, and political economic structures in which such making takes place. Applying a strategy of 'close description' as developed by craft anthropologists to processes of labour allows the intricate and mediated conditions of localized labour experiences to emerge ethnographically, and shows that labour itself can be viewed as an outcome of the affective and aesthetic qualities of production.

As artisans in San Martín Tilcajete make Oaxacan woodcarvings with their families, co-workers, or employers, they simultaneously make their social relations into labour. This labour may be marked by the payment of a wage, as it is in the case of the Garcías' workshop, or it may be concealed within the household, but in all cases, its character is entirely coloured by the social relations and ideological conditions in which their work takes form and acquires value. Workers' labour for the Garcías is inseparable from other sorts of relationships that they have with their employers and with one another; the potent, affective relations of kinship and *compadrazgo* in San Martín draw Tileños together into tightly textured lives. This multiplicity of connectedness means that working experiences of wage-labour are also emotional experiences of kinship; employing kin infuses the employer-employee relation with all kinds of other rights and obligations. As respect is required amongst kin and *compadres*, so respect is expected amongst kin and *compadres* who work together. It is not particularly rare to find that people employ their family members, especially in places where economic security may be hard to come by. However, in the Oaxacan woodcarving workshops of San Martín Tilcajete, the employment of kin alone cannot explain the character of the labour that takes place there. It is also necessary to account for the ways that these artisans understand their work and the objects that they make in order to understand why labour looks the way that it does. The schema of authorship that structures the art world and art markets for Oaxacan craft and ethnic art significantly impacts the ways that labour is both envisioned and enacted by artisans, and so must be understood as intrinsically part of their labour itself. By considering the emergent affective and aesthetic dimensions of people's work within their larger social lives, we can more satisfactorily account for both the material and social conditions under which inequalities of work are produced, and more broadly the multitude of ways that contemporary capitalism both accommodates and transforms the cultures and societies in which it unfolds (Harvey & Krohn-Hansen, this volume). Labour must remain a central concern for anthropologists addressing these issues, as it allows us to analytically connect the systemic and apparently imperative character of global capitalism with the specific histories of capital relations and the diverse personal experiences of those who 'make' capitalism itself.

NOTES

The research for this essay was generously funded by the Emslie Horniman Fund of the Royal Anthropological Institute. I would like to thank Penny Harvey, Christian Krohn-Hansen, Ingjerd Hoëm, Keir Martin, Marit Melhuus, Knut Nustad, Andrew Sanchez, Elisabeth Schober, Astrid Stensrud, and all of the participants of the Reconfiguration of Labour workshop held in Oslo in June 2015. I would also like to acknowledge the late Olivia Harris, whose quotation provides the epigraph for this essay. Her work encourages us to pay attention to the ways that belonging together affects how people work together.

[1] All personal names in this article are pseudonyms.

[2] See, for example, the *Journal of Material Culture*; 'Anthropologies of Art [A/A]' (*http://www.anthropologies-of-art.net/*); Taking Stock: Anthropology, Craft and Artisans in the 21st Century (*http://anthro.vancouver.wsu.edu/research/Takingstock/*); and the Research Network for Design Anthropology (*https://kadk.dk/en/research-network-design-anthropology*).

[3] See Chibnik (2003) for a detailed history and discussion of how the market for Oaxacan woodcarvings changed throughout the 1990s.

[4] Figure based on a survey conducted March to April 2008.

[5] As per the requirements of the North American Free Trade Agreement.

[6] Owing to a combination of ongoing economic crises and recessions in the United States and highly visible media coverage of Mexico's drug-related violence. Increasing tensions between successive state governments and various trade unions and social movements have led to frequent protests and blockades in Oaxaca's capital, creating further difficulties for the tourism industry (Howell 2009; Waterbury 2007).

[7] This art world also extends to some degree to Canada, Europe, and Japan, where artisans have also shown their work, but the United States is the most significant market for their work outside of Mexico.

[8] My thanks to Keir Martin for helping me work through this point.

[9] Currently, only the second and third generation of artisans in families are establishing themselves independently of their parents. Where children wish to pursue alternatives, such as migration, education, or the seminary, there seems little pressure from parents to remain in woodcarving.

[10] Over the course of my fieldwork, there were four to five carvers, twenty to twenty-five painters, and two people working on wood preparation, in addition to five to eight piece-rate workers doing preparation in their own homes. Since the time of my fieldwork, the total number has grown to at least sixty and they are now dispersed between two different workshop sites.

[11] This situation was not without difficulties, as the Garcías' personalized power was believed by many to undermine the traditional power structures of the community's collective governance.

[12] In cases where workshops carry the name of the family (e.g. 'workshop of the Salazar Pérez family'), the two surnames used are always those of the adult man, not his wife or other members of the household who participate in production.

[13] They are not 'forgeries' in the sense that they do not claim to be made by the Garcías, yet they are clearly appropriating the Garcías' style.

REFERENCES

CANT, A. 2015. The allure of art and intellectual property: artisans and industrial replicas in Mexican cultural economies. *Journal of the Royal Anthropological Institute* (N.S.) **21**, 820-37.
——— 2016a. The art of indigeneity: aesthetics and competition in Mexican economies of culture. *Ethnos: Journal of Anthropology* **81**, 152-77.
——— 2016b. Who authors crafts? Producing woodcarvings and authorship in Oaxaca, Mexico. In *Critical craft: technology, globalization, and capitalism* (eds) C. Wilkinson-Weber & A. Ory DeNicola, 19-34. London: Bloomsbury.
CARRIER, J. 1992. Emerging alienation in production: a Maussian history. *Man* (N.S.) **27**, 539-58.
CHIBNIK, M. 2003. *Crafting tradition: the making and marketing of Oaxacan woodcarvings.* Austin: University of Texas Press.
COHEN, J. 1999. *Cooperation and community: economy and society in Oaxaca.* Austin: University of Texas Press.
——— 2015. *Eating soup without a spoon: anthropological theory and method in the real world.* Austin: University of Texas Press.
COLLOREDO-MANSFELD, R. 2002. An ethnography of neoliberalism: understanding competition in artisanal communities. *Current Anthropology* **43**, 113-37.
CONEVAL [CONSEJO NACIONAL DE EVALUACIÓN DE LA POLITICA DE DESARROLLO SOCIAL] 2012. *Informe de pobreza y evaluación en el estado de Oaxaca, 2012.* Mexico City: CONEVAL.

COOK, S. 1990. Female labor, commodity production and ideology in Mexican peasant-artisan households. In *Work without wages: domestic labor and self-employment within capitalism* (eds) J.L. Collins & M. Gimenez, 89-115. Albany: State University of New York Press.

DE NEVE, G. 2005. *The everyday politics of labour: working lives in India's informal economy.* Delhi: Social Science Press.

ERRINGTON, S. 1998. *The death of authentic primitive art and other tales of progress.* Berkeley: University of California Press.

HARRIS, O. 2007. What makes people work? In *Questions of anthropology* (eds) R. Astuti, J. Parry & C. Stafford, 137-67. Oxford: Berg.

HERZFELD, M. 2004. *The body impolitic: artisans and artifice in the global hierarchy of value.* Chicago: University Press.

HOWELL, J. 2009. Union struggles in urban Mexico: Oaxaca City revisited. *Anthropology News* **50**, 53-4.

HUNT, R.C. 1971. Components of relationships in the family: a Mexican village. In *Kinship and culture* (ed.) F.L.K. Hsu, 106-57. London: Aldine Transaction.

INGOLD, T. 2013. *Making: anthropology, archaeology, art and architecture.* London: Routledge.

KESKÜLA, E. 2014. Disembedding the company from kinship: unethical families and atomized labour in an Estonian mine. *Laboratorium* **6**, 58-76.

KONDO, D. 1990. *Crafting selves: power, gender and discourses of identity in a Japanese workplace.* Chicago: University Press.

MARCHAND, T. (ed.) 2010. Making knowledge. *Journal of the Royal Anthropological Institute* (N.S.) Special Issue.

MOHSINI, M. 2016. Crafting Muslim artisans: agency and exclusion in India's urban crafts communities. In *Critical craft: technology, globalization, and capitalism* (eds) C. Wilkinson-Weber & A. Ory DeNicola, 239-58. London: Bloomsbury.

MORISAWA, T. 2015. Managing the unmanageable: emotional labour and creative hierarchy in the Japanese animation industry. *Ethnography* **16**, 262-84.

NASH, J. (ed.) 1993. *Crafts in the world market: the impact of global exchange on Middle American artisans.* Albany: State University of New York Press.

NUTINI, H. 1984. *Ritual kinship*, vol. 2: *Ideological and structural integration of the compadrazgo system in rural Tlaxcala.* Princeton: University Press.

ORY DENICOLA, A. 2005. Working through tradition: experiential learning and formal training as markers of class and caste in North Indian block printing. *Anthropology of Work Review* **26**, 12-16.

PARRY, J. 2013. Company and contract labour in a central Indian steel plant. *Economy and Society* **42**, 348-74.

PRENTICE, R. 2015. *Thiefing a chance: factory work, illicit labor, and neoliberal subjectivities in Trinidad.* Denver: University of Colorado Press.

SANCHEZ, A. 2016. *Criminal capital: violence, corruption and class in industrial India.* London: Routledge.

SCHNEIDER, A. 2006. *Appropriation as practice: art and identity in Argentina.* London: Palgrave Macmillan.
——— & C. WRIGHT 2013. *Anthropology and art practice.* London: Bloomsbury.

SEDESOL [SECRETARÍA DE DESARROLLO SOCIAL] 2013. *Catálogo de localidades: San Martín Tilcajete* (available on-line: *http://www.microrregiones.gob.mx/*, accessed 9 January 2018).

STEPHEN, L. 2005. *Zapotec women* (Second edition). Austin: University of Texas Press.

TOWNSEND-GAULT, C. 1998. At the margin or the center? The anthropological study of art. *Reviews in Anthropology* **27**, 425-39.

VENKATESAN, S. 2010. Learning to weave, weaving to learn . . . what? *Journal of the Royal Anthropological Institute* Special Issue: Making knowledge (ed.) T. Marchand, S158-75.

WATERBURY, R. 2007. The rise and fracture of the Popular Assembly of the Peoples of Oaxaca. *Anthropology News* **48**, 8-10.

WILKINSON-WEBER, C. & A. ORY DENICOLA 2016. Introduction: taking stock of craft in anthropology. In *Critical craft: technology, globalization, and capitalism* (eds) C. Wilkinson-Weber & A. Ory DeNicola, 1-16. London: Bloomsbury.

WOOD, W.W. 2008. *Made in Mexico: Zapotec weavers and the global ethnic art market.* Indianapolis: University of Indiana Press.

YANAGISAKO, S. 2002. *Producing culture and capital: family firms in Italy.* Princeton: University Press.

« Fabriquer » le travail dans un atelier artisanal mexicain

Résumé

L'anthropologie de l'artisanat a été redynamisée par de nouvelles approches théoriques de la matérialité, de la créativité et de la dextérité. Menées en lien avec des processus économiques et politiques plus vastes tels que le nationalisme, l'identité et le consumérisme, ces recherches ne portent pas tout à fait sur les questions concernant le travail. Basé sur des recherches ethnographiques à San Martín Tilcajete, un village de sculpteurs sur bois dans l'état mexicain d'Oaxaca, cet article montre comment le travail « se fait » dans les ateliers traditionnels, grâce aux relations sociales et matérielles qui s'y établissent. L'auteure avance que, plus que par la propriété des moyens de production, les relations de travail sont produites à San Martín par l'entremêlement de l'idéologie du « créateur », présente dans le monde de l'art, avec les relations intimes de la parenté. Le marché de l'art situe la production de valeur dans l'œuvre de ceux qui se trouvent reconnus comme créateurs, faisant l'impasse sur le travail des nombreux ouvriers qui produisent les sculptures. Les travailleurs employés par des membres de la famille ont de la peine à gagner leur indépendance sur ce marché, à cause des multiples relations d'obligation et de respect qui sont au centre des liens de parenté et pèsent d'un lourd poids social, et parce que leur propre travail créatif est assimilé au style général de l'atelier qui les emploie.

4

Recapturing the household: reflections on labour, productive relations, and economic value

MARIT MELHUUS *University of Oslo*

Labour regimes organize the economy; they also organize lives. With the continued deregulation of the labour market and the simultaneous drive to cut labour costs, there lies a challenge to grasp not only the workings of capital but also the way such processes impact on the organization of everyday labouring lives. This implies a focus that is attentive to value, combining political economy with moral economy. I suggest that household analysis represents one way to address such issues. Household analysis provides a means of ethnographic access to a particular temporal dynamic that is revealing of a layered texture of precariousness, capturing at one and the same time the material realities and the intimate relations of living. Regimes of labour and regimes of value can thus be brought into the same frame, indicating relational dependencies as well as structures of social inequality. Drawing on earlier ethnography amongst landless tobacco growers in Corrientes, Argentina, I draw attention to the potentials of a particular perspective, all the while paying attention to the specific historical and political context. Anthropology is well placed to grasp contemporary configurations of labour and how these both are framed by and contribute towards reproducing social and economic inequalities, not only locally but also at a more global scale.

Recent decades have seen a significant shift in the organization of labour and capital, where emphasis is placed on flexibility and the outsourcing of labour tasks. With increasing urbanization and a concomitant expansion of the informal economy, precarious labour is a grim reality for growing numbers in many parts of the world. However, as Millar reminds us: 'In many countries of the global South ... precarious work has arguably *always* been part of the experience of the labouring poor' (2014: 34, emphasis in original; see also Bremen 2013). And as Narotzky (this volume) reiterates: 'One may argue that dislocation is not new in the process of capitalist capitalism, nor in past historical forms of predatory conquest' (pp. 35–6). Anthropologists have increasingly documented these realties from various perspectives (e.g. Cross 2010; Goldstein 2003; Han 2012; Lazar 2008).

Nevertheless, there is great variety in how labour is configured under contemporary capitalism. With specific reference to the figuration of labour and capital, Tsing argues that 'diversity conditions the responses of both capital and labor to the problem of cutting labor costs and disciplining the workforce' (2009: 150). She shows how global supply-chain capitalism generates forms of labour that are based not only on self-exploitation but also on what she terms 'super-exploitation', drawing attention to 'non-economic factors such as gender, race, ethnicity, nationality, religion, sexuality, age and citizenship', and, I would add, kinship (2009: 158), implied in labour performance. Bringing together the economic and non-economic aspects of labour, Tsing reminds us of an important dimension of any labour configuration: that labour practices are always embedded in specific sociocultural settings.

Recent years have also seen an increased focus on affect and affective labour, in particular with regard to neoliberal transformations. The current emphasis on the non-economic factors of labour reconfigures labour practices in other terms, potentially displacing the questions tied to economic value and the very grounds for capturing labour performed as self-exploitation or even super-exploitation. With the continual deregulation of the labour market and the simultaneous drive to cut labour costs, it seems an urgent task to grasp the way such processes inflect on the organization of everyday labouring lives. As Hann and Hart point out 'Even in a post-Fordist, post-modern age, most people still have to work for a living' (2011: 170).

In their call for a rethinking of the nature of economic life, Narotzky and Besnier focus more broadly on social reproduction and those complex phenomena that come together in the way ordinary people go about making a living – or a 'life worth living' (2014: S5). They centre on the importance of worth in making a livelihood. The term 'livelihood' embraces more than labour practices, pointing to a moral dimension of economic activity and hence to relations of commitment and also dependency, such as kinship. Central to Narotzky and Besnier's approach, in addition to crisis and hope, is a consideration of value. Although accepting Graeber's reinterpretation of the labour theory of value 'that defines value as the spending of creative energy in producing and maintaining society' (2014: S6), they are attentive to different coexisting regimes of value, combining political economy with a moral economy (as well as a feminist economics). Their broad approach is an invitation to bring regimes of labour and regimes of value within the same frame. In this essay I do just that.

I suggest that the household represents a viable and fruitful analytic concept not only in explorations of contemporary, precarious labour regimes, but also in juxtaposing these regimes with coexisting regimes of value. Many of the activities that sustain people and livelihoods worldwide are household based. To the extent that household activity is productive, household analysis enables us to explore not only how labour is mobilized and deployed to make a life and create a livelihood, but also – and just as important – how economic value and sources of profit and accumulation are generated. This would contribute to our knowledge of the working and living conditions of many urban and rural poor across the world, while yielding insights into the continued reproduction of structures of inequality. Household analysis provides a means of ethnographic access to a particular temporal dynamic that is revealing of a layered texture of precariousness, capturing at one and the same time the material realities and the intimate relations of living, and how these are interlaced.

The household, in my usage, is not reserved for non-market economies. It is not a term solely applicable to pre-industrial societies. This specificity would, as Gregory (2009) points out, limit the usefulness of the concept. Nor do I consider the household to be confined to autarkic, self-sufficient peasant production. Rather, in line with Gregory, I view householding as embedded in market relations, straddling both the market and non-market domain (Gregory 2009: 144).[1] For my purposes, the household is a useful tool for particular ethnographic inquiries, and my specific focus is tied to the nature and character of household labour. However, what place the household has in an economy will necessarily be an empirical and historically contingent issue (see also Campbell, this volume).

My discussion on the household is based on fieldwork carried out in 1974-5 among landless tobacco growers in Corrientes, Argentina. In retrieving this work, I wish to draw attention to the potentials of a particular perspective. My engagement with the household, and more specifically with household analysis, was triggered by a specific research interest. That interest centred more broadly on agrarian issues related to social inequality and processes of social transformation. At the time (and especially for those working in Latin America), these questions were framed in terms of the 'peasant debate'. More concretely, my focus was on economic value, the creation of a surplus and its eventual appropriation. This demanded a more detailed examination of labour and labour practices. My assumption was that labour is the source of economic value; thus my perspective was what Gregory terms 'production-centric' (2014: 52), and my queries were directed at the ways in which economic value was created and circulated.

Wolf's now classic work *Peasants* was an inspiration, especially his discussion of surplus and 'social surpluses' (1966: 4-10). Wolf contends that peasants necessarily produce a surplus, that this surplus takes different forms, and that 'the term "peasant" denotes no more than an asymmetrical structural relationship between producers of surplus and controllers; to render it meaningful, we must still ask questions about the different sets of conditions which will maintain this structural relationship' (1966: 10). In this essay, I will not address the peasant or the peasantry as such(see Kearney 1996).[2] My point is, rather, methodological. In order to come to grips with surplus production and the nature of conditions under which it is created and appropriated, I needed an analytical framing that would allow for a detailed and systematic generation of particular data. Household analysis served this purpose well. However, at issue in the present context is whether such analysis may also be productive for contemporary labour issues, which may be far removed from rural concerns.

A time and a place

In May 1974 I set sail for Argentina, departing from the Norwegian port of Ålesund.[3] After about five weeks at sea, on a 'work-a-way' contract, we disembarked in Buenos Aires. Some days later, we arrived in Goya, Corrientes, about 1,000 kilometres northeast of the capital. Goya was a hub for the producers of black tobacco, *criollo correntino*, which was one of the main crops of that area at the time. My research was to focus specifically on the landless tobacco growers and their nascent political mobilization. My choice of this particular place at this particular time was an interest in agrarian sociopolitical movements, and not least processes of rural social transformation.

I had been spurred by the optimism that prevailed in Argentina in the wake of Hector Campora's presidency in 1973 and the return of Juan Domingo Perón from his exile in Spain and subsequent ascent to again become president of the republic. Perón's return was an extraordinary event. He encapsulated the drive for change and the hopes for a better future, while at the same time laying the ground for the troubled times that followed. There was a surge of interest for a whole range of social problems with a goal to confront and solve them. The agrarian sectors were given particular attention. The Agrarian Leagues (Ligas Agrarias), organizing peasants and farmers in the northeastern provinces of Argentina, had won wide support and their demands were in part being met.[4] The Ligas Agrarias Correntinas (LAC) were formed in January 1972. In 1973, they had organized a 'strike': that is, a refusal to deliver and market their harvested tobacco. The 'strike' lasted about a month. Their immediate demands were higher prices, a more just classification system, and a guarantee of purchase. I was going to work closely with the Ligas Agrarias Correntinas.[5]

On 1 July, shortly after my arrival, Perón died. Isabelita,[6] his wife and vice-president, took office as president of the nation. She left the reins to José López Rega (already an important confidante of Perón), and the feared 'Triple A' (Alianza Anti-Comunista Argentina) stepped up its operations. Death lists were published; people were killed or disappeared. Terror began to permeate all sectors of Argentinian society. The political momentum of the LAC was thwarted, their political activity effectively forbidden; their leaders were persecuted, jailed, and tortured. In the wake of this political violence, not only did the LAC lose their nascent bargaining power in their attempt to gather tobacco growers collectively behind particular demands, but also, and perhaps as importntly, a potential sense of community was lost that might have contained further acts of dislocation (see Schober, this volume, on the role of unions in labour struggles). This was the start of a bleak and dark period in Argentina's recent history, the dirty war, *la guerra sucia*, which only ended in 1983 with Raúl Alfonsin's election as president.

The prevailing political climate exacerbated the social and economic insecurities of these tobacco producers and the tense political situation forced me to redesign my research project. The increasing threat of state violence stopped the political mobilization of these rural poor cultivators, while simultaneously frustrating an anthropological endeavour. It was definitely not wise to study political processes; more importantly, it was not feasible. Rather than focus on political processes, I focused on economic ones. Politics and economy are intimately linked, and through a detailed study of the production and marketing of black tobacco, I was also able to get at the underlying conditions that structured this agrarian sector. Indeed, it was precisely the precarious economic situation of the tobacco growers that had spurred their truncated political involvement. The majority of these tobacco growers were landless peasants, producing a crop for one of the major industries in Argentina. Locally, the production of black tobacco was referred to as '*el cultivo de la miseria*' (the crop of wretchedness or misery), a poignant reminder not only of the labour efforts involved in producing tobacco, but also of the vulnerability of these growers, situated as they are between landowners, the tobacco industry, and the state, with a crop that is susceptible to the vagaries of the weather.[7] I chose to locate my research to an *estancia* – or large estate – that organized its economic activities around cattle and tobacco production.[8]

My framework – then
My overall research interests were related to what has been coined 'the agrarian question' (McMichael 1997), and as mentioned, my specific interests were in processes of social transformation: rural change and the potential role of a peasantry in such processes, especially as these were played out in Latin America. At the time of my study, the distinction between pre-capitalist and capitalist societies was analytically relevant, although challenged. The 'dual economy' thesis and modernization theories had been discarded in favour of dependency theories; structural inequalities were articulated through world systems theories. Politically, the term 'imperialism' was applied not only to denote the structural inequalities in the world but also as a rallying cry for

Journal of the Royal Anthropological Institute (N.S.), 75-88
© Royal Anthropological Institute 2018

struggle and international solidarity. There was an overall concern with development processes and processes of social change more generally, with a particular focus on rural development. It was within such a scenario that the peasant gained an important place and studies of peasant societies flourished.

Drawing on such scholars as Chayanov (1966), Meillassoux (1973), Mintz (1973), Sahlins (1974), Shanin (1971), Stavenhagen (1973 [1969]), and Wolf (1966), I was interested in what I then termed 'the character of integration' of what could be coined as a 'peasant economy' to society at large. Working from the premise that the basis for this particular social formation (i.e. tobacco production in Corrientes) was one of social and economic inequality, I was interested in what restricted – or generated – a process of accumulation amongst the tobacco growers, potentially allowing for a reinvestment in more expansive production. To this end, the notion of surplus – or, more precisely, economic surplus – was central. My question was not whether a surplus was produced, but rather how (or by whom) that surplus was appropriated. The problem (as I phrased it then) was not that peasants are unable to produce a surplus, but rather that they are unable to realize it.

My framework was Marxist.[9] My arguments were framed in terms of relations of production, labour, and unequal exchange. Although accepting that the dominating 'mode of production' was capitalist, I argued that this did not necessarily entail that a capitalist logic informed all forms of economic activity. Thus, my focus was on forms of labour and the way different labour regimes are subsumed under a more overarching capitalist rationality. These landless tobacco cultivators were commodity producers. Yet they were not wage earners; they were not employed (neither were they 'wageless' [Denning 2010]). In other words, they were not what would (then) be classified as rural proletarians. Rather, we could say that they were 'self-employed'. In a limited sense, their production efforts could be viewed as an example of unpaid labour. However, none of these terms fully captures their way of life and their various dependencies. With the exception of land, they did control their means of production. But most importantly they controlled their own labour. The tobacco cultivators were producers of an industrial commodity – tobacco – supplying the raw material to an industry that dominated a significant global market, namely that of cigarettes. Hence, they were totally dependent on a market in order to realize the value of their productive efforts. Moreover, they were totally dependent on a landowner in order to produce at all.[10]

Access to land was achieved through contracts of *apacería* (rent in kind) with the landowner. In my case, these *apaceros* (as they were called) paid 30 per cent of their harvest to the landowner, an *estanciero* (estate owner) whose property consisted of 3,700 hectares.[11] Insofar as a tobacco cultivator was attached to a large landowner, a producer could potentially have unlimited access to land, granted the land was suitable for tobacco cultivation, the labour power was available, and the landowner allowed access. Increased tobacco production would serve the interest of both the landowner and the tobacco cultivator: the better the harvest, the better the income for both. The opposite, obviously, also holds true. Regarding the commercialization of the tobacco, the cigarette industry was in a monopoly position. The buyers of tobacco present in the area set the terms: fixing the price and the quality criteria. Thus the demands of the cigarette industry – both in quality and in quantity – and the price it was willing to pay directly affected the incomes of both the tobacco producer and the landowner.

Configuring labour: household analysis

The labour regime that I studied is the product of a particular historical conjuncture. This history is expressed through specific relations, such as the property structure, the land tenure system, and the development of the tobacco industry in Argentina. These relations are in turn embedded in certain practices, tied to the specificities of black tobacco and its cultivation and eventual commercialization. In this labour regime, the critical factors are land, technology, and labour power. As I have already indicated, the property structure was characterized by a concentration of land in a few hands. Hence, most of the tobacco cultivators were landless.

I turn now to the way I chose to approach my fieldwork, concretely and specifically. What kind of evidence did I need to gather in order to answer the particular questions I had set for myself? How did I configure my focus on surplus? Two points are central. One has to do with the very characteristics of black tobacco. What does cultivating black tobacco entail in terms of land, labour, and technology? The other has to do with labour and how this labour was organized. Which units of analysis would work for me? At the time, and with my explicit focus on economy, the household served as my point of entry.

I had been trained in household analysis with a specific focus on household viability. A household, we were taught, is at one and the same time a unit of consumption and a unit of production. A household refers to an organized group that acts as a decision-making unit regarding production, distribution, and consumption. A household could also be considered a redistributive unit where relations of dependency and mutuality coexist. A household may be composed of members that are not family or kin. Thus, a household is not necessarily a family, but it may be. Central to household analysis, then, is household composition, and in particular the relationship between consumers and producers (non-productive and productive labour). This balance is critical for the household's viability, articulating the relationship between production and reproduction. Moreover, as this relationship shifts over time, the focus should be directed at the developmental cycle of the household, in order to capture the critical moments of fusion and/or fission (see Goody 1969 [1958], especially Fortes 1969 [1958] and Stenning 1969 [1958]). Attention was centred on the organization of production/consumption within each household, as well as an examination of the relationships between households. Thus, both intra- and inter-household relations were in focus. As a unit of analysis, then, the household captures a particular temporal and relational dynamic, which sheds light on how resources are effectively managed over time. In this framework, labour practices are crucial.

A focus on household and household viability opened two paths of exploration. On the one hand, I detailed the actual composition of each household, registering all members and their relations to each other. Among other things, this revealed strategies for extending the reproductive cycle, such as 'adopting' or incorporating children (of, for example, an unwed daughter) into the household or attaching single men (who might or might not be kin) to the household. It also revealed an extensive out-migration of household members. By combining a registering of family histories and migratory patterns, I also gained insight into the developmental cycle of each household. On the other hand, by focusing on labour practices, I was able to attend to the entire productive cycle of tobacco, the amount and kinds of labour required at each stage, as well as the technology employed. I also paid attention to subsistence production as well as other activities that sustained the household over time. A specific focus on viability also made

Journal of the Royal Anthropological Institute (N.S.), 75-88
© Royal Anthropological Institute 2018

evident the critical points that determined the amount of tobacco each household could produce. While revealing the precarious position of these tobacco cultivators, the analysis also demonstrated incipient processes of social differentiation.[12]

Black tobacco is characterized by its labour intensity. This is in contrast to light tobacco (Burley and Virginia). Black tobacco is dark and rough and relatively heavy. Its special flavour results from the drying and curing process, which (at the time) was not mechanized and therefore was dependent on sunny weather. In fact, at the time of my fieldwork, very few of the labour processes involved in black tobacco cultivation were mechanized. The technology applied was simple. For traction-power, mules, horses, or oxen were mainly used, though the tractor was gaining ground. All other operations were manual. There were two peak periods in the cycle: one at the time of transplantation of the tobacco plants from the seed-beds to the field; the other at harvest time.[13] Whereas it was possible to mobilize extra hands (from other households) during the time of transplantation, this was not possible at harvest time. All available hands in each household were needed to harvest, bundle, dry, and sort the tobacco in preparation for commercialization. In fact, it was the 'harvesting capacity' of any one household that determined the amount of tobacco that was planted; this was the crucial factor in planning the production cycle.

As mentioned, my interest turned on the notion of economic value, the creation of a surplus and its circulation and appropriation, whether as a source of profit or as potential accumulation. The challenge was to find a way to make the surplus 'evident'. With regard to the 30 per cent rent transferred to the landlord, the surplus forfeited was obvious. But what about the price mechanism? Did the price obtained for the tobacco also reflect an unequal exchange, a more covert transfer of economic surplus? If you recall, the price of the tobacco was one of the main issues that the Ligas Agrarias had raised, and which provoked the 'strike' of not delivering their tobacco for sale. (The other was the classification criteria.) Thus, with regard to price there was definitely a felt sense of injustice. Moreover, the mere fact that prices were up for negotiation (as the LAC had proved) indicated that there was a certain leeway that could be exploited. In order to make a probable argument, I needed to do a series of calculations related to the production cost and the value of labour power. I cannot render these calculations here, but refer to my original work for the details (Melhuus 1987: 180-214). Suffice it to say that through my calculations I was able to establish that the price of tobacco was such that the majority of the tobacco cultivators were producing under conditions that did not permit accumulation; they did not get their 'labour's worth'. Moreover, I argued that were there was an 'invisible' surplus, expressed through the market-price mechanism, which was transferred to the industry.

The crux of the argument lies in the fact that for these peasants labour did not enter as a cost factor. These cultivators were operating under a different economic rationality (than that of a strictly capitalist enterprise), a different labour regime which not only allows for, but is in a sense based on, a notion of unpaid labour. But the notion of unpaid labour implies more than the mere fact that they do not calculate labour in terms of cost. It also points to the issue of economic surplus – and the appropriation and realization of this surplus. Insofar as there is a relation of unequal exchange – both with regard to the land rent and with regard to the price mechanism – this surplus is siphoned off, to be realized by others, in an 'asymmetrical structural relationship between producers of surplus and controllers' (Wolf 1966: 10). My argument, then, was that the economic rationality that underpinned this production was based on auto-exploitation and it was this factor that made it profitable to maintain this particular peasant economy. And with regard to social change, my point was that any systematic accumulation that could transform the cultivators' lives and livelihoods was very difficult to achieve. The property structure and the land tenure system, as well as the tobacco industry, were conducive to maintaining the status quo.

Vulnerable lives

My systematic focus on the household and household composition, the relation between productive and non-productive labour, and household viability was directed at demonstrating how an economic unit was reproduced and how this very process of reproduction also reproduced relations of a different order. The way I framed my question with regard to surplus required a particular kind of evidence. However, this close examination of daily lives also revealed an extremely precarious situation.

These peasants were poor; they made their living on the very margins of society. There was good reason to call tobacco the 'crop of misery'. People were very conscious of their poverty and explicitly tied this to a specific morality, where being good and being poor were equated. They did not necessarily yearn for wealth, but hoped for a decent life. Their houses were made of mud or reeds, with earthen floors and thatched roofs. A family would have one main construction consisting of one room, partitioned by a cupboard or the like. Here the parents, daughters, and younger children slept, sharing beds. The older boys would sleep in a partition of the *galpon* (a larger shed for storage of equipment, drying tobacco, etc.). Cooking was done over an open fire, in a separate small construction. There was no piped water, nor was there electricity. The most usual source of water was the nearest pool of almost stagnant water, where people washed and cows meandered, and from where drinking water was fetched. A few families had constructed a well.

Most of the older people were illiterate, although extremely knowledgeable about tobacco cultivation and agriculture more generally; the women had extensive knowledge of local healing herbs. There were few local institutions. There was no church, only a small chapel that the priest attended nine days a year. There was no health centre in the rural area; for any emergency, people had to go to Goya, although transport was hard to procure. Once at the medical facilities in town, these peasants were often the last to be attended, irrespective of how early they had arrived. The local school was hard to get to, and although education was seen as important, many of the children did not attend regularly. Amongst themselves, people would often speak *guaraní*, and they listened to Radio Paraguay (*guaraní* is the official language in Paraguay, along with Spanish). The men dressed in traditional *bombachos* (baggy trousers), black sombreros, and riding boots or *alpargatas*; the women wore cotton dresses or trousers with T-shirts. At harvest time, money might be spent on one new set of clothing for each family member.

Yanagisako (1979) has pointed out that peasants are exposed to particular risks (e.g. the market, state, the weather). These tobacco producers are no exception. In fact we can deduce a layered texture of precariousness. In addition to material poverty, they lived with the insecurity and risk entailed in being landless, at the mercy of landowners. They were also subject to the vagaries of the weather in ensuring a good harvest; whether they would be able to sell their crop at a good price. At a larger scale, there was the threat that the tobacco industry might shift its priorities, with light tobacco eventually supplanting *criollo correntino*. Moreover, the institutional void implied a weak sense of community with little potential to tie these people actively together; there were no organizations that could mobilize them in a mutual cause. In fact, the demise of the Ligas Agrarias implied, *inter alia*, a cessation in the circulation of information regarding trends in the market, the debt crisis in Argentina, and other macro-economic factors that impinged on their everyday lives. Thus their very ignorance of significant contextual factors was a contributing element to their already volatile existence. Hence, many of these peasants were kept in place by both the economic and the political circumstances that framed their lives. Others had no option but to migrate. Those who stayed survived by mobilizing all available hands, irrespective of age or gender. Thus, the question of self-exploitation must also be read in light of the internal power relations and dependencies, adding yet another layer to the workings of the household and its vulnerability.

Recapturing the household

At an abstract level, labour regimes are ways to organize the economy. Yet they also do more than this: they organize lives. In this sense, any labour regime is concretely and locally manifest. I have argued that household analysis is one way of accessing specific labour regimes. Moreover, I have suggested that a household can be viewed as a site where regimes of labour and regimes of value coalesce, thus bringing economic value and moral values into the same frame. At the core of my analysis of the tobacco growers was a concept of value, explicitly related to labour and economic surplus. Thus I was mainly concerned with economic value. In his extended discussion of value, Graeber states that 'value is the way actions become meaningful to the actors placed in some larger social whole, real or imaginary' (2001: 254). This perspective, which places the power of creativity at its core, ascribes value to meaning and imagination. Although embracing a significant dimension of value, it is not very helpful in capturing forms of economic value: how these are creatively produced and circulated or even creatively usurped.

With a dual focus on economic surplus and household organization of labour, I was able to show how particular relations of social inequality were generated and reproduced. I was also able to indicate the tensions and contradictions in these relations. Holding these contradictions together were the tobacco-producing units and the way their labour power was configured within this wider sociopolitical structure. This configuration rested on the very fact that labour was unpaid and did not enter as a cost factor. That there are ways of subsuming labour that are more profitable than wage-labour is not unique to this particular case. Rather, it is probably the reality for many working poor all over the world. Hence, there is a need to document ethnographically the diverse ways in which labour costs are cut or even effectively erased (for a different perspective on the erasure of labour, see Cant, this volume). This, however, does not preclude a focus that simultaneously seeks to understand how actions become meaningful to people themselves within some larger social whole. On the contrary, insofar as we are concerned with the ways in which people survive at the margins of society, we need to hold together the intimate connections between the way people actually make a living and what makes a life worth living.

The relations that organize a household obviously consist of more than the ratio between consumers and producers. Households are also sites of deep affective attachments (Richard & Rudnyckyj 2009). The nature of such attachments will necessarily vary, depending on the kinds of and grounds for moral commitments the household is organized around, the relations of authority, and the degree of control any one member can exert. The enactment of any specific labour regime is reproduced by and dependent upon the mobilization of such particular relations. Hence, the exploitation, self-exploitation, or super-exploitation of a peasantry or urban slum dwellers might imply at a household level unequal relations of power or even coercion. To what extent such relations are the glue – or potential undoing – of the household will turn on the moral values and affective bonds that can be summoned not only within the household but also more broadly: to the people, to the place, to the land. But perhaps more importantly, the commitment of any one household member will depend on whether there are viable or desirable options. Whatever the case, affect will be at work, making kinship and gender, as well as religious beliefs or other forms of affiliations, important dimensions in securing household viability.

Households, however, are not necessarily at one and the same time units of production and units of consumption. The separation between work life and family life has been an important characteristic of modern industrial economies, and the relation between production and reproduction is a core issue for feminist studies. As Rudie (2001 [1969]) points out, households are involved in both external and internal relations, where the former has to do with economic efficiency (market transactions) and the latter with moral commitments (reciprocity). There is, according to Rudie, a tension between these two domains, reflecting the external and internal relational network in which a household is involved. In other words, the household must hold together these two contradictory operational domains. This is, among other things, what householding is also about. Rudie insists that this differentiation is most marked in Western industrialized societies, where there is an acknowledged separation between 'a market model' and a 'love model', or what we might today label more broadly an 'affective model', necessarily paying heed to kinship relations. Whether this distinction holds more generally is, of course, an empirical question, which must be examined in each case.

While ignoring the affective dimensions of labour (market relations), Rudie nevertheless alerts us to specific and at times contradictory processes that are at work within a household. Her focus is on situations where productive and reproductive labour are separate domains, while at the same time paying attention to how these domains are related. It is precisely by reading across these domains that we can bring together the efforts and creativity that go into making a life and making a living (see also McKinnon & Cannell 2013a). This will necessarily involve a double focus: on the one hand, on those relations and practices that contribute towards reproducing a particular economy (through relations of labour); and, on the other, on those relations and practices that contribute towards creating a livelihood. These two domains are mutually constitutive, if not overlapping, incorporating at one and the same time the transformative and integrative potentials of social life.

To what extent household analysis is fruitful for anthropological approaches to labour will necessarily depend on what forms of labour are being scrutinized and how this labour is organized. It seems that in those cases where the units of production and of consumption overlap, household analysis is useful. In situations where productive and reproductive labour are separate domains, while paying attention to how these domains are related, household analysis alone might not yield the fine-grained ethnography that illustrates these intimate links. Nevertheless, work life and family life are mutually imbricated and must be viewed in conjunction. Both the tension and the significance of the relationship between these domains can productively be explored by incorporating an affective dimension in the relational analysis of households, and not least by being attentive to the significance of affective labour within the family (Melhuus & Borchgrevink 1984).

Conclusion

In this essay, my overall concern has been tied to the diverse ways that labour is configured under capitalism – and anthropology's shifting relationship to examinations of labour. Assuming that labour is the source of economic value, I have argued that there is something to be gained by a continued focus on economic value insofar as we are concerned with the ways capital subsumes labour and how this affects the everyday lives of labouring people across the world. From this perspective, I suggest that some notion of the value of labour still has currency, and one challenge is to uncover the forms that this value takes, be it as 'unpaid' labour in conditions of self-exploitation, or even super-exploitation, as actors in an informal market or as outsourced self-employed entrepreneurs. All such work practices are variations of a flexible labour 'market' under uncertain conditions. They may be efficient ways of disciplining the workforce and cutting labour costs, while at the same time placing the economic risks onto an already vulnerable population, creating both ambiguity and uncertainties.

As anthropologists, we are interested in how people go about their lives, not just making a living, but making a life. We want to know what actions are meaningful to people and why. Work life and family life constitute two core domains that underpin people's lifeworlds. Both these domains coalesce around economic and moral values, and it is this very configuration that also permits certain forms of exploitation. Hence, labour practices and the concomitant regimes of labour must be seen in conjunction with regimes of value; political economy and moral economy must come within the frame (Narotzky & Besnier 2014). I have argued that the household can serve as a useful tool and significant entry point in order to capture these two dimensions of livelihood. Households straddle the market and non-market domains and householding embraces the many activities and relations, as well as intimacies, that make life meaningful. Importantly, also, households are processual entities, thus revealing of a particular temporal and relational dynamic. Household analysis may, then, also contribute to grasping emerging dislocations in time (such as that between labour time and personal time) and the way these are linked to local conditions of opportunity, a point Narotzky (this volume) makes in her discussion of Krohn-Hansen's (this volume) analysis of temporal work rhythms. Hence, I find household analysis particularly productive in our ethnographic inquiries where labour, labour relations, and labour practices are in focus, all the while keeping in mind the affective stuff that holds these relations and practices together.

If the logic of capital tends to abstract the economic from all other relations, the anthropological perspective insists that economic relations are not only embedded in but also constituted by relations of kinship, gender, ethnicity, religion, and so on. That this also holds true for capitalist enterprises has been amply demonstrated (McKinnon & Cannell 2013b; Mollona 2009; Yanagisako 2002). The current interest in labour and labour regimes invites us to re-explore the ways labour has been understood and approached ethnographically and consider these in conjunction with contemporary processes of transformation and struggle for even a minimal survival. Such efforts necessarily entail a broader scope, not least the specific historical and political context. Global inequalities have not diminished but have taken on a different character. Combining detailed ethnography of the minutiae of everyday life and

relational dependencies (labouring and otherwise), anthropology is well placed to
grasp contemporary configurations of labour and how these both are framed by and
contribute towards reproducing social and economic inequalities, not only locally, but
also at a more global scale.

NOTES

The present essay springs out of a collaborative effort by the so-called 'Labour Group' at the Department
of Social Anthropology, University of Oslo. This group was constituted in order to elaborate one of the
sub-themes that formed part of the overall project 'Anthropos and the Material: Challenges to Anthropology',
generously funded by the Norwegian Research Council (1 January 2013-31 December 2016). The group
provided a congenial atmosphere, an intellectual thrust, and an exceptional determination to bring our
collective efforts to fruition. A very rewarding experience. I especially wish to thank the editors Penny Harvey
and Christian Krohn-Hansen for careful reading and incisive comments to earlier drafts of my essay, and
to Penny in particular for the many inspired and witty conversations over the years. Thanks also to the
anonymous readers of the *JRAI* for encouraging feedback and to Justin Dyer for his meticulous copy-editing.

[1] In contrast to Guyer's (2017) historical perspective on the legacy of the household, my take is
methodological. Framing her discussion in terms of infrastructure, Guyer examines the classical elements of
the household, alerting us to the way it has been deployed over time. In this effort, she makes an interesting
analytical distinction between the 'house' (material good and container) and the 'hold' (as relations of
dependency).

[2] Although the category of the peasant may be obsolete, the '*campesino*' is still thriving. One of the major
contemporary rural organizations is La Vía Campesina (Martínez-Torres & Rosset 2010). Moreover, rural
populations are continuously facing acute problems, especially dispossession and land grabbing (Li 2009;
2011).

[3] I travelled with Svein Erik Duus. We had each received grants from the Norwegian Research Council
(then NAVF) to carry out our respective projects on tobacco.

[4] The Ligas Agrarias sprang out of the Movimiento Rural de Acción Católica and were the first independent
organizations of the peasants and rural poor in Argentina. For a brief historical overview of the development
of Las Ligas Agrarias in Corrientes until the 1970s, see Calvo & Percíncula (2012).

[5] My introduction to the Agrarian Leagues was through Eduardo Archetti. He was at the time completing
his fieldwork, together with Kristi Anne Stølen, among the *colonos* in the northern part of Sta Fé (see Archetti
& Stølen 1975). My fieldwork lasted thirteen months, from June 1974 to July 1975.

[6] Her full name was María Estela Martínez de Perón, but she was known as Isabel or Isabelita.

[7] The Argentinian state is also involved, through state policies directed at the producers, such as the
Instituto provincial del tabaco (created in 1964) and the Fondo especial de tabaco (created in 1967). For an
analysis of state policies and the development of the tobacco industry in Argentina, see Duus (1978); for a
short introduction, see Melhuus (1987).

[8] Access to this particular *estancia* was facilitated by the LAC. I also did a short comparative project
amongst small landowning cultivators (*minifundios*) in order to capture the movement between being
landless producers and being small landowning tobacco cultivators.

[9] When I wrote the preface to the published version (1987) of my original thesis (from 1978), I formulated
some of the main criticisms that had since been raised against Marxism, dependency theories, and the like.
Most importantly, these turned on the question of structure versus agency (structural determinism); the lack
of attention to the cultural dimension; and the absence of a gender perspective.

[10] At the time of my study, the Department of Goya was characterized by a concentration of land in few
hands: 56.3 per cent of the property units were less than 50 hectares, comprising only 3.7 per cent of the
total area. At the other extreme, 70 per cent of the total area belonged to estates over 1,000 hectares or more,
totalling 4.9 per cent of the property units. Moreover, of a registered 7,816 tobacco-producing units, 5,638
were landless, that is, around 72 per cent; and of these, 73.3 per cent had holdings under 9 hectares (for details,
see Melhuus 1987: 45-50).

[11] There were a total of twelve families/households living on his property. The landowner also had around
1,000 head of cattle. Of the twenty-two households, fourteen were *apaceros*; two were *peones* who worked for
a wage minding the cattle and doing general maintenance work; four were *pobladores*, who, in exchange for
their labour on the *estancia*, were given the right to cultivate some land; and two were *ocupantes gratuitos*,
occupying the land free of charge.

[12] The households varied in size from a total of four to fifteen persons. One household consisting of fifteen
persons had a very favourable composition: seven females and eight males, with nine of the members being

between 14 and 60 years of age. This household was able to cultivate 9.5 hectares of tobacco, and had been able (as the only one within the *estancia*) to purchase a tractor on credit (Melhuus 1987: 123, Table 4.3, and 135, Table 4.4).

[13] To plant one hectare of tobacco, between 18,000 and 25,000 plants were needed. The tobacco was harvested leaf by leaf as they matured; they were first dried under shelter of a roof, then moved out to dry in the sun. At the slightest sign of rain, the tobacco had to be moved into shelter.

REFERENCES

ARCHETTI, E.P. & K.A. STØLEN 1975. *Explotación familiar y accumulación de capital.* Buenos Aires: Siglo XXI.

BREMAN, J. 2013. A bogus concept? *New Left Review* **84**, 130-8.

CALVO, C. & A. PERCÍNCULA 2012. Ligas Agrarias en Chaco y Corrientes: experiencias de organización campesina en contextos de transformación territorial. *De Prácticas y Discursos. Cuadernos de Ciencias Sociales* **1: 1**, 1-36.

CHAYANOV, A.V. 1966. On the theory of non-capitalist economic systems. In *A.V. Chayanov on the theory of peasant economy* (eds) D. Thorner, B. Kerbaly & R.E.F. Smith, 1-28. Homewood, Ill.: Richard D. Irwin.

CROSS, J. 2010. Neoliberalism as unexceptional: economic zones and the everyday precariousness of working life in South India. *Critique of Anthropology* **30**, 355-72.

DENNING, M. 2010. Wageless life. *New Left Review* **66**, 79-97.

DUUS, S.E. 1978. *Tobakk og politikk.* Department of Administration and Organization Theory, University of Bergen.

FORTES, M. 1969 [1958]. Introduction. In *The developmental cycle in domestic groups* (ed.) J. Goody, 1-14. Cambridge: University Press.

GOLDSTEIN, D.M. 2003. *Laughter out of place: race, class, violence and sexuality in a Rio shanty town.* Berkeley: University of California Press.

GOODY, J. (ed.) 1969 [1958]. *The developmental cycle in domestic groups.* Cambridge: University Press.

GRAEBER, D. 2001. *Toward an anthropological theory of value: the false coin of our own dreams.* New York: Palgrave.

GREGORY, C. 2009. Whatever happened to householding? In *Market and society: the great transformation today* (eds) C. Hann & K. Hart, 133-59. Cambridge: University Press.

——— 2014. On religiosity and commercial life: toward a critique of cultural economy and posthumanist value theory. HAU: *Journal of Ethnographic Theory* **4: 3**, 45-68.

GUYER, J.I. 2017. Survivals as infrastructure: twenty-first-century struggles with household and family in formal computations. In *Infrastructures and social complexity: a companion* (eds) P. Harvey, C.B. Jensen & A. Morita, 323-34. London: Routledge.

HAN, C. 2012. *Life in debt: times of care and violence in neoliberal Chile.* Berkeley: University of California Press.

HANN, C. & K. HART 2011. *Economic anthropology: history, ethnography, critique.* Cambridge: Polity.

KEARNEY, M. 1996. *Reconceptualizing the peasantry: anthropology in global perspective.* Boulder, Colo.: Westview Press.

LAZAR, S. 2008. *El Alto, rebel city: self and citizenship in Andean Bolivia.* Durham, N.C.: Duke University Press.

LI, T.M. 2009. To make live or let die? Rural dispossession and the protection of surplus populations. *Antipode* **41**, 66-93.

——— 2011. Centering labor in the land grab debate. *Journal of Peasant Studies* **38**, 281-98.

MCKINNON, S. & F. CANNELL 2013a. The difference kinship makes. In *Vital relations: modernity and the persistent life of kinship* (eds) S. McKinnon & F. Cannell, 3-38. Santa Fe, N.M.: SAR Press.

——— & ——— (eds) 2013b. *Vital relations: modernity and the persistent life of kinship.* Santa Fe, N.M.: SAR Press.

MCMICHAEL, P. 1997. Rethinking globalization: the agrarian question. *Review of International Political Economy* **4**, 630-62.

MARTÍNEZ-TORRES, M. & P.M. ROSSET 2010. La Vía Campesina: the birth and evolution of a transnational social movement. *Journal of Peasant Studies* **37**, 149-75.

MEILLASSOUX, C. 1973. The social organization of the peasantry. *Journal of Peasant Studies* **1**, 81-90.

MELHUUS, M. 1987. *Peasants, surpluses and appropriation: a case study of tobacco growers from Corrientes, Argentina* (Oslo Occasional Papers in Social Anthropology). University of Oslo.

——— & T. BORCHGREVINK 1984. Husarbeid: tidsbinding av kvinner. In *Myk start – hard landing* (ed.) I. Rudie, 319-38. Oslo: Universitetsforlaget.

MILLAR, K.M. 2014. The precarious present: wageless labor and disrupted life in Rio de Janeiro, Brazil. *Cultural Anthropology* **29**, 32-53.

MINTZ, S.W. 1973. A note on the definition of peasantry. *Journal of Peasant Studies* **1**, 91-106.

MOLLONA, M. 2009. *Made in Sheffield: an ethnography of industrial works and politics*. New York: Berghahn Books.

NAROTZKY, S. & N. BESNIER 2014. Crisis, value and hope: rethinking the economy: an introduction. *Current Anthropology* **55: S9**, S4-16.

RICHARD, A. & D. RUDNYCKYJ 2009. Economies of affect. *Journal of the Royal Anthropological Institute* (N.S.) **15**, 57-77.

RUDIE, I. 2001 [1969]. Husholdsorganisasjon: tilpasningsprosess og restriktiv form: et synspunkt på økonomisk endring. In *Sosialantropologiske grunntekster* (ed.) T.H. Eriksen, 147-64. Oslo: Gyldendal.

SAHLINS, M. 1974. *Stone Age economics*. London: Tavistock.

SHANIN, T. (ed.) 1971. *Peasant societies*. Harmondsworth: Penguin.

STAVENHAGEN, R. 1973 [1969]. *Las clases sociales en las sociedades agrarias*. Mexico: Siglo XXI.

STENNING, D.J. 1969 [1958]. Household viability among the pastoral Fulani. In *The developmental cycle in domestic groups* (ed.) J. Goody, 99-119. Cambridge: University Press.

TSING, A. 2009. Supply chains and the human condition. *Rethinking Marxism: Journal of Economics, Culture and Society* **21**, 148-76.

WOLF, E.R. 1966. *Peasants*. Englewood Cliffs, N.J.: Prentice-Hall.

YANAGISAKO, S. 1979. Family and household: the analysis of domestic groups. *Annual Review of Anthropology* **8**, 161-205.

——— 2002. *Producing culture and capital: family firms in Italy*. Princeton: University Press.

Reconquérir la maisonnée : réflexions sur le travail, les relations productives et la valeur économique

Résumé

Les régimes de travail organisent non seulement l'économie, mais aussi les vies. Avec la déréglementation constante du marché du travail et la recherche des réductions de coûts, il devient difficile de saisir non seulement les modes de fonctionnement du capital mais aussi l'impact de ces processus sur l'organisation des vies quotidiennes au travail. Il faut pour cela prêter attention à la valeur, en combinant économie politique et économie morale. L'auteure suggère que l'analyse de la maisonnée est un moyen de relever ces défis. Elle ouvre un accès ethnographique à une dynamique temporelle particulière, qui révèle une texture de multiples couches de précarité, révélant tout à la fois les réalités matérielles et les relations intimes de la vie. Les régimes de travail et les régimes de valeur peuvent ainsi être ramenés dans le même cadre, en retraçant des dépendances relationnelles aussi bien que des structures d'inégalité sociale. À partir d'une ethnographie antérieure parmi les cultivateurs de tabac non propriétaires de leurs terres à Corrientes, en Argentine, l'article attire l'attention sur les possibilités d'un point de vue particulier, tout en s'attachant au contexte historique et politique spécifique. L'anthropologie est bien placée pour appréhender les configurations contemporaines du travail et la manière dont celles-ci sont encadrées par les inégalités sociales et politiques et contribuent à les reproduire, non seulement au niveau local mais à une échelle plus largement mondiale.

5

Wage-labour and a double separation in Papua New Guinea and beyond

KEIR MARTIN *University of Oslo*

In this essay, I explore how the idea of wage-labour is used to perform a double separation within and between persons. The first aspect of this separation is a separation of activities that are characterized as 'labour' from the person performing the activity thus characterized. This separation is the precondition for the second separation: namely a partial and often contested separation between the two parties to the contested wage-labour transaction. Ethnographically, I explore how the idea of wage-labour has been used to perform this double separation in Papua New Guinea in recent years. The analysis of these separations has a long pedigree in Western critical thought, the first being at the heart of Marx's conception of the worker as person in a capitalist political economy, for example. The second separation creates the possibility of momentary perspectives from which persons can present themselves increasingly as discrete individuals separate from the claims of others. Ethnographic analysis demonstrates how the category of 'labour' and related idioms create possibilities for the historically shifting emergence and dissolution of different idioms of the person in contemporary PNG, which is taken as a specific instance of an important global phenomenon.

In this essay, I explore how the idea of wage-labour is used to perform a double separation within and between persons. The first aspect of this separation is a separation of activities that are characterized as 'labour' from the person performing the activity thus characterized. This separation is the precondition for the second separation: namely a partial and often contested separation between the two parties to the contested wage-labour transaction. Thus labour is 'dislocated' (or, as Polanyi might have it, 'disembedded') from wider networks of relational obligation; a dislocation that then partially dislocates particular persons from such networks, whether they desire that partial dislocation or not. These separations are largely rhetorical as well as being always incomplete and potentially partially reversible. But their rhetorical expression should not be taken as a sign of their unimportance. It is through rhetorical attempts to use the category of 'labour' or related idioms, as opposed to other potential descriptions of particular activities and relationships, that the reach of moral obligations is extended or curtailed in practice.

Journal of the Royal Anthropological Institute (N.S.), 89-101

Ethnographically, I explore how the idea of wage-labour has been used to perform this double separation in Papua New Guinea in recent years. The analysis of these separations has a long pedigree in Western critical thought, the first being at the heart of Marx's conception of the worker as person in a capitalist political economy, for example. The second separation creates the possibility of momentary perspectives from which persons can present themselves increasingly as discrete individuals separate from the claims of others. Land disputes are a common arena for battles over the extent to which claims and obligations can be successfully limited and controlled. In this essay, I look at two examples of people who are using the idea of wage-labour as an attempt to curtail more enduring relations that they have with others, and in particular their attempts to use this characterization as a means of separating their land from those relationships.

Tony's block

The examples given here are based upon fieldwork conducted with the Matupit community in Papua New Guinea's East New Britain province. Until its devastation in a volcanic eruption in 1994, Matupit was well known as one of the most 'economically developed' villages in PNG owing to its proximity to the town of Rabaul. In the aftermath of the eruption, large numbers of villagers relocated to a government-organized resettlement scheme in the rainforest at Sikut, whilst others returned to the ruins of Matupit. The provincial government had given many of those willing to make the move three-hectare blocks to develop cash cropping. These blocks were given to individuals or individual nuclear families with the clear intent that they would most commonly be passed on inside patrilineal nuclear families to the head of household's own offspring, rather than being subject to the overlapping claims of matrilineal clans (or *vunatarai* in the language of Tolai people, Kuanua); a form of land tenure held by many to discourage economic investment and development (see Martin 2013: 30-99).

My first example concerns the block held by Tony Dannet.[1] Tony was the chair of the resettlement committee that directed policy and attempted to guide day-to-day affairs at Sikut. One evening towards the end of September 2002, I was at his house when the conversation turned, as it frequently did, to the future of land at the site. Other residents had often informed me that the land at Sikut was 'better because it is not customary land'. But although the majority of Sikut residents were in favour of this transformation in land tenure, they remained aware of the enduring power of the extended reciprocal obligations embedded within the idea of 'custom' (or '*kastom*' in Tok Pisin, the lingua franca of Papua New Guinea). Consequently, there was a degree of fear among some that customary obligations might establish themselves by back-door means at Sikut. According to many people, if anyone allowed custom to reappear on their land, despite the state's support to keep it out, then it would have been down to that person's weakness or lack of care in policing the borders of custom. Most people were still involved in customary practices and the keeping of customary relational obligations, but they were keen to ensure that, unlike in the past, those obligations did not interfere with their own children's access to their land and investments that they had made on it.

Tony was a well-educated man with an extensive English vocabulary. He had been a senior government official in the last days of the colonial regime and the early post-independence era of the 1970s, but was now living back in the village. It was this experience that made him a suitable occupant of his current voluntary position in the eyes of many Sikut residents. He told me how important it was to keep the clan out of bought land or resettlement land and how the clan system of land 'doesn't work in new economic situations'. He followed this up by telling me that Tolai people were moving away from the clan to the individual family, 'more like your situation'. Tony went on to explain that in the past, people were tied by 'reciprocal obligations'.[2] Now when I get people to work for me, Tony told me, I make a point of 'paying them individually'. Doing this 'negates their claim' to the land. But if you let your relatives 'help' on the land, then that is where the trouble starts. If you do that, then 'they can imagine they are part of an old system' of reciprocal obligations that includes rights to land. Tony told me that he had to get some of his relatives to help him on his new land at Sikut in the months immediately after the volcano erupted, but laid great stress again on the way in which he had 'paid them individually', and that this 'buys off any customary claim'.

Tony then told me that other people in the community were looking to educated men with some financial independence, such as himself, for leadership in this respect because 'looking after our individual families is more important now than looking after the clan. This is because of economic changes. Now the land is like an investment'.

I replied that Eli, one of the educated men whom he had mentioned, had recently told me that although some people might end up allowing the clan back on to private land, that this was simply the result of weakness. Tony agreed with this assessment. There is no need 'to let custom in through the back door', he told me, and you can 'protect your property rights through the law if you want to', although this can be difficult in practice if you have already let clan members on to the land to help and they have ended up staying. He concluded by informing me that customary land 'was the major obstacle to economic development'.

Tony's comments repeated a story about land that I was familiar with in East New Britain, but they also revealed the ways in which characterizations of land and labour were intimately linked. Linkages between human activity (which in some contexts might be characterized as 'labour') and land are often noted in the regional ethnographic literature.[3] Epstein (1969: 126) observes how original claims to land among Tolai were made on the basis of the initial effort expended on clearing an area of bush (*pui*: Kuanua). These claims to land had then to be kept alive by constant insertions of human activity. Hence a *vunatarai* might have an interest in letting its relatives use land that it currently had no use for, as it kept alive a claim over land that might be useful in the future. Epstein was describing a historical period around the time of the establishment of colonial rule in the 1880s, when the Tolai population numbered a few thousand and the situation was predominantly characterized by a shortage of persons relative to land that could be claimed. By the time of his fieldwork in the late 1950s, the condition was already being reversed owing to a population explosion and, in addition, the tendency to view land as an 'investment' as a result of developments such as cash cropping (see below).

If the problem for the Tolai Big Men of the early colonial period was how to attract the human activity on to their land that would preserve and extend their claims, then the problem for the family heads of today is how to limit the claims that can be made on their lands by those whose active engagement with the land they might occasionally require; or, more crucially perhaps, how to limit the claims that can be made on the basis of the category of '(wage-)labour'. Clearing a three-hectare block of virgin rainforest, planting it with crops, and establishing a household on that block requires a large amount of activity, and most individual families will need to bring in others at various points over the years to achieve this. The question then becomes on what basis is this done and how is it characterized: as 'work', 'help', or 'labour', for example? All of these English words were used in conversations that I had with Tolai on these issues, along with Tok Pisin equivalents, such as 'wok' ('work' or 'labour') and 'halivim' ('help'). Elsewhere (Martin 2013: 92), I have written about the way in which some Matupi described to me a past pattern of related clans gardening on each other's land as part of a network of relations organized around repeating cross-cousin marriage that was designed to keep alive claims to gardening land; a habit that has now almost totally disappeared. This labour was described to me in Tok Pisin as 'halivim' (help), but in the Tolai vernacular, Kuanua, as 'wariruru', a word that would be most accurately glossed in English as 'respect'. This is one example of the kind of 'old system' of interlocking reciprocal obligations that Tony was referring to. The issue is not simply what labour is invested in land, but also how the categorization of that labour shapes its effects as much as it describes them.

Tony was keen to stress on several occasions that he paid for the labour 'individually'. By characterizing the payment in this manner, he hoped to ensure that the payment thus described would separate the labour from the person doing it. The person doing the labour might well be a relative, but Tony's payment was characterized as a payment for that labour, not as a prestation offered to the person as a whole in recognition of that relationship. That relationship between persons might endure, but Tony was keen to at least attempt to ensure that by paying them in this context as individuals he could separate the labour out from the person to whom he was related. By separating the labour from the persons to whom he might otherwise be related, he hoped simultaneously to separate the land in which their labour had been invested from those self-same relationships.

Limiting and extending the claims of labour

The separation that Tony made was to separate a particular capacity to labour from the rest of the person who was exercising those capacities and their other activities and relations. This is the same separation that Marx (1902 [1849]) describes as being at the heart of the distinction between capitalist and non-capitalist societies: namely the separation of the capacity to labour ('labour power') from the total human person of whom it is an aspect, and the consequent commodification of that capacity (individual 'wage-labour'). And the distinction between wage-labour transactions separated from their transactors and other kinds of activity that are constitutive of ongoing relations of reciprocal obligation between them can of course be seen as a key example of the distinction between commodities and gifts drawn by Gregory (1982), which Strathern (1988) put at the heart of her subsequent distinction between Western society and Melanesian sociality. In practice, this boundary between wage-labour and other forms of activity is porous, much as Carsten (2013) describes how the boundary between labour and kinship is porous in the blood bank that she studied in Penang. But as Carsten's (2013: 122) work also illustrates, despite her informants acknowledging the porousness of that boundary, they are also keen to assert that it can never be absolutely porous any more than it can be absolutely hermetically sealed. If things are to get done and if illegitimate claims and activities are to be resisted, then the appropriate place of the boundary has to be continually reasserted and its porousness has to be policed. Tony's claim that by 'paying individually' he has 'bought off any customary claim' is like Mr Dombey's statement in the opening chapter of Dickens' Dombey and Son that making wet-nursing ' a matter of wages … brings to an end any relationship' between him and the impoverished woman whom he has hired to breastfeed his son (Dickens 1848: 12). Both are attempts to police and maintain the boundary between wage-labour and kinship and both are expressions of an anxiety that the porousness of that boundary might run out of control.

The lines between wage-labour and other kinds of relations are normally potentially blurred, and this tendency can be seen either as a problem to be purified or as an opportunity to be exploited, across the political spectrum, depending upon the context. The politically centrist UK sociologist Michael Young, who was one of the co-authors of the groundbreaking study *Family and kinship in East London* (Young & Wilmott 1957), later went on to bemoan the loss of the ways in which new labour in East End factories used to be recruited through employers' and foremen's knowledge of the young recruits' elder male relatives. In these cases, the fact that recruitment was intimately tied into kinship structures outside of the home meant that the discipline of the family was carried over into the workplace, as the elder relatives would be held responsible for the behaviour of the younger workers whom they had raised and vouched for. The deliberate blurring of a distinction between labour and other forms of relationship helped to maintain a stronger discipline inside the factory than would have been allowed by a purely 'labour' relationship based upon a strict conceptual opposition between wage-labour and domestic labour or kinship relations. The subsequent reinforcement of a separation between wage-labour and local kinship networks caused by socioeconomic restructuring is described as one of the major causes for the regrettable disintegration of the old communities romanticized by Young (e.g. Dench, Gavron & Young 2006: 123-5). The idea of wage-labour, then, acts as a powerful frame by means of which particular obligations are separated out from other obligations, but that separation is never absolutely rigid or absolutely porous. Instead, there are always different interests in having wage-labour separate or cut the chains of obligation at different points, with the result that the meaning of wage-labour, what obligations it separates from others and the degree to which that separation is absolute, is always a matter of some contestation and anxiety.

The case of Dombey in Dickens' novel illustrates this beautifully. Dombey's attempt to use the idiom of wage-labour to limit the relation between his son and his son's wet-nurse is the action that to a large extent frames the eight hundred pages that follow. But is this act of separation the outcome of the individual will of the man who invokes it, or does that act itself rely upon a series of relational entanglements that its author might only acknowledge with some reluctance? Two-thirds of the way through the book, we learn that Dombey's evil office manager, Mr Carker, has taken on one of the wet-nurse's children as an apprentice, seemingly in order to protect Dombey from the claims that the child wishes to make upon him on the basis of their families' previous relationship. When Dombey discovers this after several months, he observes that this action goes well beyond the demands that an employer should expect from an employee in return for his wages, to which Carker responds that it is a natural overstepping of the bounds of duty from someone who is honoured to serve such a great man. It is indicative of Dombey's arrogant belief in the moral superiority that his possession of vast wealth gives him over other men that he instantly accepts this explanation, failing to perceive the possibility for deceit and betrayal that is already clear to the reader. He is happy to assume that another man will transcend the boundaries of a relationship allegedly limited by the concept of wage-labour in order to protect his

Journal of the Royal Anthropological Institute (N.S.), 89-101
© Royal Anthropological Institute 2018

desire to enforce that limitation in the context of another relationship. What Dickens' intuitive genius illustrates here is that even at the heart of the most powerful commodity exchange institution in history (Dombey is head of the pre-eminent clearing house in London at a time when the city was the undisputed economic capital of the world), the limitation of relational obligations in one context can always be seen as resting upon their extension in others. And that Dombey's constitution of himself as a self-reliant individual holder of property in his person and his wealth is not an act of will expressive of the internal constitution of the man himself, but is itself reliant on relations with others that explicitly transcend the limitations imposed by their characterization as wage-labour. Dombey's separation of wage-labour from kinship relies upon Carker deliberately outstepping the bounds of his wage-labour relationship to Dombey in order to protect him from the wet-nurse's family. The idiom of wage-labour may be an attempt to separate persons and thus constitute them as distinct individuals, but that separation itself relies upon a separation of the person from their labour; a separation that may well rely upon other relational entanglements and whose effects can never be entirely safely predicted or contained.

The Wudal block

In the mid-1950s, the Australian colonial administration launched a number of smaller resettlement schemes for already overcrowded villages close to Rabaul, such as Matupit, the most notable of which was the Wudal resettlement scheme. Like the Sikut blocks forty years later, the blocks in these schemes were supposed to be held by individuals and to be passed on inside (ideally patrilineal) nuclear families, thus breaking the 'problem' of extended customary obligation associated with matrilineally reckoned clan land. But when the anthropologist Jim Fingleton (1985) conducted a survey at Wudal in the 1980s, he discovered that a majority of the blocks where the original landholder had died had ended up in the possession of one of his sister's children or another clan relative instead of his own children. As people at Sikut sometimes put it to me, 'custom had come back inside the land' at Wudal, an outcome that most were keen to avoid at Sikut. Indeed, it was the experience of Wudal that had led so many to be wary of letting relatives on to the land, whether that was described as the block holder helping the relatives by letting them stay or as the relatives helping the block holder to develop his block. Tony's wry description of how paying a wage for work was designed to stop 'labour' being thought of as this kind of 'help' with obligations attached was echoed more forcefully by other Sikut residents (e.g. Martin 2013: 59).

I was aware of three Wudal blocks that had been allocated to Matupit residents in the 1960s, and in keeping with Fingleton's observations, two of these were now occupied by clan relatives of the original block holder and only one was occupied, as it was 'supposed' to be, by one of his offspring. But in one of the two cases, there was an ongoing dispute in which one of the children of the original block holder was trying to remove the niece who currently had ownership of the block. At the time of my fieldwork, the block was inhabited by a woman who was the maternal niece of a maternal nephew of the original block holder, meaning that the block had been transmitted according to 'customary' matrilineal principles over two generations. In May 2003, I discussed the case with the son of the original block holder, who was pursuing a legal case to reclaim the block. For reasons of space and because the case is still ongoing, I have left some details unexplored, but what is clear is the way in which the idea characterizing labour is central to the outcome of the ongoing dispute.

Journal of the Royal Anthropological Institute (N.S.), 89-101
© Royal Anthropological Institute 2018

The complainant's wife began our conversation by stressing how her husband had himself worked on his father's block. Even if he could technically make a claim purely on the basis of inheritance, she was keen to stress that he had also had an input into the land on this basis. The maternal nephew of the original block holder (and maternal uncle of the current occupier) also worked and stayed on the block at this time, but she was keen to stress that he was paid to do so, 'like a labourer'.[4] Once again, it was not simply the labour but the characterization of the labour and of its accompanying payments that was important. Like Tony, the complainant's wife was hopeful that characterizing the payment as a wage payment would make clear that the labour it paid for was to be considered not as a part of a customary network of reciprocal obligations but as separate from the person to whom it related. The complainant's wife told me that this situation had 'driven a wedge' between her husband and his father's clan that was 'very hurtful'. The ways in which labour has been characterized helped to create a number of divisions. From the complainant's perspective, the mischaracterization of his relative's labour as being 'help' and not the labour of a '(wage-)labourer' helped to drive a division between him and his father's clan, meaning that some of his brothers now refused to fulfil their customary obligations to their father's clan at funerals, for example. His characterization of the labour as wage-labour provided a different perspective from which his relative was internally separated into a person to whom he was still ideally customarily related and an essence of labour from which he stood separate once the wage transaction was complete. If such a separation between the current occupant's uncle and his labour were to be accepted, then the existing 'hurtful' separation between the complainant and his father's clan could perhaps be overcome.

The situation described in this version of events was complicated in a subsequent discussion that I had with the claimant a few months later in August 2003. Here the nature of the payments made to the complainant's cousin who ended up with occupancy of the block was described a little more ambiguously. At one point, he insisted that the 'clan' did not 'help' with the development of the block, but did say that sometime 'some guys from the village' (Matupit) came, leaving it unclear as to whether or how his father was related to them. Despite this, he claimed that it was 'mostly us' (i.e. his father's nuclear family) who did the work on the block at this point. He also stressed that his father paid them Aus£6 a month, which would have been a significant sum in the late 1950s, enough to classify as a reasonable wage and not the kind of minor gift that might be conceptualized as a part of the flow of small-scale help back and forth between parties related by ongoing customary links. However, when the story moved forward to the 1970s and 1980s, the relationship between labour, payment, and land was presented in a slightly less clear-cut manner. The complainant described how his father had been sick throughout the 1960s and how he and his brothers had commuted to work on the block up until 1967, when the complainant's father had put the complainant's cousin on the block to look after it. The complainant described this situation in Tok Pisin as one in which '*papa wok long baim en wantaim sampela liklik toea long pe bilong en*' ('my father used to pay him with some small amounts of money as his pay'). This is a far less forceful statement than the one regarding the £6 a month given to guys from the village back in the 1950s. The phrase '*liklik toea*' ('few pennies') potentially implies an amount of money far below the market wage-labour value of the previous example that is intended to buy off any subsequent claim. Indeed the phrase '*liklik toea*' is one that I heard on daily basis at Matupit and Sikut to describe small gifts of money that were intended to show a degree of respect and assistance to someone who had offered some kind of help or service as part of an ongoing relationship, and ninety-nine times out of a hundred it would be succeeded by the words '*long halivim*' ('for help[ing]'). What is being described here could easily sound more like a few *toea* for help (intended both as return for the help that might have been given and as a small reciprocal assistance for the person to whom the money was being given). The complainant here is therefore unusual in following the phrase *liklik toea* with *long pe bilong en* ('for his pay'). Like Tony, he understands that you cannot be seen to be allowing the clan on to the land to 'help' as part of an ongoing relationship of reciprocal obligation, as once you do that, the land becomes a part of that relationship. He therefore describes the *liklik toea* as a 'payment', but the very phrase *liklik toea* implies a recognition that the amount of money given might characterize the nature of this transaction more ambiguously, and that, consequently, its degree of separation from other aspects of their relationship is not as absolute as he might like.

As the complainant told this story in more detail, this element of ambiguity increased. It turned out that his family were also giving the occupant food alongside the *liklik toea* (a classic illustration that the money was merely one part of what might be characterized as an ongoing relationship of mutual assistance rather than a wage), and then in 1969 his father had the idea of giving his nephew rights to the first block of cocoa that he had planted 'instead of paying him … while he looked after the whole block'. The complainant told me that his father had said that he did this to '*kompensatim em long wok*' ('compensate him for his work'), and that his nephew could harvest this cocoa for as long as he was there, but that '*graun stap yet ananit long papa*' ('the land remains under the control of its owner'). Yet the attempt to linguistically limit the expectations raised by this characterization of it as 'compensation for work' was clearly of limited effect in this instance. The very act of allowing the current occupant to settle on the land and to claim the cocoa harvest as his own was enough to permit different characterizations of the current occupant's labour, and in particular how it was embedded in ongoing relationships.[5]

Discussing the case with the niece now resident on the block unsurprisingly yielded a similar story, but told with a significantly different emphasis. She passed over a key reason why the block passed to her uncle, namely owing to the original block holder losing his mental faculties as a result of malaria. She mentioned that her uncle had planted all the cocoa on the block, but again did not volunteer any information as to when that was done or what payments may have accompanied that activity. Although she had initially received support when she took over the block from a member of her own *vunatarai*, she now worked with her children and paid local young men 10 Kina a day (at the time of my fieldwork this was around £2) for major work on an 'as needed' basis. This amount was short of what, for example, someone working in a store in town might make, but it was about the going rate for this kind of casual rural labour and was not low enough to necessarily imply an ongoing relationship of reciprocal obligation. Now, she told me, the clan did not come from Matupit at all, and she had only allowed her mother's brothers on to the block twice to collect cocoa for sale. Arguably, she could be seen as attempting to use the same wage-labour device to limit the claims of her own clan that the original block holder's son was attempting to wield against her in court. The block, she told me, was just for her family. She would not let the 'other line' (her clan) in to it. Although, given matrilineal principles of descent, her children would be members of the same *vunatarai*, she was keen to make sure that as far as possible her children gained the benefits of her work on the block in a manner that was in some regard similar to men who wished to protect their children's interests from comparable claims.

It is precisely this kind of experience that leads so many at Sikut to be very wary of allowing 'nephews' on to the land to 'help', as was the case in this block at Wudal. Many refuse to allow them on to the block or else, like Tony, are keen to ensure that any payment made is clearly characterized as an individual wage and not as help. The complainant in the second case was quite clear in his expectation that his family's experience would not be repeated this time around with the block holders at Sikut. '*Bipo mipela no bin save long holim graun* ... *case bilong mi i wanpela exception tasol*' ('In the past we didn't know how to keep hold of land ... my case is just one exception'[6]). He told me that it was true that clan members could put 'back-door' pressure on block holders to allow them use of the land, but that if it ever came to a dispute these days, the government would always back the principle that this was not customary land. He contrasted this with the situation in the 1950s and 1960s, when he claimed that this knowledge was not as universally shared and many people then thought that all land was customary land.

It will not be clear for many years yet what patterns of block occupancy will emerge at Sikut. According to Isaac ToLanger, one of the 'educated men' name-checked by Tony, to really know what had happened as a result of the volcanic eruption and the subsequent resettlement would take ongoing fieldwork until around 2050. Nonetheless, by the time of my last visit in 2010, there were signs that Sikut was not entirely following the Wudal experience. There was a tussle over some blocks, but it seemed in many cases as if the ability to keep the clan off of the block, if not total in all cases, was stronger than it had been four decades earlier (see Martin 2013). On my return to Sikut in 2010, Tony had died, but his widow and children remained in occupancy of the block and I saw little sign or expectation that his nephews would have any chance of removing his children upon his widow's death. The rhetorical attempt to use wage-labour to limit other obligations is not a magic spell that miraculously transforms those who wish to use it into the 'man in nature' who wanders the pages of Locke's *Second treatise on government* (1698). But neither is it empty rhetoric with no impact upon relational entanglements. It both reflects and is part of shaping trends that enable the increasing, if partial, limitation of such claims in some contexts.

Concluding remarks

Land was not the only context in which debates over the meaning and entanglement of labour occurred, although it was perhaps the most important. Elsewhere (Martin 2007: 291; 2013: 256), I have written about a dispute over a petrol station in Rabaul that had been destroyed in the eruption of 1994. The petrol station had been built in the late 1970s by one of Matupit's best-known and most controversial 'Big Shots' (a term for the newly emerging socioeconomic elite in post-independence PNG), who had employed many of his own clan relatives in the early years of the business. He claimed to have paid them a fair market wage and they claimed that he had paid token 'help' and that they had been assisting him as part of their clan relationship to him. Consequently, the successful business, and the profits derived from it, were not entirely to be seen as the fruits of his entrepreneurial 'labour' alone. For the relatives, the work that they did for the Big Shot was as entangled with the clan as the ritual obligations that he was still happy to acknowledge.

Likewise the idea of '*kastom*' acts as a powerful marker of the limits of reciprocal interdependence that in some respects is similar to 'labour'. Often it works by virtue of opposition to a commonplace opposite, most commonly 'business' ('*bisnis*', Tok Pisin), or on occasion a 'market' (see Martin 2013: 130). Most often, to claim that what someone is doing is business is to argue that they have forgotten about or attempted to cut themselves out of reciprocal obligations at a point where they should be remembered. The order of evaluation can sometimes be reversed, however, and at times it is the inability to distinguish business from customary relations that is held to be the sickness that holds back Papua New Guineans, whether in specific instances or in general as a nation. The importance of making this kind of distinction between business and custom is often made by the emerging elite, such as ToLanger, who no longer live in the villages, or by men who have the qualifications to be members of such an elite and occupy an economically superior position to most of the villagers whom they still live alongside, such as Tony, or Eli.

On one occasion I was having a conversation in Kokopo with a young university graduate whose job it was to promote small business development in the New Guinea Islands region. The major problem for small businesses in PNG is almost universally acknowledged to be the so-called '*wantok* system': a term for the expectation of reciprocal obligations and assistance that makes demands from relatives and those to whom one has a customary relationship almost impossible to resist. My companion that evening told me that he had boiled down what he had to impart to budding entrepreneurs into one simple message: 'You have to tell your *wantoks* that you are one thing and your business is another'. Like a reversal of Tony's desire to separate his relatives' labour from their person and hence from any ongoing relationship that they might have to him, here the advice from the emerging elite to those who wish to follow in their footsteps is to separate an aspect of their own activity, their business, from themselves so that transactions that their relatives have with it cannot be seen in the context of an ongoing relationship with the rest of their person (see also Martin 2007: 289). Both the idea of wage-labour and the idea of business introduce a separation inside the person between elements of their productive capacities and the rest of their person. Wage-labour most often acts as a means of diminishing the claims that the person so divided can make upon others, whilst business most often acts as a means of diminishing the claims that can be made upon the person divided from their business. Indeed, the reciprocal symmetry between the two separations is hardly accidental as they often help to constitute each other – separating the labour from the labourer is the flipside of the mechanism by which the entrepreneur separates themself from their business. And in both cases the separation is never as absolute as its proponents may sometimes wish. Repeated assertions as to the nature of the separation should be taken not as descriptions of accomplished fact but as expressions of an anxiety that the separation may collapse. But neither should the contingent nature of these separations be taken as evidence of their illusory or false nature. They have very real effects, and the repeated desire of people across the world to make and remake such distinctions shows the importance of their continued construction and defence.

The varying ways in which the idea of (wage-)labour is used to effect separations both between a person and part of their capacities and also between the persons related by such a partially separated capacity should remind us to be wary of universalizing assumptions about the ways in which a unitary actor who is unproblematically the owner of their own labour can use that labour as the basis of claims to property.

Strathern questions frameworks that rest on the analytical assumption of 'everyone *owning their own labor* . . . For the concept that persons own and dispose of the fruits of their labor makes them individual proprietors of it' (1988: 140, emphasis in the original).

In doing so, she is questioning the ways in which these assumptions, characteristic of what Macpherson (1962) described as 'possessive individualism', sometimes underpin even Marxist and feminist anthropological analyses of non-capitalist societies. Even if the labour described in these ethnographic accounts 'cannot circulate in commodity form', Strathern is still keen to draw attention to the 'proprietorial assumption' that she argues underpins them, namely 'the unitary identification between persons (as subjects) and the products of their activity (work)' (1988: 140). Equally, however, we should be wary of taking that critique as being the basis for dividing the world up into a 'Western' or 'Euro-American' world in which non-partible individuals own their labour and other areas in which such assumptions do not hold. What the two cases that I have outlined here demonstrate is that contemporary Melanesians are perfectly capable at particular moments of presenting a picture in which labour is a separable aspect of a person designed to construct two persons related by that labour as discretely separable individuals, in particular contexts at least.

More generally, the very idea of the individual self-proprietor at the heart of classical 'Western' theories of person and property itself often rests on particular moments of personal partibility. The idea of labour as a particular capacity at the core of the person and their rights to property in themselves and, most crucially, those external objects that they can claim property rights in itself relies on the idea that labour is a capacity of the person that can be partially detached from the person and put into relations with the outside world. Take, for example, Locke's claim, used to justify individual property, that, 'The labour that was mine, removing them out of the common state that they were in, hath fixed my Property in them' (1698: 187).

This labour is for Locke 'the unquestionable property of the labourer' (1698: 186), providing one of the key foundational statements of the kind of universalizing analytical assumption of individualism critiqued by Strathern. And it is implicitly assumed to be non-relational in origin for Locke (although not for many subsequent Western theorists who also placed labour at the core of human existence, most notably Marx), thus explaining its clearly 'natural' status as the core of the individual's self-proprietorship. In order for it to operate as such, however, it has to be described in a manner that equally strongly implies that it is a partible 'property' of the person that is separable from the rest of the person of whom it is a core constituent. Locke describes, for example, how the person who claims property in this manner '*lay(s) out something upon it* that was his own; his labour' (1698: 189, emphasis added). Likewise, we are told that the man who alters aspects of nature '*by placing any of his labour upon them*, did thereby acquire a property in them' (1698: 193, original emphasis removed, new emphasis added). Both quotes are suggestive of labour as a 'property' that is not merely a characteristic of a person, like breathing or eye colour, but also as a possession that can be held separate from the person who owns it and then 'laid out' upon the world in order to transform both the world and aspects of the world's relationship to that person, namely by transforming it into his 'property' as well. The property claimant removes something from the 'state of nature' when 'he hath mixed his labour with, and joined it to something that is his own, and thereby makes it his property' (1698: 185).

Locke's language here suggests that labour is a property that is somehow separate or separable from the person's other properties (i.e. characteristics or capacities), and that when thus put into relation or 'joined' to aspects of the external world creates a new kind of property in the sense of legal ownership.

We have been familiar, at least since Macpherson (1962), with the idea that property in one's person is the never explicitly stated yet indispensable precondition and foundational template for the rise to dominance of the mutually constituting idioms of property and individualism in the political theory of the early bourgeois age. Perhaps the quotes above suggest that we could add something to that perspective: namely that the conception of 'labour' as a 'property' – both in the sense of being an innate individual property (or characteristic) of each person and simultaneously and most crucially in the sense of being a possession of the person that has to be partially separated from that person in order for it to make fundamental transformations in the world – is itself an implicit assumption that is fundamental to the conception of self-proprietorship explored by Macpherson. Rather than living in a world in which partible conceptions of persons are counterposed to individually discrete conceptions,[7] we instead live in a world in which different kinds of partibility occur at different moments as a fundamental component of the constitution of different kinds of idioms of the person, including that of the individual who owns their own capacity to labour. Locke's person may be conceived of as ontologically individual and prior to the relations that they enter into. But their ability to enter into the particular relations with the world that constitute them as the highest form of individual, namely the modern property owner, relies upon a conception that a 'property' that is fundamentally constitutive of their person, namely their labour, can be partially detached from them and 'mixed' with aspects of the world in order to then create a relationship of property ownership with that aspect of the world. And important as this conception has been to political theory and practice since its inception, it is in no way the basis for a 'Western' conception of the person. It is entirely possible to have a 'modern' or 'Western' theory of the person that is based upon the detachability of labour that is not ontologically individualist in this manner, of which Marx is the most notable example. And even in the classic bourgeois form of the conception of possessive individualism as the ontological state of being, as described by Macpherson, such a state of being is only maintained by the minority who are able to detach their labour and use it to establish a relationship of property in external objects (whether they be inert, animal, or the bodies of other humans) and thus avoid relationships of dependence with other persons. This is a situation in many regards radically different from Strathern's (1988: 200) description of how the *moka* exchange cycle of the PNG Highlands might be seen as a means by which 'something that he [the person] made out of relations with agnates' can be reappropriated 'individually and separately' in relations with exchange partners, in which the starting assumption is a relational entanglement from which individuality has to be carved. But in both cases formations of individual autonomy are always vulnerable to other perspectives from which they can be seen to rest upon the manipulation of partible relationality.

NOTES

Fieldwork was conducted between 2002 and 2005 and in 2010. The fieldwork was supported by research grants from the Economic and Social Research Council, the Wenner Gren Foundation, and the Danish Research Council. I am grateful for comments and suggestions from the Labour Reading group at the Department of Social Anthropology at the University of Oslo, from participants at a workshop held on labour and anthropology in Oslo in June 2015, and also from Marilyn Strathern.

[1] All persons described in this account have been given pseudonyms in order to lessen the possibility that this account might be used in any ongoing or future disputes.

[2] Unlikely as it might appear, this was the exact English phrase that he used. Partly this is due to his background as an educated former member of the elite, but also perhaps to the long history of anthropological research at Matupit and surrounding villages, in particular by A.L. Epstein, whose involvement with Matupit over thirty-five years had an impact upon many Matupi.

[3] See Martin (2013: 30-99) for an overview of some of these discussions.

[4] This interview was conducted in a mixture of Kuanua, Tok Pisin, and English, and the complainant's wife switched to English at this point in order to make sure the point was totally clear.

[5] Pickles (2013: 520) discusses in another PNG context how the phrase 'liklik mani' (small [amount of] money) can be used rhetorically to demonstrate that although the amount of money given by one person to another is small, it potentially marks a large proportion of what the donor has available and should thus still be judged as generous. By this reading, the complainant here could also be attempting to stress his father's generosity at a time when the block was still being developed and money might not have been readily available.

[6] By which in this context he meant 'example' of the trend from the past, but a case that should ideally be seen as an exception from contemporary standards.

[7] Let alone a world in which some geographical regions are dominated by partibility and others by discrete bounded individuality.

REFERENCES

CARSTEN, J. 2013. Ghosts, commensality and scuba diving. In *Vital relations: modernity and the persistent life of kinship* (eds) S. McKinnon & F. Cannell, 109-30. Santa Fe, N.M.: SAR Press.

DENCH, G., K. GAVRON & M. YOUNG 2006. *The new East End: kinship, race and conflict*. London: Profile.

DICKENS, C. 1848. *Dombey and Son*. London: Bradbury & Evans.

EPSTEIN, A.L. 1969. *Matupit: land, politics and change among the Tolai of New Britain*. Canberra: ANU Press.

FINGLETON, J. 1985. Changing land tenure in Melanesia: the Tolai experience. Ph.D. thesis, Australian National University.

GREGORY, C. 1982. *Gifts and commodities*. London: Academic Press.

LOCKE, J. 1698. *Two treatises on government*. London: Awnsham/John Churchill.

MACPHERSON, C. 1962. *The political theory of possessive individualism: Hobbes to Locke*. Oxford: University Press.

MARTIN, K. 2007. Your own *buai* you must buy: the ideology of possessive individualism in Papua New Guinea. *Anthropological Forum* 17, 285-98.

——— 2013. *The death of the Big Men and the rise of the Big Shots*. New York: Berghahn Books.

MARX, K. 1902 [1849]. *Wage-labour and capital*. New York: New York Labor News Company.

PICKLES, A. 2013. Pocket calculator: a humdrum 'obviator' in Papua New Guinea? *Journal of the Royal Anthropological Institute* (N.S.) 19, 510-26.

STRATHERN, M. 1988. *The gender of the gift: problems with women and problems with society in Melanesia*. Berkeley: University of California Press.

YOUNG, M. & P. WILMOTT 1957. *Family and kinship in East London*. London: Routledge & Kegan Paul.

Travail rémunéré et double séparation en Papouasie-Nouvelle-Guinée et ailleurs

Résumé

Le présent essai explore l'utilisation de la notion de travail rémunéré pour réaliser une double séparation dans et entre les personnes. La première est une séparation entre les activités qualifiées de « travail » et la personne qui exécute ces activités. Celle-ci est un préalable à la seconde séparation, partielle et souvent contestée, entre les deux parties prenantes à la transaction travail-salaire. L'auteur explore, du point de vue ethnographique, la manière dont l'idée de travail rémunéré a été utilisée, ces dernières années, pour réaliser cette double séparation en Papouasie-Nouvelle-Guinée. L'analyse de ces séparations n'est pas nouvelle dans la pensée critique occidentale : ainsi, la première est au centre de la conception selon Marx du travailleur comme personne dans une économie politique capitaliste. La deuxième crée la possibilité de perspectives momentanées à partir desquelles les personnes peuvent se présenter, de plus en plus, comme des individus séparés, distincts des revendications des autres. L'analyse ethnographique démontre la manière dont la catégorie « travail » et les idiomes qui lui sont liés créent des possibilités d'émergence et de dissolution, fluctuantes dans l'histoire, de différents idiomes de la personne en Papouasie-Nouvelle-Guinée contemporaine, exemple spécifique d'un important phénomène global.

Disorganization, precarity, and affect

of 're-learning' working skills (Hurrle *et al.* 2012) to state work-to-deserve-welfare programmes and many other programmes that have proliferated over the last decade (Roberman 2014; Serrano Pascual & Magnusson 2007; van Baar 2012; van Berkel & Borghi 2008; Wacquant 2010).

This shift represented a new effort in managing the historically ambivalent public attitudes towards poverty and work in Slovakia, moving the emphasis on the continuum of deserving and undeserving poor towards the moralizing yardstick assessing individuals' efforts, motivation, and proactive search for formal jobs as indexed by an active carving out of entrepreneurial subjectivity. More generally, as Narotzky (2015: 180) argues, this moral(izing) shift towards personal responsibility and the entrepreneurial self of the worker can be seen as one of the constitutive aspects of flexible capitalism in general. In her ethnography of an unemployment office in Riga, Ozolina-Fitzgerald (2016) shows how the politics of activation and of waiting coexist and operate as a key mechanism of neoliberal biopolitics.

Long-term unemployed citizens in Slovakia were interpellated as passive subjects in need of 'activation' through so-called 'Activation Works', which were meant to lead to their reincorporation into the formal labour market and enhance their prospects of socioeconomic mobility. While the idea of activation promoted an image of flexible and entrepreneurial workers, its everyday practice and key components resembled the older labour regimes in its emphasis on regularity and ordered(-cum-ordering) fixity of the collective work rhythms moulding workers' bodies. This particular refashioning also contributed to reinscribing moral distinctions between 'good' and 'bad' citizens, the former seen as actively trying to find wage-labour and the latter conceived as passively waiting for different forms of state support. In Slovakia, these moral distinctions were firmly entangled within historically developed racialized hierarchies and marginalization of Roma/Gypsies, which continued to be reanimated and vested in new forms.[5]

Considering the relative overrepresentation of Roma/Gypsies amongst the poorest and most marginalized segments of Slovakian society (Filadelfiová, Gerbery & Škobla 2007; Gerbery, Lesay & Škobla 2007), the effects of these reforms were disproportionately felt by this minority population. Roma/Gypsies in Slovakia occupy locations of 'structural vulnerability' (Quesada, Hart & Bourgois 2011) reinforced by the racialized practices of discrimination experienced in their efforts to enter the labour market. With state social assistance suddenly halved and basic benefits falling under the minimum subsistence level, most of the poor had to readjust to these new conditions and alter their survival strategies accordingly. Mastering 'survivalist improvisations' (Ferguson 2015), combined with coping with lowered state support and participating in Activation Works, became crucial for the poor to survive. Since 2004, these changes have also propelled many Roma/Gypsies to migrate westwards with the prospect of greater socioeconomic opportunities and existential movement; the Slovak accession to the EU in particular brought new hopes for Roma/Gypsies to secure a better future by becoming a cheap(er) Eastern European (migrant) labour force in Britain (Grill 2011; 2012; 2015; Pine 2014). The collapse of socialist industries and collective farms and the shift towards capitalism in Slovakia led to several dislocations of labour (Harvey & Krohn-Hansen, this volume). But global capitalism, the softening of border regimes, and enlargement of the EU entailed particular reconfigurations between transnational capital, labour, and places, which turned some groupings into a mobile workforce as cheap migrant labour (in this case, in Britain).

Historical and research contexts

Once a showcase of vaunted socialist progress embodied by various factories, since 1989 the east of Slovakia has been particularly hit by the closing of various industries and companies that previously provided employment for most Roma/Gypsies. During the socialist period, the state's efforts to incorporate Roma/Gypsies into the production process via formal employment formed one of the key principles of official policy and discourse, ascribing 'citizens of Gypsy origin'[6] more equal social citizenship and making them into a working class (see Donert 2017; Stewart 1997). Nearly all Roma/Gypsies worked in construction companies, steel and shoe factories, or collective farms. Although their modes of incorporation in socialist wage-labour were carried out under highly unequal conditions, they constituted a mode of recognized social membership and belonging, and most Roma/Gypsies I spoke to today yearn for the stability associated with socialist wage-labour. The post-socialist socioeconomic restructuring was accompanied by the withdrawal of welfare-state services and the re-emergence of the racialized stigmatization of Gypsies, which overlapped with categorizations of them as workshy and (un)deserving poor. The disadvantaged structural position occupied by Roma/Gypsies was amalgamated with stigmatization and discrimination in the context of access to the radically reconfigured formal labour market and welfare state, in which an increasingly large number of able-bodied men – not only Roma/Gypsies – joined other surplus categories in need of social assistance. For Ferguson (2009; 2015: 156), these changes represent political and analytical disruptions to previous models built on the generalized figure of the wage-labouring 'worker' (together with the coupling of capital and organized labour) and its significance for the domain of 'the social'.

Roma/Gypsies in Slovakia are often classified as 'economically inactive', 'unskilled', 'passive', or located 'outside of the labour force' and dependent on social benefits or moralizingly associated with informal economies.[7] In 2004, as part of neoliberal reforms promoted under the slogan 'Work pays off', the state introduced a set of tools aimed at the 'activation' of the long-term unemployed. The policy-makers described the AW programme in terms of preserving, re-learning, and reacquiring 'working habits', professional skills, and practical experiences, as well as increasing the motivation to work.[8] AW were presented as a temporary tool to help participants to re-enter the official labour market. Officially universalist but implicitly circumscribed within the racialized imaginary, they targeted those 'who lack deep-rooted working habits, have generally lower standards of living and more numerous families than is common in society'.[9] This particular conjunction of 'lost working habits' and 'more numerous families' echoed key tropes through which unemployed Roma/Gypsies have been represented in dominant discourses as the ultimate 'scroungers' who 'take without giving back' and 'don't want to work'. This figure embodies the rupture of reciprocity between the 'giving' state and the 'receiving' citizens in need – who are expected to display not only gratefulness, but also more 'active' bodily efforts in order to manifest social membership and citizenship. For most of the unemployed Roma/Gypsies enrolled in the AW programme, in practice these efforts translate into working in low-skilled menial jobs at the local municipality level for up to twenty hours per week. This work is framed as an extra incentive to earn 63.07 EUR/month (as of 2013) in addition to receiving state unemployment benefits.

Underlying the state's 'activation' reforms was the idea that unemployed people suffered not only from deprived material conditions, but also from some kind of intellectual and psychological poverty or 'idleness' owing to their state as 'long-term unemployed'. In the discourses of the state representatives, the poorest people receiving benefits were cast homogeneously as 'passive' to their fate; dependent on benefits; not able to find themselves a job; or as living for the moment, unable to manage their livelihood. In my interviews with various social workers and state officers, these representations appeared frequently in phrases such as 'They don't know how to live' or 'They live from day to day'. Thus, the idea of 'activation' became closely associated with moralizing assumptions about the poor's 'deservingness' and 'willingness' to work.

In the rest of the essay, I will turn to ethnographic perspectives on AW. First, I will examine their everyday organization and rhythms through my own insertion in the field. Second, I will look at state agents (mayors of municipalities and AW supervisors) and local hierarchies within which these works are situated. Finally, I will discuss some perceptions from Roma/Gypsies participating in these AW schemes.

Everyday organization, rhythms, and waiting

One morning in autumn 2006, I was among the 'activation workers' lining up in front of the municipality building around 6:30 a.m. We had been asked to come earlier, well ahead of time, despite the fact that the official starting time was 7 a.m. While waiting for the distribution of daily work and for registering in the attendance sheet, the AW workers gathered in bustling, spontaneously formed groups animated by lively banter and gossip. Once registered, workers were assigned different jobs and divided into smaller groups responsible for performing a particular task or maintaining a particular territory. AW workers were tasked with cleaning several streets, cutting grass alongside the road, or doing some construction work. These divisions were organized by a person responsible for distributing the daily tasks (usually a vice-mayor or one of the permanent employees of the municipality) and then supervised and practically invigilated by a co-ordinator responsible for overseeing the workers' performance on site.

Similarly to cases in other ethnographies on waiting (Auyero 2012; Hage 2009; Ozolina-Fitzgerald 2016), the long-term unemployed AW workers were imagined as having plenty of time on their hands and were often made to wait for various reasons before being assigned tasks for the day. Somewhat ironically, making the long-term unemployed participants keep time was one of the important aspects defined within the AW programme, though occasionally this was maintained to rather extreme degrees. For instance, although the workers would frequently finish their daily tasks relatively early, they had to stay at the workplace until the time was up. However, keeping time and 'waiting/seeing out' their AW shifts were not the only practices enmeshed in politics of time and disciplining the poor. Those who were repeatedly late, absent, or failed to comply patiently with the assigned tasks risked being reported to the local unemployment office and consequently losing their AW position. Similarly to those who were caught 'working informally', the state form of punishment frequently consisted of making the poor wait a certain amount of time before regaining eligibility for the state form of unemployment support or AW benefit.

According to the official regulations, the AW participants were asked to work in the mornings up until lunchtime – that is, for a couple of hours scattered across weekdays rather than fewer days of full eight-hour shifts. In 2006, some mayors and co-ordinators were more flexible and frequently allowed AW workers to work for eight hours per day in order to come for fewer days per month. However, this practice – which allowed AW participants to search for and work at informal jobs on other days – was significantly restricted as the sites of AW became increasingly controlled and randomly checked by visiting labour office inspectors. Thus, one of the key elements of the AW scheme was articulated around the regularity of one's bodily habits and practices embedded within particular spatio-temporal rhythms aimed at mimicking the experiences of 'real work'.

At the beginning of their working day, the activation workers were given a tool (e.g. a rake, scythe, or broom) for which they were personally responsible: they had to sign off when taking this tool in the morning, as well as when they returned it upon leaving the job. This individualization of responsibilities, I was told by one of the non-Roma woman in a co-ordinating position, has the twofold role of making sure that 'nothing goes missing at the end of the day' and of instilling and creating a sense of individual 'responsibility' and 'care for things'. These two are inevitably intertwined and reflect the corrective ideological underpinning of seeing Roma/Gypsy subjects as less responsible (and thus likely to leave behind or lose their things), prone to stealing (an idea circulating in the form of stories of individual thefts of tools or gas), or having less skilful bodies (lacking or losing working habits) that might lead to breaking tools. This illustrates an important aspect of this supervisory workfare guided by the moral and practical efforts to 'correct' the conduct and behaviour of their targeted participants (Wacquant 2010: 213, 218; 2012: 242). Thus, the supervisory role in Activation Works operates simultaneously as disciplinary, corrective, and educational.

At the AW spaces of my fieldwork, the division of labour was gendered. Women were usually given the task of sweeping streets with brooms and collecting garbage on streets or in parks. The men were asked to do more physically demanding tasks, such as mowing grass with a scythe or helping with cemetery reconstruction. The activation workers had a hierarchy of more or less desirable tasks and places to carry out daily work. There was also a mutual observation of other participants' work performance so as not to work more (but also not less) than the others. Early in my fieldwork, I was working with a group of men keen to do exactly the same as the other Roma/Gypsies in AW. Ironically, my initial overzealousness to finish the tasks (stemming partly from a willingness to immerse myself more fully through bodily participation in and approximation to the lives and work of the Roma poor) was met with corrective and sarcastic remarks from some of my co-workers: 'Don't rush. Take your time!' My enthusiasm also provoked teasing from some of the women in AW, who, switching to speaking in *Romanes* with the assumption that I would not understand, suggested that I was 'being a horse' for the other male co-workers. Laughing and teasing me and my other colleagues, the women were simultaneously referring to my work dedication in contrast with the other AW workers, who seemed less 'keen', and to the extraordinary constellation of relations in which non-Roma (i.e. myself) would be willing to work more within a group of Roma/Gypsy workers (a scenario reversing the traditional racialized order of things, in which Roma/Gypsies would usually be working and following the orders of non-Roma).

The more experienced co-workers instructed me and the other AW novices, in a rather ambiguous way, that we should 'work so it's good' (*rob tak, aby bolo dobre*). This referred to a particular performance of work, understood as doing the tasks assigned by the co-ordinator/mayor, but doing them more slowly so as not to finish too early, or avoiding cleaning a larger space on the streets than was assigned for that particular day. There was also an awareness of working more in the presence of the AW co-ordinator or mayor. This focus on keeping time and working within the timeframe at an appropriate pace intersected with spatial locations and assigned tasks, which essentially allowed for controlling the pace of the AW performance with varying degrees of visibility and invisibility. Activation workers' practices and responses to this spatio-temporal framework were also shaped by the awareness that their assigned task might not take that much time to do, yet they would still have to stay at the workplace until the official end time. This might lead to them slowing down their work so tasks would appear completed by the end of the working time, diligently performing their work when a superior was present, or even taking breaks and chatting in the absence of the supervisor, who would circulate around different working groups and invigilate their work.

In the case of post-Soviet immigrants in activation schemes in Germany, Roberman (2014) discusses similar processes and calls these acts of simulation 'performances of the seriousness of work'. In his ethnography of redundant workers at a former socialist car factory in Serbia, Rajković (2018) develops a concept of 'mock-labour' to refer to the blurred lines between the category of work and the matter of social assistance in the context of unproductivity and staged simulation of work. In the case of Activation Works, workers shared a general tacit consensus about the pace of the work to make the work effort appear harder.

Activation Works in Slovakia not only entailed the simulation of work on the part of those who were enrolled in these programmes, but crucially also implicated those who had supervisory and co-ordinating roles in particular forms of complicity. This complicity lay in a paradox in which both the co-ordinator and the supposedly 'activating worker' knew that these works would not help the worker to get wage-labour. Similarly, the co-ordinators of AW were also aware of the activation workers' poorly paid conditions. Gejza,[10] a Roma/Gypsy AW co-ordinator in his mid-fifties who had only recently returned home after spending several years working in the United Kingdom, often felt like he was caught in between: between the mayor and Activation Works (and workers), between institutions of control and recognition of the 'kind of works the AW were', between (non-Roma) institutions and Roma/Gypsies. He often allowed his workers to take frequent breaks, but he was also aware of his disciplining position and the results of the work, for which he was partly responsible. His perspectives frequently showed contradictions and ambiguities regarding the conditions of AW – he would ask, 'What can you ask them to do for the [little] kind of money they get?' – but would also envision the AW participants as 'poor workers' (lacking skills and discipline).

Hierarchies of supervision, uses of 'work'

In July 2013, I found myself talking to the mayor of a local municipality, who had previously worked as its functionary and vice-mayor for the past three decades. She started our discussion by saying, 'We've got no problem here. We don't make any differences [i.e. between Roma/Gypsy and non-Roma] here. I only have good and bad people'. As I nodded, she continued:

> You know how hard-working our Roma are. We have no problems here ... I don't have here these backward and inadaptable Gypsies [as other municipalities do]. We only have a few that are problematic. But our Roma have always worked, already during socialism and after ... whether they were going to the Czech Republic, doing *fušky*[11] at home. They always wanted to work.

The mayor reiterated the same positive words when describing how Roma/Gypsies manage activation schemes and continued, almost whispering, 'I wouldn't need that many positions for the amount of work that is here [i.e. in the village], but I pity them'. Yet just a few minutes later, she switched to a more critical tone:

> But you know how they are. A person would have to stand above them, [invigilating] them all the time. They work one hour and already want to have a break. They work a tiny bit and would already

want to go home … And what kind of job you can give them to do [i.e. with their low-skilled and poor-quality work performances] anyway?

This encounter with the mayor draws our attention to ambiguities surrounding particular ways in which Roma/Gypsies are constructed as economically 'inactive' in public discourses. It highlights the denial of a 'problem', implying a 'Roma problem' or problems between Roma/Gypsies and non-Roma, and re-inscribes the dichotomous logic of two collectivities and a philosophy of moral behaviourism. On one hand, the mayor recognized the worsening prospects in everyday economic precariousness and uncertainties, acknowledging how difficult it was for the poorest to get by. She drew attention to the historical experiences and labour practices of local Roma, which points towards their constant movement to find new economic niches rather than passive 'inactivity'. She mentioned the coexistence of various informal jobs (*fušky*) as a legitimate economic strategy, and she was well aware of how most people in East Slovakia – Roma/Gypsies and non-Roma alike – frequently combine various forms of income within the blurred boundaries between informality and formality.[12]

Yet the mayor also expressed compassion for the Roma/Gypsy poor, showing an empathetic understanding of their situation and thus incorporating more people in Activation Works than she 'realistically needed' for those types of jobs. Her use of the notions of pity and compassion also reveals some of the criteria in selecting participants based on her definition of 'neediness' (as well as deservingness and proactive willingness to work). Selection of AW participants was often dependent on their material status and a certain recognition of them as 'willing to work' (*chcejú robit*), which also reflected assumptions about their perceived non-problematic status. The mayor's words also highlight her understanding of Activation Works as rather useless work that could be done by fewer people; she believed AW could not have higher criteria or requirements owing to their demotivational setup and the assumed poor quality of workers. Although pitying 'them', she also raised a moralizing critique regarding 'their' (i.e. the racialized collective of Roma/Gypsies) work ethic and working habits. In doing so, she thus inadvertently reproduced and redrew a line between the deserving and undeserving poor occupying particular subject positions vis-à-vis state structures. She clearly ascribed moral characteristics to long-term unemployed Roma/Gypsies and evoked the necessity of constant surveillance and disciplinary techniques if 'they' (i.e. 'Gypsies') were to work.

The mayor's perspective also highlights the rather contingent conditions and arbitrariness shaping the selection of people for Activation Works. Participation and continuation in AW schemes were often conditioned by their work performances, as well as by symbolic recognition of their status and circumstances in the local microcosm. These acts of recognition entailed two sets of criteria: one's perceived work performance and willingness to work; and compassion for individuals' circumstances (i.e. poor, divorced, widowed, many children, etc.). Additionally, other factors played an equally (if not more) important role, such as docile submissiveness and political loyalty to the mayor; those who did not vote for the mayor were often not accepted to AW and thus were excluded from this workfare.

However, what I want to highlight here is the idea of performance and work within the activation schemes alongside the idea of complicity. The paradoxical nature of the AW setup meant that participants had to demonstrate that they were good and willing workers, which often led to particular performances and simulating acts of 'work'. At the same time, their efforts were constantly scrutinized against the backdrop of a deeply entrenched public stigma of 'Gypsies' as 'natural performers' and thus somehow 'inauthentic' workers who are 'faking' work (cf. Lemon 2000).

Activation Works also represent particular types of work in terms of public recognition, which are not considered 'real work' by most non-Roma. Often, this vision was supported by examples of 'seeing' the Activation Works as just 'fooling around.' Non-Roma also view AW as racialized labour, performed mostly by Roma/Gypsies with little wider relevance and usefulness. At best, there was a certain recognition that AW participants helped to maintain the cleanliness of public spaces. In the words of one of the local non-Roma villagers in his mid-twenties, who worked as a truck driver, 'I'm not saying anything, they do keep the place clean ... but other than that, they don't really do much.'

However, this general public image also differed depending on particular contexts and trajectories. In some localities, mayors deployed different perceptions of and uses for the AW programme. Instead of demonstrating compassion and complicity in assigning undemanding work tasks (which to some extent resonated with some of the dominant representations of Roma/Gypsies as 'workshy'), they considered AW a good opportunity to do things for the municipality using cheap – albeit 'unskilled' – labour. Employing the logic of 'hard fist' governance, these mayors usually closely supervised AW participants and used them as cheap labour for more qualified and demanding jobs. These mayors described their use of AW as positive for both the municipality and the practices (and reputation) of the activation workers, who were able to demonstrate their skills and their willingness to work.

Those who worked in these particular AW, however, did not necessarily share the mayors' perspectives. Panka, a young woman who had not been able to work since the birth of her two sons, saw AW more like 'doing horses for' the mayor: 'What do you gain from it? Nothing! If they would give us a normal salary for this, that would be a different story!' Like Panka, others viewed mayors' (ab)uses of AW as exploitative. The idiomatic expression of 'being a horse' for someone not only referred to this perceived asymmetric and exploitative relationship, with Roma/Gypsies toiling at the bottom, but also encapsulated a more existential quandary of being acted upon rather than being an acting agent in the social world. When I worked alongside Panka one day and our discussion turned to whether she had learned some new skills and working habits that could be useful in searching for a job in the legal labour market, she replied dismissively:

> No way! It's this kind of work about nothing! At least if it would be some kind of reasonable work [it would be all right]. But this kind of work? Raking, cutting grass, and other kinds of toiling and suffering? ... The only thing I earn are calluses on my hands!

In practice, a mayor's strategy also meant that he or she could effectively replace more expensive service providers and companies with the cheap and exploitable labour force of the activation workers. The issue of exploitation and asymmetry was also highlighted by a number of activation workers, who were aware of the fact that they would be paid much better for the same jobs if they were to perform them in the context of formal (e.g. as a part of some construction company) or informal (e.g. paid in cash as *fuška*) labour markets. Thus, the use of activation workers for more skilled tasks resembles the precarious situation which Roberman aptly characterizes as '"working non-workers": those who, although employed, remain without the economic and symbolic rewards that the normative jobs provide' (2014: 335). The precarity of the AW participants' situation lies in its paradoxical nature: although they perform work, they are unable to

Journal of the Royal Anthropological Institute (N.S.), 105-119
© Royal Anthropological Institute 2018

do the same type of work in a different capacity, either formal or informal, for better financial rewards.

From 'alms' to yearnings for 'normal' jobs

The status of Activation Works as 'work' was highly ambiguous for most Roma/Gypsies (with or without AW experiences). Contrary to studies arguing that Roma/Gypsies considered AW to be the equivalent of 'normal work' and hence would not search for work in the formal labour market (Oravec & Bošelová 2006), my ethnography shows how Roma/Gypsies differed in their categorization and valuation of AW. While the poorest frequently ended up with relatively long-term participation in AW, this was not because they considered them equal to jobs on the legal labour market. Rather, given the lack of available jobs for the structurally vulnerable and racially stigmatized Roma/Gypsies, the combination of social benefits and activation allowances – and in a better-case scenario, one-off informal small jobs for those more skilful and well connected with social capital – often meant more (albeit fragile) security amidst the pervasive uncertainty of their everyday socioeconomic terrain.

Despite the popular dominant representations of Roma/Gypsies as 'illiterate' and 'workshy', they had a very clear idea of how much one could earn for another type of formal or informal work rather than 'toiling in activations for [almost] nothing'. From this perspective, AW did not appear to be 'proper work' (*poriadna robota*) and were ranked as additional and somewhat stable (though small) contributions to the family income.

The Roma/Gypsies employed through this scheme usually made a distinction between what they considered to be 'normal work' (*normálno butji*) and Activation Works. They did not call the latter 'activating works', but instead referred to them as '*butji pro výboris*' (literally 'work for the municipality'). However, many would also use the expressions 'I'm only working "as if"... I am working at the municipality' (*čak avka kerav ... kerav pro výboris*) or 'It's just that [not quite] kind of work' (*oda čak ajsi butji*), through which they differentiated Activation Works from 'normal', proper jobs. Sometimes they would rhetorically ask with a sarcastic and dissatisfied tone, 'So what kind of work is this?' This was related to the low amount of financial gain, but also the type of work that they were given, which was often stigmatizing, lacking in recognition, and even humiliating for some of the participants. For instance, some Roma/Gypsy AW participants (who considered themselves socially higher in the existing hierarchies – 'on a good level', as they put it) experienced visceral disgust, shame, and anger when being asked to clean up garbage surrounding the marginalized 'Gypsy settlement'.

Additionally, AW participants' perceptions also depended on one's prior job history, social trajectory, age, and gender. The representations of AW were often gendered, and many men did not consider watering flowers or cleaning streets to be 'proper work'. Men, especially those with previous experiences of financially rewarding work and a hyper-masculine self-understanding of being the breadwinner, found it difficult to do these types of jobs without earning any substantial amount of money. In some contexts, their sense of masculinity was compromised by participation in Activation Works, as well as by being asked to perform certain tasks they did not consider to be 'real work' worthy of men or that were well below the (skilled) labour they had previously carried out. For example, being reduced to the role of auxiliary workers in construction work during AW rather than being 'masters' – after priding themselves on being exemplary workers (such as skilled bricklayers) for socialist companies – was often accepted with ambiguity and resentment. Although in both positions (socialist wage-labourer and wageless 'activation worker') Roma/Gypsy men encountered a non-Roma supervisory gaze disciplining and regulating the display of their bodily (labour) habits and controlling the rhythm and intensity of their work, the experiences of 'work membership' (Ferguson 2015: 158) were clearly differentiated not only in terms of economic evaluation, but also, crucially, in terms of modes of recognition. Most women, in contrast, did not see their participation in Activation Works as compromising; some even found it relatively flexible, easy to do, and convenient, as it allowed them to bring some additional money to the household income while managing other roles performed in gendered family obligations. Thus, their 'work for the municipality' meant that they did not have to commute to work (which the majority of other jobs required) and still managed to allow for housework, cooking, and the ability to be home when their children returned from school.

The Roma often said that AW were 'good for nothing' (*o ničom*). At the same time, this was contrasted with 'better than nothing' (*feder sar nič*). Some would call this *žobračina* ('alms', literally money gained from 'begging'), referring to the small amount of money they earned from AW. Their critique of the AW as 'good for nothing' reflected what they perceived as the practical meaningfulness of these types of jobs and ritualized forms of work performance.[13] Indeed, those who could find alternative forms of income-generating strategies (formal or informal work at home or away during their labour migration journeys) would avoid participating in AW. The majority of Roma/Gypsies shared a rather widespread feeling of resentment towards shrinking forms of state support and new forms of poverty- and unemployment-reduction programmes, most clearly embodied in the form of AW. As men often remarked in relation to the unworthiness of one's efforts, characterized by 'so much endurance [suffering] for such alms', there was a pervasive sense of discomfort and injustice over being forced into a relationship as a recipient of the state's alms (cf. Han 2014: 73), which was somehow conditioned by the humiliating prospect of 'works for the municipality'. And yet for many, especially those disconnected from other sources of income and avenues of social mobility, the extra income obtained through the docile submission to AW was considered 'better than nothing' – or at least 'something' – in the context of pervasive poverty.

Conclusion

The changing forms of social assistance for the unemployed poor, illustrated here through ethnographic focus on AW, show a recent convergence of socioeconomic crisis, state reforms, and shifts towards disciplinary workfare and punitive penalization that render illegal various informal economic strategies of the poor. Previous combinations of survivalist improvisations and unemployment benefits have become increasingly harder for the poor to realize. This, in turn, has produced more everyday uncertainty and precariousness, which has left many Roma/Gypsies with a sense of growing disconnection, insecurity, and hope for migration. In the context of shrinking forms of state support, the AW programme has come to mean an additional amount of money that has contributed to the fragile balance of household income in such precarious conditions and allows for the redistribution of state social assistance among other kin members. At the same time, the AW programme – originally envisaged as a 'temporary' tool for 'activating' citizens expected to be re-entering the official labour market – has failed in one of its key objectives: practically none of the Roma AW workers I encountered managed to get wage-labour given the extreme scarcity of productive work opportunities and their racialized subjection in Slovakia.

Owing to the increase in poverty and the lack of other possibilities following the economic crisis and downsizing of state support, the structural vulnerability of Roma/Gypsies has intensified in the last few years; in many localities, the demand for Activation Works exceeds the actual amount of available posts (Kureková & Konsteková 2013; Kureková, Salner & Farenzenová 2013). The heightened competition makes the selection process for AW a site of struggle for imposing a particular vision of oneself – of proving and performing one's worthiness and morality – implicated in the figure of a 'good worker' to be considered for Activation Works and to maintain the position once secured. These contexts have become conducive to performances of a certain subjectivity and forms of care, carried out to elicit pity and recognition in the eyes of state representatives as one who endures material hardships, has many vulnerable dependants, deserves to be chosen according to one's active willingness to work, and/or has proven to be a 'good worker'.

The AW programme envisions citizens-cum-individuals as rational actors with individualized responsibilities aimed at cultivating particular strategy-making agency, skills, and dispositions. Simultaneously, however, it reinscribes subjects' practices within the highly moralized landscape of citizenship, in which the collective of those 'actively searching' is valorized against all those who are cast relationally as uselessly passive. Yet if, as Narotzky shows (2015; see also this volume), we consider flexibility and adaptability as two of the key components in the making of an entrepreneurial subject, the relative fixity of ordering and orchestrating the collective rhythms of AW highlights contradictions between ideological calls for an entrepreneurial self and practices of AW embedded within racialized hierarchies and politics of waiting. While in theory the AW programme aims to produce a particular 'activated subject' through sets of spatial and temporal arrangements, rhythms, and socio-political organization, its social effects vary in relation to a set of factors, positions, and fields (such as a mayor's vision, local hierarchies, historical trajectories, and other socioeconomic avenues of social mobility), but practically never propel its participants towards more 'activated' upward mobility.

In her study of voluntarism in post-Fordist Italy, Muehlebach (2011) shows how forms of public volunteerism and relational labour contribute to public recognition and valorization of 'active' citizenship. In contrast to her work, my ethnography has focused on spaces and Roma/Gypsy participants' labour, in which their enforced and performed willingness to work and modes of affective labour are situated in the context of everyday precariousness and conditioned by the extra financial incentive of the state. It has highlighted how the valorization of 'active' citizenship must be positioned within the economy of racialized stigma and labour attached to Roma/Gypsies. Unlike the Italian citizens described by Muehlebach, Slovak Roma/Gypsies participating in AW struggle for their 'work' to be publicly recognized as 'valuable' and usually do not see it as a valid avenue for approximating the modes of social belonging associated with past labour regimes. I have attempted to show how, under certain conditions, their labouring bodies and the material outcomes of their work could gain particular forms of differentiated recognition and social membership while simultaneously allowing for possibilities of a reconfigured grey zone of exploitation under the auspices of state welfare.

NOTES

This work was supported by the ERSTE Foundation Fellowship for Social Research, the Re:Work Fellowship, the Simon Research Fellowship, the University of Manchester, the Economic and Social Research Council, the United Nations Development Programme regional centre in Bratislava, and the Wenner-Gren Foundation. I would like to express my sincere gratitude to the families who have hosted me during my fieldwork, and to all who allowed me to tell their stories and experiences. I am grateful to ERSTE Foundation Fellows, Re:Work Centre Fellows, and to Daniel Škobla, Martin Fotta, and Catalina Tesar for comments on early drafts of this essay, and to seminar and workshop participants in Turin, in Berlin, in Exeter, and in Oslo for their helpful questions and recommendations. I am particularly grateful to Penny Harvey and Christian Krohn-Hansen, the *JRAI* Editor, and two anonymous reviewers for their feedback.

[1] Throughout this essay, I use the term 'Roma/Gypsies' rather than the singular 'Roma' or 'Gypsies' in order to bypass some analytical and political struggles and critiques. While 'Roma' would be deployed as a self-referential category in *Romanes*, many of my interlocutors would also use the externally ascribed Slovak category of 'Gypsies' (*cigáni*), which can carry a derogatory meaning in certain contexts.

[2] Aside from in-depth fieldwork in one locality, I also carried out ethnographic research in a neighbouring village and conducted interviews with AW participants and state officials in a number of other localities (as part of other research projects, see Hurrle, Škobla, Ivanov, Kling & Grill 2012).

[3] As part of wider neoliberal socioeconomic restructuring and forms of governance (see Jurajda & Mathernová 2004; Marušák & Singer 2009; van Baar 2012), Slovakia incorporated in a global capitalist economy through the privatization of previously state-owned companies. Thus, throughout the 1990s and early 2000s, foreign investors and capital were attracted by the hope of creating job opportunities in a labour market stricken by rising unemployment. This was most clearly demonstrated in eastern Slovakia, where many industrial factories and companies closed following the end of socialism. These processes, characterizing the development of the Slovak economy in the last decade, can be analysed with reference to David Harvey's concept of 'accumulation by dispossession' (2003), in which the state creates conditions and provides assets (such as cheap land or a cheap labour force) in order to instigate the accumulation of capital. For instance, Slovakia has recently become one of Central Europe's largest producers in the car industry. For a historical overview of Slovak industry's 'national trajectory', see, for example, Buzalka & Ferencova (2012).

[4] These policies can be seen as part of 'governance of activation' (van Berkel & Borghi 2008), in which 'activation' refers to a mandatory part of workfare for the long-term unemployed, who must participate in various (often unpaid and voluntary based) programmes designed by the state in order to be eligible for receiving social assistance or benefits (van Berkel & Borghi 2008: 332). For an interesting critical assessment of 'activation', see Lødemel & Trickey (2001); Newman (2007); Serrano Pascual & Magnusson 2007; van Baar (2012); Wacquant (2010).

[5] Although these programmes were not explicitly defined as primarily targeting Roma/Gypsies, since public debates and discourses surrounding their introduction rested primarily on *socially* defined rhetoric regarding the general characteristics of the unemployed and their conditions, their frames and representations overlapped with the historically ethnicized vision of those seen as 'lacking working habits', which in the Slovak context was the case for the Roma minority (see Drál', 2008).

[6] This was an official state category deployed during socialism.

[7] These categorizations can be found in the dominant narratives not only of policy-makers, but also of international organizations (UNDP 2004; 2007; Duell & Kureková 2013) and NGOs.

[8] The programme's overall aim was formulated as being to 'support acquirement, maintenance, deepening or enhancement of knowledge, professional skills, practical experiences, working habits in order to enhance (chances in) work careers on the labour market' (*Predpis č. 417/2013 Z. z. Zákon o pomoci v hmotnej núdzi a o zmene a doplnení niektorých zákonov*: available on-line: http://www.zakonypreludi.sk/zz/2013-417/suvislosti, accessed 16 January 2018).

[9] Act on Assistance in Material Need No. 599/2003; Act on Subsistence Minimum No. 601/2003 Coll.

[10] All names are pseudonyms.

[11] *Fušky* is a generic term that refers to all kinds of one-off informal types of jobs outside of the official labour market.

[12] It must be noted that the possibility of simultaneously working at AW and working informally at various one-off jobs and short-term work has become increasingly difficult in recent years as state institutions operate with heightened alertness, enacting greater control and possible punitive sanctions.

[13] Their claim resonates with what Larsen (2001) described as 'empty ritual acts' in his study of labour activation projects among marginalized residents of one deprived neighbourhood in Copenhagen.

REFERENCES

ANDERSON, B. 2013. *Us and them? The dangerous politics of immigration control.* Oxford: University Press.

AUYERO, J. 2012. *Patients of the state: the politics of waiting in Argentina.* Durham, N.C.: Duke University Press.

BUZALKA, J. & M. FERENCOVA 2012. National trajectories – Slovakia. MEDEA Project (http://www.medeasteelproject.org/sites/medea.localhost/files/National%20trajectories%20-%20SK.pdf, accessed 20 March 2013, no longer available on-line).

DONERT, C. 2017. *The rights of the Roma: the struggle for citizenship in postwar Czechoslovakia.* Cambridge: University Press.

DRÁL', P. 2008. Symbolic processes of social exclusion of Roma in Slovak public policy discourse. *Ethnicity Studies* **1-2**, 85-116.

DUELL, N. & L. KUREKOVÁ 2013. *Activating benefit in material need recipients in the Slovak Republic.* The Central European Labour Institute Report for the World Bank, Bratislava.

FERGUSON, J. 2009. The uses of neoliberalism. *Antipode* **41**, 166-84.

——— 2015. *Give a man a fish: on the new politics of distribution.* Durham, N.C.: Duke University Press.

FILADELFIOVÁ, J., D. GERBERY & D. ŠKOBLA 2007. *Report on the living conditions of Roma in Slovakia.* Bratislava: UNDP.

GERBERY, D., D. LESAY & D. ŠKOBLA (eds) 2007. *Kniha o chudobe: společenské súvislosti a verejné politiky.* Bratislava: Priatelia Zeme-CEPA.

GRILL, J. 2011. From street busking in Switzerland to meat factories in the UK: a comparative study of two Roma migration networks from Slovakia. In *Global connections and emerging inequalities in Europe: perspectives on poverty and transnational migration* (eds) D. Kaneff & F. Pine, 79-103. London: Anthem Press.

——— 2012. 'Going up to England': exploring mobilities among Roma from Eastern Slovakia. *Journal of Ethnic and Migration Studies* **38**, 1269-87.

——— 2015. 'Endured labour' and 'fixing up' money: the economic strategies of Roma migrants in Slovakia and the UK. In *Gypsy economy* (eds) M. Brazzabeni, M. Cunha & M. Fotta, 88-106. Oxford: Berghahn Books.

HAGE, G. (ed.) 2009. *Waiting.* Melbourne: University Press.

HAN, C. 2014. The difficulty of kindness: boundaries, time, and the ordinary. In *The ground between: anthropologists engage philosophy* (eds) V. Das, M. Jackson, A. Kleinman & B. Singh, 71-94. Durham, N.C.: Duke University Press.

HARVEY, D. 2003. *The new imperialism.* Oxford: University Press.

HURRLE, J., D. ŠKOBLA, A. IVANOV, J. KLING & J. GRILL 2012. *Uncertain impact: have the Roma in Slovakia benefited from the European Social Fund?* Roma Inclusion Working Papers. UNDP Europe and CIS: Bratislava Regional Centre.

JURAJDA, S. & K. MATHERNOVÁ 2004. *How to overhaul the labour market: political economy of recent Czech and Slovak reforms.* Paper for the World Development Report 2005 (available on-line: http://www-wds.worldbank.org/servlet/WDSContentServer/WDSP/IB/2005/01/31/000090341_20050131092037/Rendered/PDF/314330Jurajda11oWDR050bkgd01public1.pdf, accessed 16 January 2018).

KUREKOVÁ, L. & J. KONSTEKOVÁ 2013. *Examining specific labour market policies aiming to foster labour market integration of Roma and vulnerable groups in Slovakia.* NEUJOBS WP **19**(2). Bratislava: Slovak Governance Institute.

———, A. SALNER & M. FARENZENOVÁ 2013. *Implementation of Activation Works in Slovakia: Evaluation and Recommendations for Policy Change.* Bratislava: Slovak Governance Institute and Open Society Institute.

LARSEN, J.-E. 2001. The active society and activation policy. Paper presented at the Cost A13 Conference: Social Policy, Marginalization, and Citizenship, 2–4 November 2001, Aalborg University, Aalborg, Denmark (available on-line: http://citeseerx.ist.psu.edu/viewdoc/summary?doi=10.1.1.198.2636, accessed 16 January 2018).

LEMON, A. 2000. *Between two fires: Gypsy performance and Romani memory from Pushkin to postsocialism.* London: Duke University Press.

LØDEMEL, I. & H. TRICKEY 2001. *'An offer you can't refuse': workfare in international perspective.* Bristol: Policy Press.

MARUŠÁK, M. & L. SINGER 2009. Social unrest in Slovakia 2004: Romani reaction to neoliberal 'reforms'. In *Romani politics in contemporary Europe: poverty, ethnic mobilization and the neoliberal order* (eds) N. Sigona & N. Trehan, 186-208. Basingstoke: Palgrave Macmillan.

MILLAR, K. 2014. The precarious present: wageless labor and disrupted life in Rio de Janeiro, Brazil. *Cultural Anthropology* **29**, 32-53.

MUEHLEBACH, A. 2011. On affective labor in post-Fordist Italy. *Cultural Anthropology* **26**, 59-82.

NAROTZKY, S. 2015. The payoff of love and the traffic of favours. In *Flexible capitalism: exchange and ambiguity at work* (ed.) J. Kjaerulff, 173-206. Oxford: Berghahn Books.

NEWMAN, J. 2007. The 'double dynamics' of activation: institutions, citizens and the remaking of welfare governance. *International Journal of Sociology and Social Policy* **27**, 364-75.

ORAVEC, L. & Z. BOŠELOVÁ 2006. Activation policy in Slovakia: another failing experiment? *Roma Rights Quarterly* **1**, European Roma Rights Centre (ERRC).

OZOLINA-FITZGERALD, L. 2016. A state of limbo: the politics of waiting in neo-liberal Latvia. *British Journal of Sociology* **67**, 456-75.

PINE, F. 2014. Migration as hope: space, time, and imagining the future. *Current Anthropology* **55: 9**, 95-104.

QUESADA, J., L.K. HART & P. BOURGOIS 2011. Structural vulnerability and health: Latino migrant laborers in the United States. *Medical Anthropology* **30**, 339-62.

RAJKOVIĆ, I. 2018. For an anthropology of the demoralized: state pay, mock-labour, and unfreedom in a Serbian firm. *Journal of Royal Anthropological Institute* (N.S.) **24**, 47-70.

ROBERMAN, S. 2014. Labour activation policies and the seriousness of simulated work. *Social Anthropology* **22**, 326-39.

SERRANO PASCUAL, A. & L. MAGNUSSON (eds) 2007. *Work and society: reshaping welfare states and activation regimes in Europe*. Brussels: Peter Lang.

STEWART, M. 1997. *The time of the Gypsies*. Boulder, Colo.: Westview Press.

UNDP [United Nations Development Programme] 2004. *Unleashing entrepreneurship: making business work for the poor*. New York: United Nations Development Programme.

——— 2007. *Report on the living conditions of Roma in Slovakia*. Bratislava: United Nations Development Programme.

VAN BAAR, H. 2012. Socio-economic mobility and neo-liberal governmentality in post-socialist Europe: activation and the dehumanisation of the Roma. *Journal of Ethnic and Migration Studies* **38**, 1289-304.

VAN BERKEL, R. & V. BORGHI 2008. Introduction: the governance of activation. *Social Policy & Society* **7**, 331-40.

WACQUANT, L. 2010. Crafting the neoliberal state: workfare, prisonfare, and social insecurity. *Sociological Forum* **25**, 197-219.

——— 2012. The wedding of workfare and prisonfare in the 21st century. *Journal of Urban Poverty* **16**, 236-49.

Réapprendre à travailler ? « Travaux d'activation » et nouvelles politiques d'aide sociale : le cas des Roms de Slovaquie

Résumé

A partir d'une enquête de terrain menée parmi des groupes de Roms et de Gitans de Slovaquie, l'article explore le concept « d'activation par le travail », suivant les lignes mouvantes de la précarité économique et des nouvelles politiques d'aide sociale qui, dans le contexte d'un État en pleine mutation néolibérale, visent les personnes officiellement sans emploi. Axé sur la manière dont les nouvelles idéologies et les politiques d'activation agissent sur les pratiques quotidiennes, il dissèque les expériences vécues et les formes de sociabilité qui naissent dans les espaces créés par ces forces centrifuges de l'État. L'article accorde une attention particulière aux significations contestées, aux politiques d'attente et aux actes de compassion suscités par le travail des sujets et leurs emplois simulés.

7

Interrupted futures: co-operative labour and the changing forms of collective precarity in rural Andean Peru

PENNY HARVEY *University of Manchester*

Sociological interest in precarious labour has focused on the existential insecurity associated with the discontinuous work relations of contemporary modes of production and the difficulties produced for the formation of effective modes of social and political solidarity. This essay, by contrast, explores the continuities of precarious living in the Southern Peruvian Andes over the past century, with a focus on how the affective force of social obligations and responsibilities to wider collectives (such as the family, the peasant community, or the co-operative) both support and interrupt the search for more stable personal and collective futures. Approaching precarity as a relational condition, the essay traces how precarity takes form in the movements between formal and informal labour practices.

This essay focuses on the ambiguities that inhere in agricultural labour regimes (historical and contemporary) in the Southern Peruvian Andes, and the shifting forms of precarity to which these ambiguities give rise. I am particularly interested in thinking through how the legacies of the hacienda system and of the Peruvian Agrarian Reform continue to shape the livelihoods of small-scale farmers. Sociological interest in precarious labour has focused on the existential insecurity associated with deregulated and decentralized production processes: the increase in zero-hour contracts, the demand for flexibility, the out-sourcing of risk, and the dismantling of labour unions.[1] Such conditions certainly affect the lives of many Andean farmers who supplement their agricultural work with migrant and contract labour and with small independent businesses. However, few Andean farmers would see precarity, vulnerability, or uncertainty as a specifically contemporary condition.[2] Andean livelihoods have always been subject to the fluctuations of economic and environmental forces, to political violence[3] (most recently in the protracted war between the state and Shining Path), and to the systematic social inequalities and entrenched hierarchies that place particular existential burdens on the poor. In this respect, precarious living is routine for many, if not most, people in the world today (Muehlebach 2013; see also Grill, this volume).

Taking a position at a tangent from the concerns with the demise of wage-labour in Western economies, Kathleen Stewart is more interested in the affective force of precarity, which she refers to as a form that takes place through 'attachments, tempos, materialities and states of being' (2012: 524). Such a sense of precarity can be both powerful and elusive. As she writes: 'Precarity can take the form of a sea change, a darkening atmosphere, a hard fall, or the barely perceptible sense of a reprieve' (2012: 518). Stewart's focus on precarity attends to a basic human existential condition of vulnerability and uncertainty, and connects to the distinction that Judith Butler (2009) draws between precariousness and precarity, where the concept of precarity is deployed to name the *differential* distribution of precariousness by such factors as class, citizenship, and race (Allison 2016). For the purposes of this essay, I narrow the reference still further following Kathleen Millar's insistence that 'precarity (unlike the precariat) is not a category but a relationship, ... a concept that examines how insecure conditions of labor intersect with fragile conditions of life. Precarity is a beginning point of analysis – less a label or diagnosis than a method' (Millar 2016). And in particular it is a concept that points specifically to the analysis of labour. Nevertheless, it was Stewart's articulation of precarity as 'a form that takes place' that suggested a direction for my analysis, and the possibility of drawing connections to another debate on labour and form: namely discussions of the distinctions between formal and informal labour.

Informality in Keith Hart's original discussion (1973) refers to a specific relationship between work practices and the formal, state-regulated economy. Informal work, in this reading, is work that is not recognized by the state. It is not captured in formal accounts of a national or regional economy. It is thus, by definition, not regulated, not calculable, and, from the perspective of state actors, not predictable. In her recent discussion of informal commerce in Lima, Peru, Daniella Gandolfo (2013) notes a tension between informality as that which is unrecognized (lacking in a legal and/or social status), and informality as an escape from the constraints of recognition (a *modus operandi* that works against state imposition of form). The entrepreneurial traders of Lima's vast contraband markets evade formality, and resist attempts by state bureaucracies to draw them into regimes of regulation. Their resistance carries costs and risks, not least the difficulty of getting access to credit, but the freedom and autonomy that informality affords is valued more highly.[4] Of relevance to the following discussion of rural labour practices is Gandolfo's claim that one of the key freedoms of informality is to subsume profit to particular modes of sociality. Wealthy traders give time and money to 'reciprocal obligations and forms of consumption that limit the accumulation of wealth' (Gandolfo 2013: 280). They invest in their market colleagues, in family relations, in saints and in earth forces: that is, in the conditions of possibility for a productive life. The state, by contrast, is apprehended as a deadening rather than as a life-giving force, and, as far as possible, it is kept at a distance.

In Southern Peru, rural livelihoods also depend on the generative force of the land, on saints, and on kinship, but the desire and willingness to engage the state also remain important. Increasingly, rural livelihoods depend on the ability to access state (and NGO) resources while also retaining the capacity to mobilize collectives that ultimately defend access to land against the incursions of private investment and of state extraction. The argument I seek to pursue in this essay is that precarity takes form at the interface of formality and informality, in the desire and need for official recognition and for the autonomy afforded to those who remain below the radar of state controls. In contemporary Peru, long-established social collectives such as agricultural co-operatives and peasant communities that until recently were afforded a

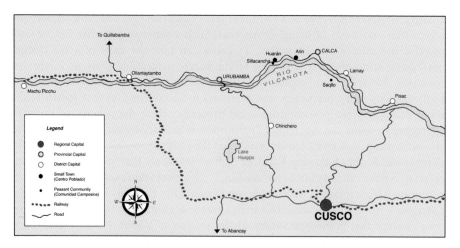

Figure 1. The Vilcanota Valley, Peru.

degree of autonomy (even if born of neglect and disinterest) have been visibly undone by an aggressive liberalization of the economy, the disruptions of war, and the state-supported impetus towards entrepreneurial over social initiatives. Nevertheless, long-established co-operative labour practices remain highly visible as a means of negotiating the uncertainties of rural life. Communal work parties are routinely enacted to forge relationships between communities and the state, while informal co-operation remains fundamental to the reproduction of both community and kinship as autonomous spheres of action. Outcomes are, however, always uncertain, the boundary between formal and informal labour unstable and open to retrospective interpretation. These tensions that appear in the movement back and forth between formal recognition and informal flexibility articulate a sense of precarity that is not fully captured by discussion of dispossession. Rather it is the affective force of dislocation that I seek to articulate in what follows.

The material at the core of this essay is drawn from a project on decentralization and regional government in Peru that I have been carrying out in Cusco's Vilcanota Valley in collaboration with Deborah Poole. The Vilcanota Valley (Fig. 1) is known to millions of tourists as the Sacred Valley of the Inkas. It lies between the city of Cusco, with its imperial and colonial heritage, and the UNESCO World Heritage site of Machu Picchu. The valley has its own historic attractions: ancient terraces, much fine stonework, and the Inka fortress of Ollantaytambo. Colonial churches and the lavish buildings of the hacienda estates also attract visitors. Some have been restored and converted into expensive hotels, or tourist centres. Others, somewhat dilapidated, remain under the control of the co-operatives and communities that emerged in the wake of the Agrarian Reform of 1969. The architecture leaves no doubt that this valley has long been an area of state intervention, of accumulated wealth, and of international circulation. Today, the valley has two sizeable administrative centres – the provincial capitals of Urubamba and of Calca – and many smaller communities where people make their living in a mixed economy of subsistence agriculture, small-scale businesses, and migrant labour.

Journal of the Royal Anthropological Institute (N.S.), 120-133
© Royal Anthropological Institute 2018

Reciprocal labour and the mobilization of a precarious collective

In 2010 there were terrible floods in the valley. The Vilcanota River burst its banks. Houses and above all crops were washed away. Thus it was that in 2011 Deborah Poole and I found ourselves walking along the river bank with an inspection team comprised of representatives of the regional water authority and various functionaries of the provincial government of Calca with responsibility for civil defence, environmental protection, town planning, and infrastructural development. In was in the context of this expedition that we first visited the community of Saqllo. We learned, over the course of that day, that Saqllo was a complex irritant for the authorities. We were told that the residents of Saqllo were fierce defenders of their autonomy, constantly lodging complaints with the Town Hall, consistently refusing to collaborate, although always quick to claim their rights. The municipal authorities were particularly aggrieved by Saqllo's withdrawal of an agreement to a plan to locate a rubbish dump on their land. The agreement that had been entered into with representatives of the community had met with opposition at a subsequent meeting of the community assembly, despite the fact that the works had already been initiated and preliminary excavations completed. Furthermore, the refusal of the community assembly to endorse the agreement had been followed by a fierce opposition movement contesting the legality of the construction. There were also problems with the river. The maize fields of Saqllo had been very badly damaged by the floods. The community were looking for support and compensation from the provincial authorities. This juxtaposition of requests and refusals were clearly on the minds of the inspection team as we made our way up-river, attending to the effects of the flood damage, and the diverse ways in which residents had tried to protect land, or to take advantage of the changing topography as the river ate away some areas while opening up new spaces elsewhere. There were many problems and irregularities to attend to as we walked. After some while we realized that a man from Saqllo had attached himself to our party. He kept gently urging us to keep moving and reminding us that the community had gathered and were waiting to discuss their problems. When we finally got to Saqllo, the community were indeed gathered on the edge of the river bank. At this time of year the river was dry. There was clear evidence of gravel extraction, which, we were informed, was being undertaken by the provincial government, who needed the materials for a road construction project. The inspection team stood together down on the river bed and a fractious discussion emerged as to the causes of the particular flood damage, and the reasons why the river had surged into their fields.

The engineers asserted that the community only had themselves to blame. They had been extracting sand and gravel from the river bed without authorization. The experts should have been consulted to ensure that these extractive processes would not adversely affect the course of the current. The residents countered that they had only extracted small amounts, in accordance with their legitimate rights. There was a heated argument about who was authorized to do what in relation to the river bed. Ambiguous and competing competencies between national bodies, provincial authorities, and local communities were clearly intersecting in this space. At some point the conversation was interrupted and we were ushered over to an adjacent space where it finally became clear why our human shadow had been doggedly encouraging us to keep moving for the past couple of hours. The community had prepared a large communal meal for the authorities. Anxious that we should arrive at the optimal moment to eat the meal, the man had been sent to keep us moving, and to ensure that we did not stop elsewhere. All the households of Saqllo were involved, each contributing food (potatoes and guinea pigs), money for alcohol, and the labour required to prepare and serve the meal. We ate the meal together. The offering of food in Andean communities, as elsewhere, implies quite specific relational effects. Communal meals such as the one we participated in that day are central to Andean practices of reciprocal labour, routinely enacted in relation to one of two dominant forms of exchange, *ayni* and *mink'a*. *Ayni* is a form of short-term reciprocal exchange, associated with the circulation of energy (Allen 1988), directly connecting the consumption of food, alcohol, and coca leaves with bodily effort: agricultural work, building work, cooking, ceremonial tasks, and so on. *Ayni* exchanges are affective forms of labour, orientated to the completion of specific tasks, but also, and as importantly, *ayni* labour generates a sense of collective endeavour. In agricultural communities, *ayni* labour implies the opening of one's body to flows of energy that routinely extend to the sentient forces of the environment, the mountains, and the earth. *Ayni* contrasts with non-reciprocal labour, or *mink'a*, where labour is compensated with food, festivities, alcohol, and produce, but where there is no expectation that the exchange will forge an on-going relationship. Like *ayni*, *mink'a* labour elicits payment in kind. The exchange is concrete and avoids translation into the abstract value of a wage. However, it carries the same connotations of wage-labour in the sense that the exchange is orientated to the closure of relational obligations rather than the on-going formation of social collectives (see Martin, this volume). *Ayni* is thus a forward-orientated exchange that seeks to activate on-going relations, whereas *mink'a* is compensated by the offerings of food, drink, and sociability as a form of closure. Traditionally, labour exchanges in the harvest season took the form of *mink'a* rather than *ayni*, as the fruits of the earth were appropriated by individual households, in contrast to the extensive ethos of *ayni* exchanges that characterized the sowing season (Gose 1994; Harris 2000).

Ayni exchanges have long been understood as constituting the fabric of the Andean *ayllu*. The *ayllu* is a social rather than a legal figure, denoting the configuration of 'community' as co-constituted in the active engagements with kin and with land – through this specific form of labour exchange. *Ayllu* is a concept that incorporates human and nonhuman being, encompassing environmental forces as integral to the time/space of the collective.[5] As Marisol de la Cadena (2015) has recently argued, *ayllu* can usefully be conceptualized as event, rather than identity. The *ayllu* is an emergent and achieved collective, the affective entanglement of persons and energies (including the life-giving energies of the land, of water, and of the mountains) that root human collectives in specific times and places, but which nevertheless have to be constantly made and re-made in the circulations of reciprocal exchanges. The sharing of the meal that day raised the possibility that an *ayni*-'style' exchange had been initiated. The meal was prepared in relations of *ayni*, and incorporated foods such as the guinea pig, raised in the intimate space of household kitchens, and only acquired through *ayni* (as they cannot be bought or sold in the market). It thus carried a potent sociality. At the same time the meal did not constitute a classic *ayni* exchange, which involves not just reciprocity but a direct equivalence of return such as a specific number of hours in labour exchanges, or the return of the same produce in material exchanges. However, the invocation of *ayni* that the communal meal carried was there in the sensibility of future return, of the gift given in explicit expectation of a future return. Over the course of the meal this expectation took on a more specific form. It turned out that what the people of Saqllo wanted at that point was for the Calca authorities (the over-arching provincial authority) to come with them to the adjoining town of Lamay (a district of Calca). They claimed that the Lamay authorities were to blame for the unregulated extraction. The people of Saqllo needed the support of the Calca authorities to ensure those upstream would not be allowed to interfere in the river. If they could arrive in Lamay with the visible backing and support of the provincial authorities and the representative of the regional water authority, then they were sure that their complaint would be recognized as legitimate, and their up-stream neighbours would be obliged to respond. The strategy was not without risk, for as Michael Sallnow noted back in 1987, 'ayni is more an ideological category than a transactional formula' (1987: 109). Furthermore, an *ayni* exchange should ideally both be short term and involve equivalence of reciprocation, emphasizing horizontality, rather than the capacity to draw another in through the force of hierarchical relations.

The authorities and the anthropologists had not contributed to the preparation of the meal, and the meal did not, as yet, incorporate our labour. However, by eating this meal, we were drawn into the logics of exchange that would (ideally) compel us to act *with* the people of Saqllo rather than simply on their behalf. None of these details were made explicit, and they did not need to be, because the community were engaging people practised in the arts of local administration. The inspection team understood the deal. One of the engineers told us that he was known locally as 'The Exterminator' (of guinea pigs) because of the way in which people consistently elicited his help through the gifting of this ritually potent food. The mobilization of the authorities worked, and shortly after we had finished eating, our newly formed collective climbed into the available vehicles: two spectacular old trucks, the men in one, the women in another, the engineers and the anthropologists joining the convoy in the municipal 4 × 4. We thus arrived in the square of the small sleepy town of Lamay in a demonstrable show of force that the river inspection team found themselves rapidly having to back away from so as not to alarm the local authorities. The confrontation was managed effectively; the engineers took control of the meeting, regained a position of authoritative neutrality, and negotiated a date when the residents of Lamay and of Saqllo would come together in a communal work party (*faena*) to re-orientate the course of the river.

We were thoroughly intrigued by the event, not least by the capacity of the people of Saqllo to move seamlessly from their condition of recalcitrant trouble-makers to a collective entity with whom the state authorities could actively and positively identify. The visibility of communal labour (*faena*) and *ayni* exchange was central to this move. The production of the meal, the collective journey to the neighbouring town, and the agreement to the communal work party enacted Saqllo as a community that could be both recognized (by state officials) and granted a degree of autonomy. The capacity to organize in this way was fitting to the legal figure of the 'peasant community' that was set up in 1974 in the wake of the Agrarian Reform. Over the years, subsequent governments have gradually eroded community autonomy, particularly with respect to the inalienability of land, a clause that was fully rescinded in the 1993 constitution, under the presidency of Alberto Fujimori. Nevertheless, the notion that the integrity of the peasant community is forged in the combination of communal labour (*faena*) and *ayni* exchange remains a powerful mobilizing trope that contemporary communities can use in their attempts to engage state agencies as autonomous entities. *Faena* has a quite different resonance to *ayni*. *Faena* is the demand of corvée or tributary labour made on communities for the furthering of public works. Nevertheless it is also constitutive of community, as those who work in this way, as collectives, register their presence and their rights in relation to the state. Contributions in kind (notably in labour and in the provision of materials) are a common feature of agreements for state support (which most commonly takes the form of technical expertise and machinery). The mode of collaboration is important because the unit of engagement with the state is the community, rather than the individual citizen. Indeed, the tensions between the Calca authorities and the residents of Saqllo over the rubbish dump and the extraction of gravel from the river tacitly revolved around the moral distinction between collective and self-interested action. In both these disputes the common good was invoked at a scale that enacted the local community as self-interested, while the resolution of the joint working party that came out of the Lamay meeting conjured a wider and more inclusive sense of community.

The capacity to define the emergent effects of specific relational forms retrospectively has always been an arena for the exercise of power. Sallnow (1987: 109) drew attention to the etymology of *ayni* by way of a reminder that the term also denotes contradiction and incompatibility. His systematic analysis of exchange relations in the late 1970s, in a community located in this same region of Cusco, showed the ways in which relations of class differentiation were routinely enacted through the manipulation of the ambiguities of demand and expectation inherent in the entanglement of labour obligations in these diverse modes of exchange (Sallnow 1989).

Narratives of dislocation

We returned to Saqllo at a later date to find out more about the place. The president of the community suggested that we take a walk with a young man whom we will refer to here as Pepe. It soon became clear why he had been chosen as our guide. Relaxed and articulate with foreigners, Pepe walked with us along the banks of the Vilcanota and told us about himself, and about the community of Saqllo. He had been admitted to the University of Cusco to study agronomy, but his studies were constantly interrupted by the need to work to help support the family back home. He valued what he had learned at the university nevertheless, but so too what he knew from his work on and with the earth. At one point he had taken up an opportunity to travel to the United States, where he had worked in Humboldt County in California in illegal marijuana cultivation. There was no sense in his conversation with us that the illegality of this flourishing transnational economy had generated any sense of precarity for him; indeed he never even mentioned the illegality, and the instability of his labour status was not voiced as a concern. What he did talk about was the opportunity to learn, and the fact that he was called home. The interruption to deal with the needs of his family in Saqllo was the issue that structured his narrative. Pepe was not married, but he had siblings and a mother to care for. His siblings all worked, on and off, in white-collar jobs in urban areas. He had yet to finish his studies, but he was attentive to the need to ensure a continuity of land cultivation in Saqllo. He was occasionally offered work by NGOs to deliver courses, and had even been invited to visit Ethiopia in this capacity. His trips abroad were always short term, and he knew that he had no idea what the future might hold. He would come and go depending on what was offered and what was needed back in Saqllo. His story was not recounted as a drama. It was simply a life story marked by interruption.

He suggested that we walk along the river to the house of the former *hacendado* – the landowner in the times of the haciendas – which after the Agrarian Reform had become the administrative centre for one of the largest agricultural co-operatives in Southern Peru. These co-operatives had been set up under state-controlled administrations to manage the expropriated lands. As we walked and talked, Pepe showed us how we could read local history from the diverse ways in which river defences had been constructed over time. He pointed out the structures that the hacienda owners had built, and others that the co-operative had put in place: good defences where rocks and willow trees were lodged together to form barriers that the river could rise over but not destroy (so the banks at least remained intact). There were also less successful concrete structures that had been built more recently by the regional government and had not lasted. It seemed as if the hacienda and the co-operative had cared more directly for the land as a continuous ecology, and knew better how to manage the course of the river in relation to the land. Or, perhaps, it was simply that they were more able to manage the social conflicts that underpinned the current problem. Pepe not only showed us where the fields had been eaten away by the river, he also described some of the complex and conflictual relationships between communities that centred on the struggle for land. These struggles that were fostered by both the hacienda and the co-operative regimes, as I detail below, had become more visible, and more threatening with the removal of legal community status, and the subsequent limited ability to control those who set out to alter the course of the river. And these were not just community rivalries. We were told that one of the main culprits was an individual on the far side of the river: an ex-minister of state, armed and determined to defend his right to do as he pleased on the land that he had acquired when in office. We walked past the spot controversially designated for the rubbish dump and could see why the people of Saqllo were not keen. It was located away from the river on the far side of the community's maize field. However, this was not to be a technologically controlled space. All the toxic effluent would run back to the river through their fields.

Our walk elicited a growing sense of the histories of dislocation, interruption, and contestation that marked the course of the Vilcanota River. Finally we came to the house of the hacienda. It was abandoned now, but there were traces of its previous uses. Most recently the building had housed an orphanage. There were still children's drawings on the walls. But the fancy materials and elegant proportions of the *hacendado*'s residence were also visible. It was in the gardens that Pepe began to talk in more detail about the co-operative. His father had been a key figure in this organization before the war with Shining Path in the 1980s that all but put paid to its existence. Pepe talked about what had been cultivated there in the past and how production right along the valley had been co-ordinated from this place. This sense of the productive and social power of the co-operative was quite surprising to us. We had already encountered its current administrative centre in the ex-hacienda of Huarán, down-river from Saqllo. There the co-operative had been introduced to us in a very different light. We had interviewed the current manager, but he had systematically evaded our attempts to elicit anything beyond the short and potted history of how the peasants had heroically occupied the hacienda and evicted the landlord. We talked with people who had lived and worked on the hacienda, and watched Federico García's film *Kuntur Wachana* (1977) with one of the protagonists who had been involved in the take-over. And we had talked with many others in Huarán, members and non-members of what was left of the co-operative. We learned that this once 'model' co-operative had become a secretive and conflict-ridden organization that draws much criticism from local people. As an economic enterprise it retains some relevance locally (it still owns some land and a small meat-processing plant), but these activities are of minimal significance when compared to the organization that Pepe was invoking. Their income now appears to come principally from the rent of a large field to the controversial Camisea gas pipeline project. Nevertheless, the fact that the co-operative does control access to productive land and generates some income from the pipeline is enough to ensure that many families keep up their dues to ensure a foothold in this controversial and dispersed property regime, to which I will return shortly.

As we stood in the grounds of the old hacienda, Pepe said that what he really wanted to do was to set up an agricultural college in this building. It would be perfect. He wanted to recover the spaces that were already proven to be productive and create a community-based centre where local people would learn through experimentation and from each other, and thereby gain both a certain technical autonomy and a reliable and sustainable source of good food. It seemed a great idea, but there was a problem. Pepe thought it unlikely that he would ever be able to raise the funds for such an initiative because it was not clear whom he represented, or whether he was capable of conjuring a 'collective' that could be recognized by potential outside donors as a 'community'. Here the salience of formality returns. Pepe had no formal relationship to this place. It turned out he was not a 'socio' (member/associate) of the co-operative, nor was he a 'socio' of the community of Saqllo, although his mother was. To be a 'socio' is a legal status – one that is surrounded with rules, prerequisites, and an obligation for continual payments in money and/or in labour. Membership in the co-operative is inherited but still has to be paid for – and membership is actively maintained through work. The skills and experiences from which Pepe's dream had grown were obtained from living in faraway places that had precluded his formal inclusion in these corporate bodies. Thus Pepe can support his mother by helping to meet her obligations, and thereby ensure that as and when appropriate, somebody else in the family could assume membership and thus ensure continued access to the land. As far as his dream was concerned there was a further problem with the building. It belonged to an organization (the co-operative) that was in decline and fraught with tensions. Its membership (the socios) was drawn from diverse communities, communities often at odds with each other. To take on the building would require an on-going engagement with the co-operative and all its competing interests and agendas. Formal status, that supported by the kind of mid- to long-term stability that any lending or donor institution would be looking for, would be extremely hard to come by.

The historical background that underpins this example of layered dislocation is complex. In what follows I trace some of the ways in which precarity has taken form in Saqllo at the interface of formality and informality – with respect to the flood damage, to access to agricultural land, and to the thwarted possibilities of Pepe's vision for the future. A key dimension of this account is the shifting and equivocal understandings of co-operative labour – and the tension between the modes of co-operation that secured the collective force of Andean peasant communities, and the debilitating effects of the state-controlled co-operatives that were instigated by the Agrarian Reform. In the tension between these two modes of co-operation it is possible to trace how collective social entities have been rendered ever more 'informal' in recent Peruvian history – in ways that allow for autonomy but also leave people highly vulnerable.

The politics of formalization

The Peruvian Agrarian Reform, which followed a military coup in 1969, imposed a far-reaching expropriation of hacienda land. The regime was responding in part to organized rebellions against the haciendas. The Cusco region was particularly strong and well organized, under the leadership of the charismatic peasant leader Hugo Blanco, based in the fertile lowlands of La Convención. The land reforms of 1969 were extensive but were not intended to hand land over to the peasant workers. This was the same military regime that smashed unions, cancelled elections, and shut down parliament. What they did was impose a top-down reform, implemented through a new regime of collectively managed co-operatives. SINAMOS (the National System for Social Mobilization, which in Spanish produces an acronym that translates as 'without masters') was the government-imposed structure for reform and for participation. The structure was not open to negotiation and in many cases posed huge logistical barriers to productive success. Land was frequently expected to support many more co-operative members than had previously been supported under the hacienda regime. The requirement to take out and to repay loans meant that for some the regular income from hacienda labour disappeared as co-operatives struggled to maintain productivity levels under the new system of distribution. The Reform also legislated against any form of private investment in or sale of agricultural land (Mayer 2009).

In the Vilcanota Valley the expropriations were slow to take off. These lands were valuable and the landowners were well connected. In Huarán the landowner had the support of the Ministry of Agriculture. However, SINAMOS was backing the organized association of peasant and urban union activists, encouraging them to invade the land. Two communities in this area (Arín and Sillacancha) had lost nearly all their productive land to the hacienda, and the *hacendado* had also denied water to the people of Arín as they were seen as trouble-makers. These acts of direct dispossession had created a highly politicized community, increasingly forced to work in contract labour. Many travelled to Quillabamba and beyond into the lowlands province of La Convención, where they came into direct contact with Hugo Blanco and his associates. The Sillacancha community, on the other hand, while utterly dependent on the landlord, also enjoyed his favour, and were never politicized to the same extent as their neighbours in Arín. After expropriation, through a land invasion that was led by the people of Arín, the distribution of land, and of membership rights in the newly formed co-operative, replayed these established inter-community tensions that the landlord had fostered in a policy of divide and rule. The activists were highly organized and the co-operative flourished. Unlike the situation in many other co-operatives, productivity increased, and at the height of its strength in the mid- to late 1970s this venture was one of the largest and most successful highland co-operatives in Southern Peru – stretching down the Vilcanota Valley into the province of La Convención.

However, by 1980 a post-revolutionary government had allowed co-operatives to officially parcel out the land between their members. The Morales Bermudez government (1975-80) that came to power five years after the Agrarian Reform also withdrew technical support from Huarán. Its political antagonism had not been forgotten. In Huarán the *socios* divided the land between themselves according to a formula that favoured the activists from Arín, over the people of Sillacancha. Even within Arín, plot sizes and the value of plots varied considerably. The retrospective logics of accounting that produced this highly differentiated formula for land distribution drew directly on Marxist theories of labour in the calculations of how value had been extracted from those who worked the land. Endowed with a sense of their right to the property that they had fostered over the years without the compensations afforded to the people of Sillacancha, the people of Arín made their demands in ways that were difficult to contest at the time. The current co-operative, however, suffered from the

Journal of the Royal Anthropological Institute (N.S.), 120-133
© Royal Anthropological Institute 2018

long-term effects of this mode of land distribution, which was seen to favour older generations over the young, and established residents over those who had arrived more recently. These movements and inter-generational tensions were exacerbated in the war years of the 1980s and 1990s, a time of huge violence and destruction for this region that removed the last semblance of possibility for running a co-operative of this size. In the 1990s the Fujimori government fully reinstated the market in land as an integral part of its efforts to liberalize the economy and attract foreign investment. As the violence of the war with Shining Path receded, many foreigners began to buy land in the Huarán area, and a new wave of middle-class investors came to dominate the best agricultural lands in the valley, particularly those producing large-kernel maize for export. In many cases the co-operatives found themselves obliged to sell land to avoid the other option of bankruptcy and appropriation by banks that were no longer offering state support, but which still required the payment of outstanding debt.

The dispossession enacted in the 1970s and 1980s was indirect. In many cases the military regime had relied on the active role of the labour unions and peasant federations for the removal of the landowners. Thus despite the heavy top-down nature of the reform, the taking of hacienda lands by local people was lived as part of a radical and organized peasant movement that ensured that the reform law was enforced, often via open conflict with powerful and deep-seated regional elites, as was the case with Huarán. But by the mid-1990s, when Enrique Mayer and his assistant Danny Pinedo were doing their research, the co-operative had almost fallen apart, and when we visited it in 2010 it was in a sorry state. Many of the local residents were not *socios* and had no interest in the success of the venture. When we talked to younger people about the co-operatives that their grandparents had fought for and worked to sustain, we were almost always met with expressions of distrust and disappointment. Nobody believed in the co-operatives any more. Their leaders were thought to be corrupt, interested only in lining their own pockets. People complained that the co-operatives had not succeeded because the *socios* had systematically stolen from them. They had exploited a formalized version of community life without recognizing the politics of formalization.

Building collective futures

This history of struggle and contradiction that characterizes the state-sponsored co-operatives in Peru has had a very debilitating effect not just on the co-operatives themselves but on the communities that existed alongside them – independent but entangled, with overlapping memberships, with adjacent land, with many common problems but no stable basis on which to build collective futures. The effort to survive fosters competition between communities. The arguments over the course of the river and competing claims to rights to extract materials from the river bed are key concerns for the people of Saqllo. So too the arguments over the siting of the rubbish dump. In Huarán, Arín, and Sillacancha water remains at the centre of their struggles as the state seeks to impose business-orientated models of water administration that take control out of the hands of community assemblies. These are difficult issues to resolve as it is never entirely clear who has the right to agree or to refuse access to resources, and on what grounds. Beyond the ambiguities in the law that allow different entities to act in ways that cross-cut each other's spaces of legitimate action, there is also no clear view of who has rights in which collectives.[6] As we have seen, not everybody who lives in a community is a *socio* of that community. Not all members of a *socio*'s family will be a member of the co-operative. When there are struggles over how to regulate the channel of the river there is always a question of whose rights will win out: the community, the co-operative, the individual landowner, the district municipality, the province, or the region? The national body that has the ultimate regulatory authority is rarely there on the ground to enforce the law. People live in the material and regulatory spaces that carry the traces of previous state interventions and withdrawals, just as the hacienda building carries the traces of its former inhabitants, and the river the layered attempts to shore up the bank. Pepe talked to us of how the peasants had been undone (*desorganizados*) by the laws. The ways in which the rights to own and to sell land were imposed enacted not just the dispossession of land, but also the dislocation of co-operative labour as the affective grounds of social community.

These are the circumstances in which families routinely fragment and distribute their efforts to claim the footholds they can in both community and co-operative, to educate the young so that they can find work in the urban centres, or travel abroad, as Pepe has done. These distributed families are clearly still connected in some cases, as needs require family members to circulate in order to fulfil the labour obligations and payments that allow others to remain in place and maintain the land. In this way they keep options open in the face of uncertain futures. In these circulations of care and effort, interrupted futures are all too common, as Pepe's case exemplifies.

Current state policy increasingly requires local people to organize through the model of entrepreneurial governance, as in the case of the control of water resources mentioned above. State services now have to be delivered through enterprises required to engage layers of regulatory complexity – as we found in our original inspection of the flood defences of the Vilcanota River. The achievement of autonomy (the right to manage one's own resources and services) requires communities to address the barrages of regulation, and the audit and transparency protocols that keep all local initiatives firmly tied to centralized modes of state control. In these circumstances, communities struggle to assume the appropriate, legitimate form – as required by law – to operate their own services. There is a constant need for aggregation across community boundaries in ways that require people to establish collectives across differences that have long been established as divisions of competition and conflict. Pepe realized this as he tried to explain to us the impossibility of producing a coherent collective subject for the receipt of a donation or a loan to embark on his agricultural project. The authorities of Huarán, Sillacancha, and Arín also realized this as they struggled to mobilize an effective collective to take control of water distribution and to protect their autonomy by assuming the form of a public enterprise.

Conclusion

I hope to have shown that the precarious condition of Andean rural life is distributed in the bodies of those who travel and those who stay, in those who keep a foothold in the formal collectives that give access to land and those who move out to learn other things, to improve their life chances and to find the means to support those who remain. Following Stewart's suggestion that we look at precarity as a form that takes place through specific attachments, tempos, materialities, and states of being, I have traced how the histories of Saqllo and Haurán play out in the responses to environmental threat and to legal complexity at both the individual and the collective level. Labour practices are central to these endeavours. Ways of working can suture together the possibility of ensuring a collective future. *Ayni* and *faena* exist in tension as modes of co-operative labour. *Ayni* is productive work that engages the land, produces food, nurtures the local earth forces, and, on occasion, gathers state authorities into a space of community, as a mode of autonomous action. It thus constitutes a still compelling institution of relational productivity. State agents willingly engage the logics of *ayni*, but the collectives that *ayni* produces are not formally recognized by the state. *Faena*, by contrast, is a formalized labour agreement, often involving an exchange of community labour for infrastructural provision. *Faena* is the dominant form of collective labour used to build roads, schools, water systems, and so on, and the form of labour that effects the recognition of community and collectives of citizens with the rights to make claims on the state. Furthermore, as we have seen, both *ayni* and *faena*, as modes of collective working, can enact differences and exclusions. The possibilities that these forms of labour afford are in turn vulnerable, as collectives are rendered ever more informal by those agencies of the state focused on the support of corporate extraction and the health of the macro-economy. To these diverse instances of community dislocation we also have to add the effects of a state structure that is itself internally differentiated, its diverse laws working against each other, creating spaces that are simultaneously threatening and replete with possibility. My argument has been that it is in these spaces where formality and informality are mutually constituted, and mutually undermining, that precarity takes form in contemporary Peru.

NOTES

This work draws on a collaborative ethnography carried out with Deborah Poole, Jimena Lynch Cisneros, Annabel Pinker, and Teresa Tupayachi Mar, with support from the NSF, the AHRC, the ACLS, and the Wenner-Gren Foundation. The ethnography presented here was collected and discussed together. The framing of the argument is mine and all errors should be attributed to me. We could not have done this research without the support of the Centro de Estudios Bartolomé de las Casas, Cusco, or of the municipalities of Calca and Urubamba. We are also very grateful to the people of Saqllo, Arín, Huarán, and Sillacancha for their patience and hospitality. I have tried to take on board the very helpful comments from colleagues from Social Anthropology in Manchester and in Lund: many thanks to you all. Thanks also to Maria Kartveit, University of Oslo, for her help in producing the map.

[1] The work of Hardt & Negri (2004) and of Standing (2014) were influential in these discussions. Their work also provoked energetic responses, such as Breman (2013), or a more diffuse sense of suspicion within the discipline for over-generalized, or universalizing, concepts that erase the cultural and historical specificity on which ethnographic insight depends (Muehlebach 2013).

[2] The interplay between local and external forces of differentiation has been central to discussions of inequality for many decades. See, for example, the study by Norman Long and Bryan Roberts (1979) of economic differentiation in the Mantaro Valley in the central highlands of Peru.

[3] See Poole (1987) for the changing forms of violence that marked the herding economies of the highlands of Cusco from the 1830s to the 1930s.

[4] Kathleen Millar's (2014) ethnography of the *catadores*, the urban poor who collect, recycle, and sell what they find in Rio de Janeiro's garbage dump, follows a similar line of argument.

[5] These concepts are the basic building blocks of anthropological studies of Andean rural life. Key ethnographic elaborations include Allen (1988), de la Cadena (2015), Gose (1994), Harris (2000), Harvey (2001), and Sallnow (1987; 1989).

[6] In similar vein David Mosse (1997) has described the neoliberal expansion of rule-governed behaviours over previous expressions of symbolic capital and power relations.

REFERENCES

ALLEN, C. 1988. *The hold life has: coca and cultural identity in an Andean community*. Washington, D.C.: Smithsonian Institution Press.
ALLISON, A. 2016. Precarity: commentary by Anne Allison. *Cultural Anthropology* website (available on-line: *https://culanth.org/curated_collections/21-precarity/discussions/26-precarity-commentary-by-anne-allison*, accessed 19 January 2018).
BREMAN, J. 2013. A bogus concept? *New Left Review* **84**, 130-8.

BUTLER, J. 2009. *Frames of war: when is life grievable?* New York: Verso.

DE LA CADENA, M. 2015. *Earth beings: ecologies of practice across Andean worlds.* Durham, N.C.: Duke University Press.

GANDOLFO, D. 2013. Formless: a day at Lima's Office of Formalization. *Cultural Anthropology* **28**, 278-98.

GOSE, P. 1994. *Deathly waters and hungry mountains: agrarian ritual and class formation in an Andean town.* Toronto: University Press.

HARDT, M. & A. NEGRI 2004. *Multitude: war and democracy in the Age of Empire.* London: Penguin.

HARRIS, O. 2000. *To make the earth bear fruit: ethnographic essays on fertility, work, and gender in highland Bolivia.* London: Institute of Latin American Studies.

HART, K. 1973. Informal income: opportunities and urban employment in Ghana. *Journal of Modern African Studies* **11**, 61-89.

HARVEY, P. 2001. Landscape and commerce: creating contexts for the exercise of power. In *Contested landscapes: movement, exile and place* (eds) B. Bender & M. Winer, 197-210. London: Bloomsbury.

LONG, N. & B. ROBERTS (eds) 1979. *Peasant cooperation and capitalist expansion in Central Peru.* Austin: University of Texas Press.

MAYER, E. 2009. *Ugly stories of the Peruvian Agrarian Reform.* Durham, N.C.: Duke University Press.

MILLAR, K. 2014. The precarious present: wage labor and disrupted life in Rio de Janeiro, Brazil. *Cultural Anthropology* **25**, 7-33.

——— 2016. Precarity: interview with the authors. *Cultural Anthropology* website (available on-line: *https://culanth.org/curated_collections/21-precarity/discussions/27-precarity-interview-with-the-authors*, accessed 19 January 2018).

MOSSE, D. 1997. The symbolic making of a common property resource: history, ecology and locality in a tank irrigated development in South India. *Development and Change* **28**, 467-504.

MUEHLEBACH, A. 2013. On precariousness and the ethical imagination: the year 2012 in sociocultural anthropology. *American Anthropologist* **115**, 297-311.

POOLE, D. 1987. Landscapes of power in a cattle-rustling culture of Southern Andean Peru. *Dialectical Anthropology* **12**, 367-98.

SALLNOW, M. 1987. *Pilgrims of the Andes: regional cults in Cusco.* Washington, D.C.: Smithsonian Institution Press.

——— 1989. Cooperation and contradiction: the dialectics of everyday practice. *Dialectical Anthropology* **14**, 241-57.

STANDING, G. 2014. *The precariat: the new dangerous class* (Revised edition). London: Bloomsbury Academic.

STEWART, K. 2012. Precarity's forms. *Cultural Anthropology* **27**, 518-25.

Futurs interrompus : travail coopératif et formes changeantes de précarité collective dans les régions rurales des Andes péruviennes

Résumé

L'intérêt de la sociologie pour le travail précaire se concentre habituellement sur l'insécurité existentielle associée à la discontinuité des relations de travail dans les modes de production contemporains et sur les difficultés que pose la création de modes efficaces de solidarité sociale et politique. Par contraste, le présent article explore la continuité d'une existence précaire dans le sud des Andes péruviennes au fil du siècle passé. Il se concentre sur la manière dont la force affective des obligations sociales et des responsabilités envers les collectivités au sens large (famille, communauté paysanne ou coopérative) soutiennent la recherche d'un futur personnel et collectif plus stable, et l'interrompent en même temps. En abordant la précarité comme une situation relationnelle, l'article retrace la formation de la précarité dans les mouvements entre les pratiques de travail formelles et informelles.

8

Working (wo)man's suicide: transnational relocations of capital – repercussions for labour in South Korea and the Philippines

ELISABETH SCHOBER *University of Oslo*

In South Korea, 2011 was marked by the rise of a social movement against precarity, the emergence of which was dependent upon effective and affective mobilizing strategies amongst workers. The impetus was provided by a struggle at a shipyard in Pusan, where an activist held a crane occupied for 309 days. The role of affect in constituting neoliberal workplaces has recently received much attention in anthropology. The question of how emotions figure into the mobilizing efforts of labour, rather than those of management, however, has been overlooked. Hope and despair are two emotive themes amongst activists involved in the Hanjin dispute that are closely linked to the practice of suicide amongst unionized workers in the country. Since the 1997 Asian financial crisis, suicide has also become an all-too-ordinary response to pressures imposed upon an increasingly precarious Korean workforce. I look into the affective mobilizing cultures that have allowed the 'Hope Bus' movement to excel in Korea, and explore the less successful efforts that were made by Korean and Filipino activists to link up their struggles.

Introduction: what the future might bring

'The future?' The eighth president of the Hanjin chapter of the Korean Metal Workers' Union (KMWU)[1] broke into laughter once he had heard my question concerning forthcoming activities at the Pusan shipyard of Hanjin Heavy Industries and Construction (HHIC).[2] 'There is no future!' His two companions exchanged looks, and then intervened: 'President, why are you saying this?' After a moment of silence, the president began with a more measured reply: a list of things the trade unionists would do to get their association back on track. Though it was once several thousand people strong and had throughout 2011 been at the heart of the nation-wide 'Hope Bus' movement against precarity, it was rapidly losing its members to a new 'yellow union'[3] and only a few dozen members were left when we talked in November 2013. The president had clearly put much thought into how things could be turned around once again; but his outburst was what stayed with me, long after our meeting had come to an end.

It did not help that we had just spent hours talking about the deaths of various members of this union. As we walked into the Pusan headquarters of the Korean Confederation of Trade Unions (KCTU), where our encounter took place, the prominence of suicide in what was to follow had already been foreshadowed: a makeshift memorial, featuring a large poster of a smiling man, had been erected at the entrance to commemorate yet another dead worker involved in the ill-fated struggle at Ssangyong. Amidst the desperation after a defeated strike and plant occupation that had been led by the KMWU Ssangyong Motor Company Union in 2009, Ssangyong workers began to kill themselves, with over two dozen of them committing suicide until now. While the death toll at KMWU's Hanjin union was not quite as large as the one amongst Ssangyong, over the years quite a few bodies had accumulated in this shipbuilding chapter of the KMWU, too.

The most recent incident had occurred just eleven months prior to my visit, when Choe Kang-seo, the Organizing Director of the KMWU Hanjin chapter, hanged himself at the union's office inside the shipyard. Choe thereby became the latest casualty among a series of union leaders who died owing to their organizing activities at this workplace: Park Chang-soo (†1991), Kim Joo-ik (†2003), Kwak Jae-yoo (†2003), and now Choe (†2012) – a list of names I was to become familiar with that stood for a chronology of despair. While Park Chang-soo, then union president, was allegedly murdered by secret police in 1991, Choe killed himself in December 2012, shortly after it had become clear that Park Guen-hye, the daughter of South Korea's former dictator Park Chung-hee, had won the presidential elections (see Kim 2013). Choe's death by suicide, as much as it had to do with national politics, also needs to be read against the backdrop of a prolonged labour dispute at the shipyard that had stalled relations between management and the workforce since the early 2000s. It was also part of a more extensive strategy deployed by activists affiliated with the KCTU and KMWU – that is, mobilization through suicide.

HHIC, an offshoot of the powerful Hanjin *chaebol*,[4] acquired the shipyard in question in the late 1980s. In the wake of the Asian financial crisis, HHIC would begin to drastically downsize its workforce, with thousands of jobs eventually lost. Having been subjected to this restructuring, by 2010, the traditionally militant workers at the shipyard were disorganized and fragmented. In an attempt to cut through the infighting, in early 2011 a labour activist called Kim Jin-sook, a Direction Committee member of the Pusan branch of KCTU and former welder at the shipyard herself, sneaked onto Hanjin premises and climbed atop a crane. This particular machine was of major symbolic significance to local unionists: in 2003, it had been occupied by union president Kim Joo-ik, who committed suicide on it at the end of a failed strike, with another worker (Kwak Jae-yoo) then jumping off a dock as well. Kim Jin-sook's 2011 protest on the same crane thus tapped into this history of local struggles that had earlier cost the lives of Park Chang-Soo, Kim Joo-ik, and Kwak Jae-yoo. Incidentally, her nearly one-year-long occupation also inspired the Hope Bus movement – a broader coalition that took off across Korea in a concerted effort to support Kim, and that temporarily managed to bring the issue of precarity onto the national agenda.

Following key inputs by Hardt and Negri (e.g. Hardt 1999; Hardt & Negri 2000), the role that affect plays in constituting neoliberal workplaces has recently received much attention in anthropology (e.g. Muehlebach 2011; Richard & Rudnyckyj 2009; for a critique, see Yanagisako 2012). The question of how affect figures into the mobilizing practices of *labour* rather than management, however, is still understudied. We have learned from the anthropology of emotions, and in particular from Lutz (e.g. 1988) and Rosaldo (e.g. 1984), that emotions are a deeply social and collective experience and also serve as normative devices allowing for the judgement of others, particularly in cross-cultural encounters (Lutz 1986). The fundamental tension in much of this older

Journal of the Royal Anthropological Institute (N.S.), 134-147
© Royal Anthropological Institute 2018

literature, as Boellstorff and Lindquist (2004) have pointed out, is the question as to whether emotions are the property of persons, or are to be situated in larger collectives instead.

These debates on the individual versus the communal in the study of emotions (for an overview, see Beatty 2014; Lutz & White 1986) have recently been revived and reconfigured with the rise of the term 'affect' (e.g. Berlant & Greenwald 2012; Ramos-Zayas 2011; Stewart 2012). Affect, Mazzarella (2009) has argued in a major intervention, is best kept conceptually apart from emotion, where the latter is understood as a personalized experience that is simultaneously culturally/semiotically mediated. Affect, in contrast, highlights involuntariness and an anchoring in pre-linguistic, non-conscious, and pre-subjective experiences of the often collective kind, and significantly impacts the way we make sense of the world. Affect, Mazzarella argues, is a crucial component in the workings of structures of power in the sense that 'any social project that is not imposed through force alone must be affective in order to be effective' (2009: 299). While this certainly rings true, such a post-structuralist focus may not necessarily invite us to look into how radical social movements *resist* those very same structures: namely by deploying mobilizing strategies that are equally as much 'affective in order to be effective'.

Here, I shall propose a somewhat different distinction between emotion and affect. Significantly, if we view emotions as anchored in the bodies of already socialized individuals, then perhaps affect should be more firmly conceptualized as pertaining to the workings of larger collectives – Mazzarella himself seems only to suggest affinities between affect and crowds, rather than actually to situate it in the larger collective *per se*. Additionally, if we want to understand the role of affect in labour politics, we also have to pay attention to how embodied emotional experiences are being re-scaled into matters of affect that are then mobilized with the purpose of swaying larger (imagined) units such as a class or a nation in new directions. Hope versus despair are two interlinked emotive themes that I have identified amongst Korean labour activists involved in the Hanjin dispute, which these actors – by teasing them out of the stories of a handful of labour activists who have sacrificed themselves – have sought to utilize time and again in their effort to mobilize crowds into political action.

Suicide is considered an extreme but legitimate action among leftist actors in Korea. Regardless of the motivation, the act of killing oneself is a singular and violent event which tends to have major social ramifications in itself, as the self-targeted physical aggression it involves often causes many negative ripple effects that impact on the lives of others.[5] Since the days of the military dictatorship (1960-93), arguably *because of* its capacity to impact the emotional composition of others and thereby disturb the social codes normally at play, suicide has repeatedly been used to conjure up mass support.[6] Incidentally, in the post-Asian financial crisis era, suicide has also become an all-too-ordinary, quasi-apolitical response to market pressures imposed upon an increasingly precarious Korean workforce. In light of this increasing prevalence of suicide, I will show how Kim Jin-sook's struggle on the crane created emotive resonances that reverberated far beyond the walls of the shipyard to then become a major affective force. Through the usage of social media and other technologies, Kim and her comrades tapped into and amplified the strong emotions around the issue of suicide and work. In such a way, they both exhumed a history of activist martyrdom and simultaneously highlighted a disturbing suicide trend amongst an increasingly precarious workforce. Hanjin's shipyard in Pusan, I will argue, was moved into the spotlight because the dispute

Journal of the Royal Anthropological Institute (N.S.), 134-147
© Royal Anthropological Institute 2018

unfolding there allowed the participants of the Hope Bus movement to engage with a number of large-scale politico-economic changes that have recently impacted South Korean labour.

HHIC, like other players in shipbuilding, has reacted to Chinese competition by steadily laying off permanent employees and hiring new workers through subcontractors instead. This company, however, has also chosen simultaneously to offshore much of its production to a new shipyard in the Philippines, where 34,000 Filipino workers currently produce ships at a much lower cost. While the main focus here will be on how emotions around suicide were utilized as a mobilizing force that has allowed the Hope Bus movement to excel in South Korea, I will also briefly outline the less successful efforts that were made by Korean and Filipino activists to link up their struggles. My argument here is that the mobilizing cultures of affect that were employed in Korea could not entirely be translated to the Philippines. Filipino trade unionists, in their conversations with me, have on occasion stressed how differing cultural traits come into play when it comes to questions as to why such drastic techniques did not 'catch on' in their country. Before delving into this, I shall investigate what 'precarity' might mean in a South Korean and Philippine context. In the final sections, I shall give an overview of the history that preceded and enabled the Hope Bus movement, and the particular emotive elements that allowed this movement against precarious work to emerge.

The rise of precarity

The notion of precarity has gained much traction in anthropology over recent years (e.g. Allison 2013; Millar 2014; Molé 2010), with ethnographers increasingly becoming alert to the many ways in which labour, the state, and perhaps even 'the possibility of life itself' (Muehlebach 2013: 298) are becoming eroded in our most recent round of 'overheated' globalization (Eriksen 2016). The related concept of 'the precariat' (Standing 2014) has also started to enjoy popularity in the social sciences at large. Standing has argued that in order to understand the reality of contemporary labour, 'we need a new vocabulary, one reflecting class relations in the global market system of the twenty-first century' (2014: 8).

Standing's term, understood as referring to working populations that lack a list of securities, has been heavily critiqued for being ahistorical and Eurocentric (e.g. Breman 2013). To be sure, the notion of the precariat has some analytical drawbacks if conceptualized in the way Standing has proposed. At the same time, both 'precarity' and the 'precariat', if situated in a global framework and with longer histories of capitalist accumulative cycles in mind, may still open up opportunities to ethnographers. If we do take the premise seriously that workers in one location are only *made precarious* in relation to cheaper workforces elsewhere, the actual historical processes behind the most recent wave of labour depreciation could then come to the foreground of our investigations. And Hanjin's offshoring of capital and production from Korea to the Philippines may serve as a good case in point.

What is more, these debates around precarity have not stayed confined to academic realms, but are simultaneously negotiated amongst labour groups in many locations. In South Korea, for instance, the question of '*pijeonggyujig*' (non-regular work)[7] has taken centre stage since the mid-2000s. South Korea, *the* poster-child of rapid development, built up its economy during the 1970s and 1980s while a succession of military regimes (with which conglomerates like Hanjin were closely associated) kept wages artificially low. After initial successes were made through the promotion of the garment sector, it was strategic state investments in heavy industries like shipbuilding that allowed South Korea to prosper (see Chang 2010). The steep ascent that followed, coupled with the onset of democratization in the 1990s, also gave rise to higher labour standards, and wages have in the meantime risen exponentially.

The move to partially dismantle these achievements for labour again, however, followed rather quickly, namely in the wake of the Asian financial crisis of 1997. The rise of atypical labour regimes can be directly traced to this period, when the country's elites were pressured by the IMF to deregulate its labour market (see Schober in press). With workers in South Korea having made gains in labour-related securities only during the decade before the crisis, they now saw these privileges rapidly disappearing again, a fact that can also be traced in data made available by the Korea Labor Institute: while the proportion of non-regular workers in the total working population stood at 27.4 per cent in 2002, it increased to 37 per cent by 2004, and has since stabilized at around 34 per cent (see Shin 2013: 336).

The uneven burden-sharing that the 1997 crisis triggered subsequently led to many bankruptcies of small business owners, and to far-reaching lay-offs that came to impact ever larger numbers of only recently securely employed workers. Such livelihood losses, which continued for many years after the crisis, often led to the most tragic of all outcomes, with the available suicide figures telling a clear story: while in 1997, 13 per 100,000 people in South Korea committed suicide, by 2011, this number had grown to 33.3 per 100,000 (Min, Park, Hwang & Min 2015: 75). Although these dreadful statistics are unarguably also the outcome of a bundle of other social, cultural, and historical factors (with suicide being the most severe, yet somewhat socially acceptable, response to personal tragedies in the country), South Korea today consistently makes it into the top three lists of OECD countries that hold the record of having the largest numbers of people taking their own lives.

Korean shipbuilding is an industry that was even more dramatically affected by the precarization of previously secure jobs. Today, more than 50 per cent of the approximately 100,000 jobs at Korean shipyards are filled by irregular workers, who typically earn much less than their co-workers who hold regular positions. And while this process began shortly after the 1997 crisis, it only gained in speed during the recent global recession. Shipbuilding, which of course is closely tied to the shipping industry, is nearly seismographic in the way it responds to global market troubles. Consequently, the whole sector took a deep hit after 2008/9, which eventually cost South Korea its world leadership role. Until 2011, South Korea's powerful shipbuilding industry was still the global leader, with ships also representing the country's number one export item until 2008. But in recent years, the pressure from China, with its lower labour costs, has transformed the situation. As a direct response to this, Hanjin, like other major players in Korean shipbuilding, has been steadily increasing the number of workers hired through subcontractors to stay competitive.

Hanjin, however, has also utilized another strategy to keep up with the Chinese: in 2006, it began the construction of one of the world's largest shipyards in the Philippines, where 34,000 Filipino workers are currently employed who earn a fraction of what a Korean worker at the old Pusan shipyard makes. Nearly all of Hanjin's workforce in Subic are recruited through a complicated network of subcontractors, and the company takes a 'hands-on' approach towards dealing with labour, which, for instance, involves an informal ban on unions at the yard (see Schober 2018). And indeed, while Korea has, in a rather uneven fashion, recently made its entry into the capitalist heartlands, the Philippines is a country whose economy is characterized by only a small, rather undeveloped formal sector. Home-grown industries are stagnating at best, and the agricultural sector is much on the decline. Additionally, the small formal labour market is currently being subjected to new forms of precarization (see Ofreneo 2013), a development that is often summarized as 'labour contractualization' amongst Filipino labour activists. Today, up to 77 per cent of Filipinos are working in the informal sector (Ofreneo 2013: 424). In such an environment of massive under- and unemployment, unionism, a very weak form of organizing in the Philippines to begin with, is massively on the retreat (Espejo 2012). Before looking into unionization attempts at Hanjin's shipyard in the Philippines, however, let us now return to Korea, where increasingly entrenched labour activists have taken a number of drastic measures to counter management.

'Until you win this struggle'

> Dear Comrades! No matter how I die, my dead body must be placed on Crane No. 85. The crane must be my grave until you win this struggle. I will guard the square of the struggle and the victory of union members, even when dead.
>
> Kim Joo-ik's suicide note (Jang 2004: 272)

Kim Jin-sook is an unassuming woman in her early fifties, and sitting across from her at a coffee shop nearby KCTU's Pusan office in 2013, it was easy to nearly forget that her one-woman strike on a crane moved a country into debating a labour issue that had been a distinctly local matter at first, but eventually sparked nation-wide discussions on the rapid informalization of labour. I had met Kim in Berlin the year before, when an NGO I was involved with collaborated with IG Metall (the German metalworkers' union) to organize a speaking tour. I had been impressed by her energy back then, which she displayed even though she was still ailing from many physical problems after her year on the crane, entirely dependent upon the protection provided by her union friends who defended her from the ground. That crane, she told me during our second encounter, was now a thing of the past. Too old, management had said in a public statement as to why they had it dismantled, but many suspected the events of 2011 had more to do it with it than the machine's age.

Kim Jin-sook, originally from Seoul, came to Pusan in the early 1980s to look for work in the city's flourishing heavy industries. In the past, she had worked at a garment factory. What made her switch from this rather female kind of labour into the highly masculine domain of welding was that the pay was much higher in shipbuilding. In 1981, she graduated from Korea Shipbuilding and Engineering Corporation's training institute for women and got a job at the shipyard shortly thereafter. That facility, originally built in 1937 by Japanese, was a state-run enterprise until the late 1980s. Kim 'was one of about a hundred or so women who were hired as welders or metal cutters at the yard between 1977 and 1981. During that period the company opened these skilled production jobs to women for the first time because of acute shortages in the skilled workforce following the *chaebol* companies' entrance into the shipbuilding industry' (Nam 2009: 211).

Kim gradually becoming involved in labour activism, and in 1986, senior workers at the yard encouraged her to become the first female union representative. The union, which used to be a haven for militants in the 1960s, had in the meantime become a rather typical yellow union that was more concerned with collaborating with management than with workers' grievances. Kim's bid to join the union assembly was controversial, and she won her seat only after sneaking to the top of a crane, from where she gave a speech to the assembled workers (Nam 2009: 212). The company found an excuse to fire her soon thereafter. Over the years, practically all of her fired trade union friends were re-hired, but Kim found herself permanently black-listed. She would stick around, however, a permanent fixture at any labour event related to the shipyard, but no longer with official ties to the workplace.

As noted above, in 1991, Park Chang-soo, union president at that time, died a suspicious death that would turn him into a martyr for the movement. Park had joined the workforce in 1981, the same year as Kim, and had quickly made himself a name as a charismatic leader. Park was then arrested, and after three months of imprisonment he was moved to a hospital on 4 May 1991. Two days later, he was found dead, having succumbed to the aftermath of a window fall. Hundreds of students and workers then occupied the hospital, demanding his body back for an independent autopsy. Eventually, the family was handed over a corpse that had been chopped into pieces, making further examination impossible. The authorities then issued the statement that the autopsy had shown signs of a suicide, but activists insist to this day that he died at the hands of the KCIA, the Korean secret police, allegedly as part of their attempt to crush the union at Hanjin (see Presidential Truth Commission on Suspicious Deaths 2004: 262ff.). Park's legacy, Nam has argued, 'deeply etched its place on the Hanjin unionists' collective memory. The union has kept the memory of his sacrifice alive, and the union's reputation as being one of the most militant and democratic unions in the post-1987 union movement in South Korea remains strong today' (2009: 215).

Consequently, when twelve years later, in 2003, a strike broke out at the shipyard, Park's death was still a living memory amongst the activists involved. In the post-crisis era, Hanjin, now owner of the shipyard, was pushing for a restructuring of its workforce, and voluntary retirement programmes had slowly brought the number of workers down. With 650 layoffs announced in 2003, the union president at that time, Kim Joo-ik, announced a strike, climbing on top of crane 85 to pressure management to re-hire the workers. HHIC, however, countered by utilizing a new legal weapon: a recent amendment to the labour law had significantly narrowed the scope of what constituted a lawful labour dispute, and a court now declared the strike at Hanjin illegal, with the company threatening unionists with a seizure of their personal assets.

Four days before Kim Joo-ik's suicide, Hanjin sent out a notice to the workers that 'If you do not stop the illegal strike and return to the workplace, we will place your deposit, house, and wages under provisional seizure and we will bring a compensation suit for the damages caused' (Jang 2004: 275). Threatened in such a way, numerous union members abandoned the strike. As Kim Jin-sook explained in an interview in Berlin 2012 at which I was present:

> The apartments and cars of people were to be seized. Under such pressure, [most of] the strikers were giving in to the pressure: 2,400 gave up, only 60 remained. Kim Joo-ik ... occupied the crane and protested on it for 129 days, until he finally hanged himself in the crane. His salary at that time was less than 10,000 won [= €70], because everything else had been temporarily seized. That's how workers were ruined.[8]

After the suicide of the president, his comrades, according to his wishes laid out in his suicide note, prevented his body from being taken down from the crane. For two weeks, Kim Joo-ik's body stayed there packed in ice, an undertaking that the conservative press of the country described as 'taking a corpse hostage' (*Dong-A Ilbo* 2013). The dreadful tug-of-war between workers and management over the body of Kim was finally brought to a tipping-point when, as noted above, another unionized worker, Kwak Jae-yoo, followed Kim's example and jumped off a dock. Faced with two deaths and mounting public pressure, HHIC gave in and took the lay-offs back. The funeral rites for the two deceased that were held by the union at the shipyard then turned into a much publicized event. Incidentally, it was Kim Jin-sook who held the eulogy at the ceremony, giving a long, tear-filled speech in which she apologized repeatedly to her dead comrades for having let them down by not fighting hard enough for their cause.

The Hope Bus movement

> The voices of Kim and the Bus of Hope transcended the boundaries of HHIC's shipyard as an individual workplace, and echoed throughout the nation.
>
> *Kyunghyang Shinmun* 2011

Eight years after Kim Joo-ik's suicide, Kim Jin-sook would make her way up the crane. On 6 January 2011, she climbed up the machine, leaving a message to her friends that 'this was the hardest choice for me to make because I knew what Crane #85 means to us. I will step down from this crane alive, which is what Joo-ik could never do but desperately wanted to do'. By protesting the latest round of dismissals in such a way (this time affecting 430 workers), Kim Jin-sook literally followed in Kim Joo-ik's footsteps. Thousands of jobs had already been lost over the course of a decade – 7,000 regular workers were still employed at Hanjin in 2003, Kim Jin-sook told me, while the number was down to 1,500 by late 2013.

The first few months on the crane were rather quiet for Kim Jin-sook – her battle-experienced comrades had found ways to defend the crane from below from the onslaught of riot police and hired thugs, and managed to supply Kim with food to get her through the first few days that quickly turned into weeks. Significantly, they had also smuggled a cellphone up, which allowed Kim to communicate with the world through Twitter. Tweeting during nearly every waking hour, Kim slowly built up a large number of followers, with this technology allowing her to create a wider audience than many labour activists before her. With some of her tweets being shared by Kim Yeo-jin, a famous actress sympathetic to her cause, tens of thousands of people eventually became followers. Other civil society actors outside of the labour movement slowly began to pay attention, too, and a first caravan of Hope Buses would then make its way on 7 June 2011. On that day, 750 participants were bused to Pusan, where they joined nearly 7,000 local protesters. Two days later, a second Hope Bus event involved 175 buses and 50 vans, which carried approximately 12,000 people from various regions of South Korea to Pusan (see Robinson 2011). Five such Hope Bus events would be organized, which, over the course of the next few months, brought tens of thousands of protestors together, who came to catch a glimpse of the lonely female figure on top of the crane.

The individual motivations that drove students, housewives, religious leaders, day labourers, migrant workers, and university professors to join these buses were immensely diverse; but the affective dimension of being swayed by a collective attempt to prevent Kim from taking a most desperate measure was certainly crucial. After all, it was specifically the implicit danger that Kim, too, could lose her life that made her gesture to re-take crane 85 so powerful and that grabbed the attention of people near

Journal of the Royal Anthropological Institute (N.S.), 134-147
© Royal Anthropological Institute 2018

and far. By backing her demands up with the unspoken threat that her death could be the ultimate outcome if negotiations broke down (an issue that did not have to be directly communicated by Kim, given the widespread circulation of the history of crane 85 through left-wing social media and the press), Kim not only tapped into a labour history of self-sacrifice; her posture at the top of the crane also made her the seemingly unlikely heroine for a rising army of Korean precarious workers. In such a way, she 'emerged ... as the champion of irregular workers [in South Korea], the majority of whom are women' (Robinson 2011).

The fact that Kim is not your typical male industrial worker (a social figure that has come under as much criticism in Korea as elsewhere) may be one of the main reasons why she was so successful in eliciting solidarity. To be sure, suicides are a rather widespread method amongst activists in Korea, and many unionists have died without ever conjuring up as much support as Kim did. Her exceptionalism as a female activist operating in such a male-dominated world as shipbuilding, who was perhaps seen as particularly in need of support, was also communicated to her supporters during repeated public screenings of her highly emotional eulogy held at Kim Joo-ik's and Kwak Jae-yoo's double funeral. Parts of the eulogy were eventually even shown during a parliamentary hearing in August 2011, where Cho Nam-ho, HHIC's chairman, was forced to appear. After the footage ended, representative Chung Dong-Young used the silence to point at Cho Nam-ho, arguing that '[he] murdered his employees with massive lay-offs' (Ser 2011). Cho thereby became the first head of a *chaebol* to be summoned to appear before the Korean parliament in fourteen years (Santi 2011), with precarious workers viewing him as a member of the economic elite who could be blamed for some of the developments in their country (see *Kyunghyang Shinmun* 2011).

It was interesting that it was 'hope' (Korean: *huimang*) that became *the* central term around which various social strata gathered in an attempt to prevent yet another worker's death. Poet Song Kyung-dong, who was also one of the main organizers of the movement, had suggested taking the term '*huimang-twaejig*' – i.e. 'voluntary redundancy' – and reappropriating some of its hidden meanings: a suggestion that readily caught on amongst an increasingly disenfranchised working population. The first section of the word (i.e. '*huimang*') can also mean 'hope', and it was this sense nestled in the bleak prospects that came with voluntary redundancy schemes that was now to be teased out. Hope, labour activists and civil society members could agree upon, was indeed much needed in today's Korea, so the individual tragedies that stood behind the Hanjin lay-offs were now recast as signs that a possibility for change could still be discerned on the horizon, if enough people took such labour restructuring as a wake-up call for action.

At the end of 2011, and after mounting pressure from many sectors of Korean society, Hanjin declared defeat, and an agreement was reached to reinstate the ninety-odd laid-off union members who were still part of the strike. HHIC's management thus gave in to the intense public pressure that had built up (see Baca 2011). The gains made for Korean labour were certainly of significant symbolic value; but the spillover to HHIC's other shipyard in the Philippines was preciously small, as we shall see.

From Pusan to the Philippines: offshoring resistance?

> They don't want unions. Because it's a headache for them ... That's why it's hard to have unions here in Subic, because the unions in Korea, they are very strong. The workers, they died for the unions, that's why they don't want that here. My [Korean] manager told me that. I asked him, why don't you

allow unions here? And he said, because in Korea, the unions, they are giving their lives. They go on a strike for hundreds of days, and the union won.

Lauren, a former Hanjin employee

During the year of solidarity actions, violent clashes, and parliamentary debates in Korea, the controversy in Pusan also brought attention to Hanjin's second shipyard in the Philippines. At the centre of these Korean discussions was the issue as to whether Hanjin's financial status at that time warranted the mass dismissals of unionized workers. Hanjin claimed that the global recession hit the company so hard that cutbacks were inevitable. However, while at Hanjin's shipyard in Pusan not a single shipbuilding order came in between 2009 and 2011, dozens of deals to build vessels were signed at its other shipyard in Subic Bay, raising suspicions in Korea that the company was re-locating orders to justify its restructuring plans in Pusan (see Lee 2011). All the while, some labour activists used the commotion created by the Hope Bus movement to forge ties with labour groups in the Philippines, as they believed that the offshoring move by capital could only be tackled by globalizing the labour struggle.

The year 2011 consequently also saw activities nearby Hanjin's shipyard in the Philippines, a high point of which was reached when Filipino labour activists organized a 'Caravan for Decent Work and Human Working Conditions'. Modelled after the Hope Bus movement, this event brought hundreds of participants together, who drove fifty vehicles from Manila to Subic Bay. In Subic, the caravan was then met by 600 workers who joined the participants in protest, with a representative of KMWU, a dismissed Hanjin worker from Pusan, and several Korean journalists also being present during the event. Much of the connecting work between different actors involved in this protest was undertaken by representatives of Building and Woodworkers International (BWI), a global union that provided some project funds to local organizers in Subic around that time. The alliance forged during those days, however, fell apart relatively quickly once the international spotlight was no longer on the Hanjin case.

The reasons for the breakdown of this budding transnational movement linking Hanjin's two shipyards are multifarious. The company, for instance, fired dozens of workers in Subic whom they suspected of unionizing, and had their careers at the shipyard stalled once they were identified by management as potential trouble-makers. Philippine labour law only allows company-based organizing (i.e. it prohibits organizing at an industry-wide level), which had far-reaching consequences here. In 2008, a coalition of labour groups filed a claim with the Philippine Department of Labour to form an official union at Hanjin. However, their request was denied, with the group being told to organize at the various subcontracting companies that actually provide Hanjin with labour. At that time, Hanjin still had approximately 100 subcontractors, 'but all the machines, all the stuff, it's all Hanjin', as local labour activist Dan of unofficial union Samahan explained to me. Hanjin in such a way had successfully utilized its elaborate subcontracting system to limit its social obligations towards labour and prevent unionization. Finally, dynamics within the Philippine labour movement also played a detrimental role: once project funding provided to local organizers had to be cut at BWI, labour activists attached to two different groups could no longer agree over how to connect diverging ideological approaches.

Finally, the question of how emotion is re-scaled into affect may have also played a role in the vastly different outcomes in the Philippines. As Tes Borgoños, a representative of BWI, explained to me:

It was in 2011 that we really had these big campaigns. And it was written about in the international papers. And I think it also helped the Korean unions a lot … to win their case. But yes … we're back to zero. Still organizing. Because we cannot do what the Korean unions did in South Korea, you know. I see their mobilization; and I was really very impressed.

She directly attributed the successes of the Korean workers to a difference in organizing cultures: 'Of course, you know, Korean workers [*laughs*] – they are really very aggressive. They can mobilize thousands of people. And they won! They are able to win issues! We cannot do that here in the Philippines'. Life-or-death strategies like Kim's were nothing that unionists in the Philippines would be able to deploy in order to gain larger support, she believed:

I cannot imagine that any the workers in Hanjin Philippines [would] do [what Kim Jin-sook did]. I'm really amazed by what Korean workers can do. Of course, there's lots of history. There are lots of stories … For instance, they burn themselves in one of the [garment factories].[9] Of course, there are a lot of questions about that, too – if you are a good worker, why do you waste your life … And you can still do a lot of good things while you are alive, you know. But this kind of culture, although some [of it is] extreme, but some [aspects] of the culture in [the Korean] trade union movement, they can still win issues …

The story of Kim Jin-sook's struggle on the crane is certainly exceptional in the way it tapped into the dormant emotions of many around the issue of work-related suicide and recast them into an affective force that gradually came to engage with ever larger social circles in South Korea. At the same time, the company that Kim and her comrades were contesting proved rather adept at using offshoring as a strategy to de-mobilize labour in the longer run, with workers seemingly unable to keep up with the gradual cheapening of their worth at this work-site. The possibility needs to be considered that the lengthy struggles at the shipyard in Pusan were also a learning opportunity for the corporation, which used the latest round of crisis-ridden globalization to take its investments elsewhere: that is, to a location where labour's attempts to organize could be stifled from the start. The factors that have contributed to this outcome in the Philippines, as we have seen, were manifold. One significant aspect, I believe, was that the emotive content of a struggle like that of Kim Jin-sook perhaps cannot indefinitely be scaled up (going from local to national to international). In this particular case, the nation proved to be a boundary that was rather hard to overcome for labour actors, with Tes Borgoños pointing to differing cultural traits that supposedly divide Filipino and Korean activists in the way they understand suicide, which may be a reason why this form of mobilization catches on only in certain settings, while it is a no-starter in others.

The widespread relocation of capital across national borders that the Hanjin case exemplifies has consequently often had dire outcomes for labour – a social force which finds itself increasingly dislocated from its older mobilizing strategies, and at a loss when it comes to countering the detrimental effects of globalization. While offshoring capital was indeed a possible (and profitable) feat for Hanjin, connecting labour at the two shipbuilding sites, as of today, is proving a hard task indeed for those on the ground, who have been left struggling to catch up with the move that capital has made. The histories are too different, the movements too split, the obstacles too large, the sentiments too diverging, and the numbers of people involved too small. But the continued attempt is nevertheless of crucial importance, as Kim Jin-sook pointed out in 2012. 'The only way to fight [the internationalization of capital]', she said, 'is to strengthen the international solidarity amongst workers'.

NOTES

[1] The Korean Metal Workers' Union is a sub-division of its larger umbrella organization, the Korean Confederation of Trade Unions (KCTU). KCTU is one of two national trade union centres in South Korea. KCTU's beginnings are closely tied to the country's democratization movement that ended the dictatorship, with KCTU still endorsing a left-wing agenda. The organization is comprised of 677,790 members who are organized in 1,768 affiliated unions, chapters, or branches. Membership rates have been declining, with South Korea in general having a low organization rate (11 per cent) today.

[2] The interview I describe here took place during a two-week research trip to South Korea in 2013. At the Pusan branch of KCTU, my research assistant Yu CheongHee and I met up with three members of the Hanjin chapter. This essay also draws on two encounters with Kim Jin-sook, one taking place during the same November 2013 visit, another occurring a year earlier. In May 2012, Kim and another KCTU representative visited Germany for a speaking tour, which I was involved in co-organizing as a representative of Korea Verband – an NGO that collaborated with IG Metall to bring Kim to Europe at that time. Additionally, I conducted seven months of ethnographic fieldwork in the Philippines in 2013/14 (as part of the ERC-advanced grant funded 'Overheating') – a fieldwork project that allowed me to engage with Philippine unionists, workers, and other community members in Subic Bay, where Hanjin owns a second shipyard. I wish to extend my gratitude to the activists who have given me their time in Korea and the Philippines, and to Yu CheongHee for her support. I am also grateful to Christian Krohn-Hansen, Penny Harvey, Keir Martin, Marit Melhuus, Ingjerd Hoëm, Thomas Hylland Eriksen, and Mao Mollona for their comments and suggestions, and would like to thank the participants of the 'Reconfiguring of Labour' workshop for their helpful input.

[3] A non-independent trade union in which labour representatives collaborate closely with management.

[4] A *chaebol* is a South Korean conglomerate that is typically run by members of a founding family.

[5] For recent anthropological writings on the topic of suicide, see, e.g., Broz & Münster (2015); Chua (2014); Livingston (2009).

[6] The first waves of politically motivated suicides in modern Korean history were in protest at the annexation of the country through Japanese imperialist forces. The most famous suicide of a labour activist occurred in 1970, when Cheon Tae-il burned himself to death during a protest against conditions in the garment industry, which caused a ripple effect throughout Korea at that time (Jang 2004: 271f.).

[7] Non-regular work is a contested term in the Korean context. In 2001, the 'Economic and Social Development Commission' (an advisory body to the South Korean president that was founded in the wake of the 1997 crisis) established a 'Special Committee on Non-regular Workers'. The commission proposed a definition that encompasses limited-term workers (i.e. on fixed-term contracts), part-time workers (working less than thirty-six hours a week), and atypical workers (i.e. an umbrella term that encompasses subcontracting workers, special independent workers, home workers, and daily workers) (see Shin 2013: 337-42).

[8] Author's translation. See *http://end7.labournet.tv/video/6355/interview-kim-jin-suk* for full interview (accessed 19 January 2018).

[9] A reference to the suicide of Korean activist Cheon Tae-il (see note 6).

REFERENCES

ALLISON, A. 2013. *Precarious Japan.* Durham, N.C.: Duke University Press.
BACA, G. 2011. Resentment of neoliberals in South Korea. *Journal of Eurasian Studies* **8**: 4, 125-40.
BEATTY, A. 2014. Anthropology and emotion. *Journal of the Royal Anthropological Institute* (N.S.) **20**, 545-63.
BERLANT, L. & J. GREENWALD 2012. Affect in the End Times. *Qui Parle* **20**: 2, 71-89.
BOELLSTORFF, T. & J. LINDQUIST 2004. Bodies of emotion. *Ethnos* **69**, 437-44.
BREMAN, J. 2013. A bogus concept? *New Left Review* **84**, 130-8.
BROZ, L. & D. MÜNSTER 2015. *Suicide and agency: anthropological perspectives on self-destruction, personhood, and power.* London: Routledge.
CHANG, H. 2010. *23 things they don't tell you about capitalism.* London: Penguin.
CHUA, J. 2014. *In pursuit of the good life: aspiration and suicide in globalizing South India.* Oakland: University of California Press.
Dong-A Ilbo 2013. Exploiting a corpse in a labor protest? *Dong-A Ilbo,* 12 February (available on-line: *http://english.donga.com/List/3/all/26/405614/1,* accessed 22 January 2017).
ERIKSEN, T.H. 2016. *Overheating: an anthropology of accelerated change.* London: Pluto.
ESPEJO, E. 2012. Analysis: Trade unionism in the Philippines is gone (almost). *Asian Correspondent,* 1 May (available on-line: *http://asiancorrespondent.com/81540/trade-unionism-in-the-philippines-is-gone-almost/,* accessed 29 January 2018).

HARDT, M. 1999. Affective labor. *Boundary 2*, **26**: **2**, 89-100.

——— & A. NEGRI 2000. *Empire*. Cambridge, Mass.: Harvard University Press.

JANG, S. 2004. Continuing suicide among laborers in Korea. *Labor History* **45**, 271-97.

KIM, K. 2013. Former Hanjin unionist driven to suicide. *The Hankyoreh*, 11 January (available on-line: *http://www.hani.co.kr/arti/english_edition/e_national/569276.html*, accessed 29 January 2018).

Kyunghyang Shinmun 2011. Unrepentant Hanjin Chairman Cho's alliance with GNP. *The Kyunghyang Shinmun*, 11 August (available on-line: *http://english.khan.co.kr/khan_art_view.html?artid=201108111344047&code=990101*, accessed 29 January 2018).

LEE, S. 2011. Hanjin boss apologizes for dispute. *Korea Herald*, 18 August (available on-line: *http://www.koreaherald.com/national/Detail.jsp?newsMLId=20110818000777*, accessed 22 January 2018).

LIVINGSTON, J. 2009. Suicide, risk, and investment in the heart of the African miracle. *Cultural Anthropology* **24**, 652-80.

LUTZ, C. 1986. Emotion, thought, and estrangement. *Cultural Anthropology* **1**, 287-309.

——— 1988. *Unnatural emotions: everyday sentiments on a Micronesian atoll and their challenge to Western theory*. Chicago: University Press.

——— & G.M. WHITE 1986. The anthropology of emotions. *Annual Review of Anthropology* **15**, 405-36.

MAZZARELLA, W. 2009. Affect: what is it good for? In *Enchantments of modernity* (ed.) S. Dube, 291-309. London: Routledge.

MILLAR, K. 2014. The precarious present. *Cultural Anthropology* **29**, 32-53.

MIN, K., S. PARK, S. HWANG & J.Y. MIN 2015. Precarious employment and the risk of suicidal ideation and suicide attempts. *Preventive Medicine* **71**, 72-6.

MOLÉ, N.J. 2010. Precarious subjects. *American Anthropologist* **112**, 38-53.

MUEHLEBACH, A. 2011. On affective labor in post-Fordist Italy. *Cultural Anthropology* **26**, 59-82.

——— 2013. On precariousness and the ethical imagination. *American Anthropologist* **115**, 297-311.

NAM, H. 2009. *Building ships, building a nation*. Seattle: University of Washington Press.

OFRENEO, R.E. 2013. Precarious Philippines. *American Behavioral Scientist* **57**, 420-43.

PRESIDENTIAL TRUTH COMMISSION ON SUSPICIOUS DEATHS 2004. *A hard journey to justice*. Seoul: Samin Books.

RAMOS-ZAYAS, A.Y. 2011. Affect. In *A companion to the anthropology of the body and embodiment* (ed.) F.E. Mascia-Lees, 24-45. Oxford: Wiley-Blackwell.

RICHARD, A. & D. RUDNYCKYJ 2009. Economies of affect. *Journal of the Royal Anthropological Institute* **15**, 57-77.

ROBINSON, T.K. 2011. South Korea's 300 day aerial sit-in strike highlights plight of precarious workers in Korea and the Philippines. *Asia-Pacific Journal* **9**: **4** (available on-line: *http://www.japanfocus.org/-tammy_ko-Robinson/3644*, accessed 22 January 2018).

ROSALDO, M. 1984. Toward an anthropology of self and feeling. In *Culture theory* (eds) R.A. Sweder & R.A. LeVine, 137-57. Cambridge: University Press.

SANTI, R. 2011. Hanjin workers and KMWU continue fight. International Metalworkers' Federation, 26 August (available on-line: *http://www.imfmetal.org/index.cfm?c=27385&l=2*, accessed 22 January 2018).

SCHOBER, E. 2018. The (un-)making of labour. In *Industrial labour on the margins of capitalism* (eds) C. Hann & J. Parry, 197-217. London: Berghahn.

——— in press. Destabilizing the European austerity debate via an Asian detour. In *The global life of austerity* (ed.) T. Rakopoulos. London: Berghahn.

SER, M. 2011. Hanjin 'murdered' workers, pols say. *Korea Joongang Daily*, 19 August (available on-line: *http://mengnews.joins.com/view.aspx?aId=2940436*, accessed 29 January 2018).

SHIN, K. 2013. Economic crisis, neoliberal reforms, and the rise of precarious work in South Korea. *American Behavioral Scientist* **57**, 335-53.

STANDING, G. 2014. *The precariat* (Revised edition). London: Bloomsbury.

STEWART, K. 2012. Precarity's forms. *Cultural Anthropology* **27**, 518-25.

YANAGISAKO, S. 2012. Immaterial and industrial labor. *Focaal: Journal of Global and Historical Anthropology* **64**, 16-23.

Le suicide au travail : les relocalisations transnationales du capital et leurs répercussions sur la main-d'œuvre de Corée du Sud et des Philippines

Résumé

En Corée du Sud, 2011 a été marquée par la montée d'un mouvement social contre la précarité dont l'essor doit beaucoup aux stratégies de mobilisation efficaces et affectives des travailleurs. Le déclic a été produit par un conflit social sur un chantier naval de Pusan, où un activiste a occupé une grue pendant 309 jours. L'anthropologie s'intéresse beaucoup, depuis peu, au rôle de l'affect dans la constitution des emplois néolibéraux ; elle néglige cependant le rôle que jouent les émotions dans les efforts non pas de gestion, mais de mobilisation de la main-d'œuvre. Les activistes du conflit de Hanjin se sont beaucoup servis des thèmes de l'espoir et du désespoir, étroitement liés aussi à la pratique du suicide parmi les travailleurs syndiqués du pays. Depuis la crise financière asiatique de 1997, le suicide est devenu une réponse (bien trop) ordinaire aux pressions imposées à une main-d'œuvre coréenne de plus en plus précaire. L'auteure examine les cultures de la mobilisation affective qui ont permis au mouvement « Hope Bus » de triompher en Corée et explore les efforts moins aboutis d'activistes coréens et philippins qui cherchent à créer des liens entre leurs luttes.

Shifting relations between state, capital, and place

9

Moral ecologies of subsistence and labour in a migration-affected community of Nepal

BEN CAMPBELL *Durham University*

Labour migration from subsistence households in Tamang-speaking communities of Northern Nepal heralds their transition from an agrarian to a remittance economy. This migration entails the abandonment of subsistence labour processes that once wove households together in reciprocal mutuality. Migration thus dislocates persons from moral economic institutions and norms, and reciprocity is replaced by cash-calculative decisions about food systems. However, migration is a broader sociocultural response to historical precarities and struggle over de-territorializing effects of state development. Moving beyond standard 'peasant economy' forms of analysis, and domestic autarky in particular, this essay explores neglected areas of the comparative anthropology of subsistence labour, and situates the ethnography of work and power relations in indigenous and other critiques of development nationalism in Nepal. Redirecting labour abroad creates tensions in domestic reproduction. These surface in intra-clan gift exchange, in managing agro-pastoral viability, and in the ritual maintenance of order among humans and nonhumans that invokes ancestral migrations for dealing with dilemmas about contemporary dispersals.

Decades of globalization have changed moral economies of subsistence agriculture in once-remote locations. The reorientation of local-and-national frameworks of production to global markets sucks out labour power and commodities from previously peripheral societies and territories. Labour markets in emerging economies in the Gulf States and Malaysia have dislocated old production logics and dynamics of rural social differentiation in far-flung transnational hinterlands. This destabilizes the institutional ground for quasi-autonomous, culturally distinctive livelihood systems in communities that historically reproduced themselves at a distance from national regimes by working through tributary and co-operative labour processes. This is a much-overlooked theme of economic anthropology, which is distracted by notions of the primacy of kinship and domestic autarky. People's new contexts of life and work bring a problematic dependence on the cash nexus. The newly distributed domestic networks struggle to maintain relational threads of extended moral obligation.

This longitudinal study traces steps in the move to work abroad that concern the problematic inclusion of marginal ethnic groups in Nepal's project of national modernization. Incentives to intensify production and become market actors were constrained by the many ways in which caste and ethnic status mediated market access. Tamang cultural difference (language, kinship, Buddhist religion) was tolerated by a hierarchization in which archaic economic exchanges operated through creative misrecognition of status, and coercion, rather than via a Polanyian embedding of roles and complementarities. Tributary labour was marked by uneasy and provisional moral economic inflections, periodically erupting into violence. As the Tamang did not properly belong to the core of Nepalese society and economy, and they were not among the favoured ethnicities recruited by British colonial powers into Gurkha regiments, their economic practice was often a brokering of regimes of value, which literally involved doing the heavy lifting of others' property. Asian neoliberal capitalism now gives these people minimal rights as migrant labour, playing off pre-modern structures of socioeconomic inequality to realize value from workers whose national economies fail their households and communities.

'Chasing hunger uphill and downhill'

During my first fieldwork (1989-91), agro-pastoral subsistence livelihoods in Tamang-speaking communities of Nepal's Rasuwa district consisted of periods of intensive cultivation of a number of staple crops, and managing domestic herds of livestock to supplement the diet with meat and milk and fertilize fields with manure. Most households owned fields in a vertical scattering across the mountainside, offering possibilities for growing various crops at different altitudes. The growing season around the villages (between 1,700 and 2,100 metres above sea level) began with maize and potatoes sown by early March. Seedbeds for finger millet were prepared in April. Over-wintered wheat and some barley was harvested in late April and May. Then the monsoon rains came in June.

The most labour-intensive times of year were transplanting and weeding finger millet to grow through the monsoon and be harvested in November. Finger millet makes good beer and distilled alcohol. Its flour is cooked into a thick porridge eaten with a sauce, which is far more sustaining for a worker than a meal of rice. In 1990 and 1991 I followed the work groups starting with the transplanting of *blu chida* ('small grain') finger millet on the higher slopes with the first rains, descending to lower fields and the transplanting of varieties such as *tar sanga* ('white finger millet'). Inter-planting of finger millet into growing stands of maize was feasible on terraces below approx 1,700 metres. The first cobs of maize would be brought into the houses by early July. Then came two rounds of weeding. By this time of the season, plates of newly dug, boiled potatoes would greet workers at the end of the day.

Most of the work just described was not performed by households on their own, but in different forms of mutual assistance (Campbell 1994). The interactive component of subsistence practice among groups of households made the daily labouring less of a chore. Songs, jokes, cigarettes, and snacks would be shared. As one woman told me back then, 'You cannot survive alone. There is too much work on your own'. The ways to avoid being on your own were organized by clearly understood forms of reciprocity. The most common form of co-operation was the balanced-reciprocal exchange labour group (*nangba*).[1] This functioned on the egalitarian principle of every participating household sending one person (male or female between the age of 12 and 70) to work for a pre-set full day (starting about 8 a.m.) or half day (starting about 11 a.m.) continuing till about 4 p.m. While those joining the groups were all kin to each

Journal of the Royal Anthropological Institute (N.S.), 151-165
© Royal Anthropological Institute 2018

other, their participation was not due to the moral commitments of kin relatedness. The *nangba* was an organization founded not on kin ties but on arranging horizontal commitments among a set of similar land-owning households for a fixed, short-term period (cf. Bloch 1973; Erasmus 1956; M. Moore 1975; Sallnow 1989). The underlying principle of labour co-operation was voluntary association of equal turn-taking in a limited time schedule, not the enduring kinship hierarchies of age, gender, and affinal deference.[2] However, while keeping to the reciprocity-sustaining principles of equality in labour processes, an important variation happened in relation to inequalities of labour and landholdings among these participating households.

If a household did not have as much land as other *nangba* group participants, and its own task of transplanting or weeding was already completed, it could convert labour days owed into cash. This household would call in the credit days from having worked rotationally at the other households' fields and take the group's labour for their own turn to another household willing to pay the day labour rate. Back in 1990, the rate was 15 rupees per person-day. This was the same price as a heaped measuring container of potatoes (roughly a gallon), which some people preferred to cash. People sought to bridge the opportunities of reciprocity, barter, and cash according to need and convertibility. By households organizing in mutual association, there was no grand opposition between kinship and cash.

Subsistence labour in reciprocal exchange groups made 'the domestic' an arena for inventiveness and negotiation. This happened over the relations between different households, in the manipulation of boundaries between them, and in strategies for claiming alliances across them.[3] Movements through and across domestic hearths were vital tactics for realizing productive work and the sourcing of food, land, livestock, and labour. Especially at the most labour-intensive moments of the agricultural year, kin ties did not provide a clear-cut programme of work. It was organized reciprocities of balanced exchange that gave equitable form to the subsistence task-scape. An alternative institutional pattern to kinship and clan framed the organization of labour, and accomplished the critical phases of transplanting finger millet and weeding maize on an equitable basis of symmetrical households not determined by kinship obligations.

Kinship was thus not a commanding institutional mechanism for regulating expectations in the daily flow of mountain farming. However, kinship with its asymmetrical gender and age criteria did provide for long-term transfer of land. Labour from 'wife-taking' in-laws could be called on, but it was the alternative ethics and symmetrical sociability of short-term co-operation that gave impetus to each growing season (Campbell 1994). To say that production and consumption are simply 'left to kinship ties' (Hart & Hann 2009: 2) does not stand up to scrutiny when looking at the array of strategies in Tamang agro-pastoral production. Kinship's time depth and relational expansiveness provide very different frames of reference and moral inflections from those relevant to fulfilling immediate claims for domestic provisioning, or for calling on help with standing crops in the fields in need of harvesting and lugging up hill.

The creative overlaps between kin and house provide alternative institutional groundings that are rhetorically manipulated. Lineage 'sons' from poorer households would get invited to take up residence and look after a richer household's herd. They would be spoken to as 'son' by 'father' without metaphorization, as shared agnatic bone makes a classificatory body of kin, and father's brothers are all 'father'. Such arrangements for squaring immediate needs and opportunities across different households' subsistence profiles can be made to coincide in the short term with enduring bonds of kinship among 'our own people'. This does not mean, however, that kinship presents a subsistence imperative, or a constitution for regulating labour processes between property-owning domestic units. Neither extensive kinship nor the delimited material interests of domestic resourcefulness can provide sufficiency. People need to switch creatively across these modalities.[4] Most domestic subsistence labour was enacted not in autarkic isolation, as Sahlins' (1974) domestic mode of production would have us think, but in contexts of collaboration with members of other households.

Household subsistence was backed up by access to forest produce to overcome villagers' domestic insufficiencies (most households only produced enough food for six months) – until the creation of the Langtang National Park in 1976. The park banned all trade in forest products, along with hunting and swidden farming, and imposed a system of licensing for cutting timber. My first fieldwork was fifteen years after the creation of the national park. I asked older villagers if there was not previously some regulation on bartering bamboo or taking planks of wood to market. They replied that the headman (*mukhiya*) had charge of the local territory, including the forest and its pastures, and when people needed to barter or sell produce from the forest to meet a domestic shortfall 'the headman said nothing'. Conversations on the subject would discuss demands on villagers' labour by the headman to perform services for the state and for cultivating his own fields. If a household resorted to selling planks of wood in Kathmandu at the end of a week's walk across the mountains, it was made clear to me that this constituted an entitlement of moral economy counterbalanced by the demands put on villagers by the headman. There was thus a mix of redistributive and citizenship rights in this villager-headman relationship. The headman played a secular role in a moral ecology of justice and responsibility, alongside ritual specialists showing respect for territorial fertility gods, who were attributed with local sovereign powers (Campbell 2013).

The park's regulation of access to forest produce and pastures increased households' need for cash from other sources, and reduced their ability to barter independently to feed hungry mouths at home. There was a shift from occasional petty commodity transactions of forest products as foods, medicines, craft and construction materials, and animal parts to a licensed commodification imposed by national park bureaucracy. Regulation of forest access still rankles. The imposition of park regulation coincided with out-migration of several villagers for work in India as road labourers and miners in the 1970s. These India-bound migrants were not so dissimilar from seasonal labour gang migrants, who would return after two or three months.[5]

Revaluing subsistence in the light of migrant labour
The houses of migrant labourers now have linoleum floors, steel-reinforced concrete pillars in their walls, and DVD players in the treasured displays of domestic furniture. The parents and daughters-in-law struggle to grow what food they can. Several family herds of cattle and flocks of sheep have been replaced with pigs, which are less time-consuming. New kinds of low-labour high-value crops now appear in fields, such as the medicinal herb chiraito (*Swertia chirayita*). Most significantly, much less finger millet is being grown. The role of cash has increased for buying in work groups, as people don't have the dependable numbers of household personnel to commit one person day after day for reciprocal labour. The logic of food-growing activity on family fields has become selectively financialized. A woman told me when she did the cash accounting

for a typical area for growing finger millet, it costs 3,000 rupees (spent on ploughing and preparing seed beds and fields, transplanting, weeding, harvesting, and carrying). The cash value of the end-product was hardly 1,000 rupees, competing against shop-bought finger millet. In place of finger millet in the less productive upper elevations, many people are growing potatoes and fodder mixes, including some wheat. Raising factory-farm chicks with proprietary feed and electric light bulbs has become common during warmer months. Others have invested in trout farms.

Meanwhile, when the migrants do return, they expect to socialize, and plan further trips abroad. They do not rejoin the domestic food-growing labour force. They are an agriculturally non-productive class, creating an emerging dislocation (Melhuus, this volume) between themselves and their siblings and parents. They leave wives behind with babies they may not see for two years or more. The disembedding of labour from subsistence value regimes entails a financialization of livelihoods, but the cold rationality for labour migration also poses excessive risks to personal and collective interests.[6]

The levels of debt people get into to fund the overseas travel include *say ko panch* (5 per cent interest *per month*). This results in cash servitude in enclaves of unfreedom, threat, and violence (see, e.g., Kesang Tseten's 2009 film *In search of the riyal*). It is not a global marketplace of free exchange. There is no simple economic rationale for poor people's out-migration from rural Nepal: conflict, climate change, economic failures of the state, consequences of state assault on customary subsistence patterns (e.g. national park regulations), and prospects for modern consumer lifestyles all enhance the allure of Kathmandu airport's departure lounge. The massive uncertainties and indebtedness produced by out-migration searching for livelihoods elsewhere are being dealt with by inventive, handmade making-do at the village level.

It is notable that as it is mostly men who are migrants, women are increasingly left with proxy roles in keeping up their husbands' public reputation as dutiful kinsmen and household heads. Clan gender identities are performed in life-cycle rituals. A marriage was traditionally marked by dowry gifts of livestock. Seasonal exchanges of wool passed from clansmen to clanswomen, who gave home-brewed alcohol in return. Supportive relations between same-clan women and men (*busing* and *phamyung*) are morally and ritually contrasted to the erotically charged relations between different clans. Migration now presents occasions of moral economy hiatus in the proper conduct of these spheres of clan-based gender exchange. People are never just householders, and their fuller relational lives are dramatized in moments of public performance, which require negotiation of appropriate roles and duties. The visibility of status and relationships becomes problematic when migrants who are central to a household's well-being, and relational embedding are missing from symbolically marked exchanges (Barber & Lem 2008). A husband's absence often leaves a woman having to beg for money on her husband's behalf to maintain his reputation in the eyes of his clan sisters.

From this ethnographic perspective, the story of the domestic is not a focus on the smallest unit of a society that encounters complexity at higher orders of integration, or that presents a singularity of moral values and relationships radically opposed to cash calculation. The domestic is already given life and dynamism via relational complexity (Donham 1981). Ethnographic attention to the switching between household and kinship frames unsettles analytical assumptions about fixed institutional patterns for livelihood activities, and reveals complex levels of moral economy at work.

Thinking about changes in domestic life-ways affected by people migrating out of subsistence, how would the artistry of householding differ, or the activities that make foods visible, and visibly effective, as objects of giving and receiving? There is still a strong sense of resilient autonomous production in cycles of ecological practice adjusted to new circumstances. Anxieties over the absence of household members are not simply allayed by the remittance economy because in many cases the cashflow is not reliable, and does not satisfy immediate needs. Some people adapt old subsistence knowledge and habits to make do and fill the gaps (such as boiling nettles to feed pigs). Others adopt more commercialized versions of the agro-pastoral economy, and keep yak-cow hybrids to supply yak cheese factories.

Householding is to hand-craft a world (terraced fields, pastures, and forest) where accommodation to place involves engagement with domestic animals, wild creatures, different clans, territorial deities, and temperamental spirits. Achieving personhood in the domestic orbit consists in rounds of hard work, shared meals, gifted foodstuffs, and encounters with human and nonhuman visitors.

From the moral economy angle, there are new anxieties that accompany the migratory flows of people and things and their effect on ethical subjectivities. The anxieties are not simply to do with the social ravages of the global economy. There were ten years of insurgency and conflict in Nepal, followed by years of civil instability. The younger Tamang generations have been damaged and traumatized, making compliance with old forms of public ritual difficult. They question the vernacular subject positions for evaluating what can be fulsome or abundant, what is regarded as depleted and scrawny, or what is capable of being suitably restored or healed. Signs of personal and relational well-being are realigning to new desires and subjectivities. The following three ethnographic vignettes explore these impacts of migration on the domestic moral economy in more detail.

Phoning home

The first vignette describes a telephone conversation recorded when filming in 2007.[7] A young wife deploys rhetorical skills to get her husband to realize that while he is away in Malaysia, and has not been sending money regularly, she has to look after his clan relatives. The responsibility falls on her to entertain his clan sisters at the festival of Tihar, presenting them gifts of money on his behalf. The husband responds over the phone that she should ask his father and uncles for money to tide her over this period, and insists he has sent money that she should have received. She vigorously dismisses his responses as lies, and condemns his suggestion of approaching his uncles as pathetic, belonging to a by-gone era of ancestral wealth and lineage solidarity. In this classificatory rationale, one agnate stands for another in public ritual and livelihood support. She screams down the phone, 'What good will it do asking your dead grandfathers for money at Tihar? In what country has your arsehole money got lost?'

An appropriate performance of kinship obligations at Tihar should involve being able to receive visits from the clan sisters and daughters, who bring offerings of home-cooked doughnuts and home-distilled *raksi*. How the clan women present and lay out their special food and drink for the clan men is closely observed. The quality and quantity of the display is assessed to calculate how much money should be given to them. For this young family, the priority is to maintain its reputation in public displays of domestic obligation, despite the husband's absence. The reality is that the woman's natal family is wealthier than her husband's or any of his clansmen. However, she cannot

Journal of the Royal Anthropological Institute (N.S.), 151-165
© Royal Anthropological Institute 2018

ask her father to support her husband in this ritual context, which focuses on morally bounded circuits of intra-clan prestations. The wife cannot get a loan from her own father to help with her husband's obligations to his own clanswomen. This would put into question the entire support logic of gift exchange in the solidarities among men and women of the same clan. The telephone conversation was conducted on the one village landline (prior to mobile ownership), with a considerable audience listening in. The wife ends by rebuking her husband for unbelievable stories of remittances gone astray, and implores him not to spin yarns about sending money if he cannot actually send any.

Dairying dilemmas

The next example takes us to a sector of the pastoral economy that provided good cash-generating livelihoods for people with big enough families to dedicate a specialist herding camp to breeding yak-cow hybrids, or to milking them to supply seasonal cheese-making units. Five contiguous village areas had cheese-making units of this kind. I made acquaintance in 2011 with a herding woman in her late sixties by her camp fireside, while numerous chickens ran about the herd shelter. She began talking about the economic dilemmas she and her husband faced, and she expressed worry about the long-term viability of their herd enterprise. The woman said she didn't know what to do. Should she buy more milking animals or sell up? Her concerns were in part due to the absence of her children and their labour. One son had died in a factory accident in Malaysia, another son was in Kathmandu, and a daughter was in Malaysia. The old woman's train of thought was diverted by interruptions to her preparations of food around the fire-pit. Conversations in herding camps are often interrupted by animals, and in the course of shooing the chickens away from the raised sitting area by the fire, the woman expressed annoyance at her chickens acquiring social airs and graces. They had grown to prefer rice instead of maize, just as spoilt children do. In the era of migration, this rejection of dependable, old strength-giving foods, in contrast to which boiled rice is a delicacy, is a very common complaint by the older generation. 'These times are topsy-turvy', the old woman said. The fabric of values organizing everyday life – investing time and work in the care of animals, and appreciating subsistence staples – was visibly unravelling.

Interactions between humans and animals, plants and processes of material transformation, brings into view distinct ways of being human. Migration renders uncertain the roles and expectations of shared activity for the production of everyday life. Habits of a lifetime are disembedded from their obviousness in the way of things. The old woman herder faces selling up in the light of her children having died abroad or not wanting to follow a life so tied to caring for the needs of thirty cattle. The dilemmas she confronts look terminal for her domestic dairy enterprise, which is unlikely to be passed on to another generation. The disturbance to normal sequences of expectation for family roles in this way of life can understandably get projected onto the precocious dietary tastes of the hens pecking on the floor, as if they too aspire to a better life of eating rice rather than home-grown staples.

Hereditary housework

The third ethnographic vignette leads into the terrain of domestic intimacy that the Tamang-speaking communities make visible through 'winnowing tray' rituals conducted by village priests (*lhaben*). They call into play the common world of humans, animals, spirit beings, and foods across thresholds of domestic fortune. Witnessing one of these rituals in a house with migrant absentees made me reflect how the ritual's intimations of pathways and relationships did not simply index a traditional world losing relevance, but also provided linkages to migratory genealogies from the past to inform the present.

One morning in 2011, a village priest was invited to perform a minor domestic ritual of purification. He took up a position in the centre of the room facing the door, and proceeded to fill the winnowing tray with tiny piles of fermented grain, uncooked rice, a boiled egg, a piece of iron, a tobacco leaf, and a chilli pepper. In this house, two young women were raising children while their husbands were abroad. They did not pay much attention to the priest mumbling over his tray. The morning's slow pace continued. It is the general role of the priest to address the pragmatic cosmic vulnerabilities of households, and attend to fears about unwanted spirit beings that will cause disharmony, sickness, and niggardly bad words in houses. He takes onto himself the risk-laden dimension of dealing with malevolent forces. These presences will also crave and spoil the quality, the storage, and proper fermentation processes that the foods of the fields and animals furnish for human domestic residents.

As the priest organizes and recognizes the various substances on the winnowing tray through chanting, he invokes a world order that locates people in a precarious condition of needing continual replenishment, and protection from accident and harm. He reminds humans, gods, and spirits where they are in relation to the directions north, south, east, west, and centre to negotiate a *modus vivendi* with the benign presences of the local landscape, and literally to show the door to nefarious nonhumans with unwelcome cravings and desires. These nonhumans provoke irritations and squabbles among people of the house. The priest works back in time to the ancestral migrations of the Tamang and Ghale clans from Tibet who took up residence in their current homes. Primordial Buddhist Rimpoches are invoked to convey blessings for household fortune in crops, livestock, and monetary valuables. Two spirit sisters accompanied the ancestral migrations, and on different sides of the valley have to be given either eggs or chickens to appease their hunger for human foods. These spirits are lured by chanting over the tempting array of domestic materials in the winnowing tray: grains, eggs, butter, beer, incense, and a lump of iron. The priest rhythmically dips a ladle into a bowl of rice beer. Eventually he stands, takes the tray through the door, and expels the unwanted spirits, shouting and upturning the winnowing tray, much to the excitement of nearby chickens that come running to this sudden feast.

The priest himself had children and grandchildren working abroad, and in these days was sporting an elegant jacket over his traditional Nepalese man's clothing. I knew him well fifteen years previously, when he had fallen onto hard times through debt, and had taken off with his old parents to find work in another district, cursing his village as backward and undeveloped. Here he was restored to his hereditary priestly role, with a new sense of duty in modern times to keep malign influences away from human affairs. His own home was newly constructed and had linoleum on the floor, presenting a picture of domestic achievement that he was never able to aspire to before his children went off to labour in Malaysia. In this case the migratory experience has converged with forms of domestic cosmology, in which disturbance, awkward tensions, and problematic materialities of livelihood are explicitly dealt with. Indeed, the ancestral migratory mythology lays down something of a template for contemporary excursions, and makes explicit each household's routedness in movement up and down the mountainside in the cycle of agro-pastoral renewal, and between the towns of Nepal and Tibet for trade (Campbell 2013). Through chanting place names and pathways, the priest enunciates a sentient ecology of connection by imaginatively moving and recognizing distinct landscapes in passing. He makes visible in the winnowing tray the ingredients of raw, cooked, and fermented life-bringing foods. He focuses attention on domestic space and time and asks, 'Who is missing? Who needs to be remembered?' while attracting the greedy, harming, lurking spirits of malice to guzzle the contents of the tray outside, beyond the domestic threshold.

Homesteads under threat

These three vignettes concur with other research on Tamang communities on the new discrepancies between handcrafted and monied worlds (Steinmann 2016), and the new antinomies of gender and person (March in press). My first two examples portray women who find themselves in positions of not knowing what is the right thing to do, and feeling unable to act properly.[8] Migration impacts both the institutional landscapes of extended kinship ties and the composition of domestic residence and sustenance practices. It creates disjointed expectations and tensions when the social and economic ends of domestic livelihood fail to meet up. If conditions for gender and generational complementarity have been shaken up, however, certain elements of the cosmic embedding of domestic realities speak across generations, as shown in the third vignette.

When migrants return from periods abroad, they are scrutinized not only for signs of wealth brought back, but also for evidence of the toll taken by estrangement. Village women, and especially the clan sisters, will declare whether the returnees are physically plump (*tsojim*) or thin (*chipjim*). It is not just bodily condition that marks a difference from the migrant's previous persona. The crisis facing middle-aged householders is of their migrant children's self-description as global proletarians, having no interest in helping out with tasks of agro-pastoral economy when back home. A class has been formed, some of them aided by literacy, with no intention to respect outmoded norms of work that now appear as self-exploitation. Not just the work itself, but the very foods of subsistence, such as maize and finger millet, are being rejected for purchased rice.

Hierarchies of dislocation

In thinking how to explore labour dilemmas facing the community I once knew as busy with subsistence work teams, I look to Narotzky (this volume; 2015), who provides some useful pointers in her approach to moral economy, and recommends anthropologists bring into view lived dilemmas, perturbations, and conflicts as capitalism remakes personal and public interests. Tamang villagers suffer shortfalls both in subsistence output and in capacities to conduct inter-domestic exchange. Squeezed by the effects of state environmental protection, those left supporting migrant workers' households face heightened subsistence anxieties. The migrants are institutionally problematic, proxy persons as they leave social responsibilities and relationships in the hands of others, to make do and rethink the possibilities for subsistence and social reproduction. There is turmoil in the order of roles and activities for people of different clans, genders, and generations. Public and reciprocal dimensions of domestic moral economy have been challenged and transformed by the role of cash-calculative decisions over food systems and the relationships that sustain them. These are tied to the presences and absences of people in new accommodations of value. In the lived worlds of the Tamang, this is not a purely human affair, and calls attention to the animals and spirits that move in, and need removing from, the domestic orbit. For this reason and the link of iconic foods with collective fates, I contest Graeber's (2009) term 'human economy'. While understandable as a counter to the impersonal market, it is too anthropocentric for attending to how people's livelihoods are networked through conviviality with nonhumans, and are imbricated in local and global political ecologies.

Perspectives from Tamang homelands cut through the idea of economic processes embedded in stable institutional regimes of value. Livelihood practices are indeed embedded in ethical concerns and reciprocities as proper transactions in meeting everyday needs of household residents, but these are frequently in conflict and people are mindful of misuse.[9] The principles for the conduct of conduct are not the same for everyone, especially in the intermixtures of Himalayan frontier society. Paradoxical elements of the caste system, contested state control of forests, and the ideological essentialization of patrilineality result in a grand instability of moral regimes concerning the status of 'human economy'.

The commercial adaptation of the yak-cow pastoral economy to supply cheese factory units provided a version of development for the mountain economy from the 1970s. It enabled production based on new technical processes, and a degree of wealth and aspiration for communities to imagine themselves living well. This source of wealth accumulation was put in jeopardy with the creation of the Langtang National Park and the challenge conservation presented to livelihood development, restricting movements of livestock and produce in the park area. New conservation priorities for protecting musk deer, red pandas, and the high forests confronted market logics and state support for national economic development. Moreover, there is ethnic differentiation in the dairying moral economy. This region produces the largest quantity of yak cheese in Nepal, and underlying this specialization is the fact that unlike other ethnicities, Tamang clanspeople will eat the meat of stillborn calves and cattle that die of disease or from falling down landslides. Status discrimination and economic advantage converge as the Tamang will put cow meat into the pot which is taboo to other clans and castes. Hindu high castes hierarchize this dietary practice, but the Tamang have more food available as a result. Some herders allegedly kill male calves by feeding them salt to increase available milk. Moral guilt over this illegal and sinful practice causes herders to donate conspicuously at pilgrimage sites of the mountain god.

Questions about the status of 'the human' in this scenario raise broader issues of comparative ontologies of human and nonhuman interaction. In Descola's (1996; 2013) terms, the cosmology of 'naturalism', which informs humans' protection of nature in national parks, presents utterly different terms of engagement compared to the animistic perspectives of Himalayan yak herders, who maintain intimate relations with territorial spirits of the mountains to protect their families and livestock. Caste also essentializes different orders of humanity in endogamous groups analogous to species, marked by unequal dietary taboos. These discrepancies of human status and subject positions on nonhuman ethics and moral ecology defy institutional resolution. In this mountain crossroads of religion and ontologies, an economic niche has made keeping yak-cow hybrids more substantially nourishing and advantageous to the beef-eating Tamang clans than to others. Tamang villagers centre their worlds and livelihood practice in knowing contradistinction to other ways of doing things, with different outcomes for the kinds of persons and bodies that are thereby produced for labour of various sorts.

New adaptations of subsistence resourcefulness, such as keeping pigs and fattening them by boiling cauldrons of nettles, maintain the appearance of households coping while their sons go abroad in search of value in the status of migrant labourer. In the countries to which they travel, their lack of rights and freedom of action within the market make their lives as migrants massively dependent on social support networks sustained by phoning home and watching DVDs in their native languages. Migrants' accounts of working in the Gulf express both the wonder and the horror of the experience (such as the annual death toll in Qatar of some 600 Nepalis). But there is hope in the oral contact maintained through mobile phones that contrasts with earlier migration. There has also been a political imaginary of hope for a Tamang homeland in an anticipated federal constitution for Nepal, enhanced by cultural products of songs and DVDs in Tamang and other indigenous languages, recovering a sense of 'going somewhere' in a collective project of transformation, rather than being left stuck in place.

Conclusion

Capital penetration into Tamang regimes of domestic value is a story of a labour force created at the expense of subsistence viability. Roads and national parks undermined subsistence economies that had been partially integrated into national production logics through labour service and employment. Agrarian productivist logics were displaced by a re-territorialization of rural areas into conservation zones spurred on by environmental crisis narratives. Rights to forest provisioning were denied to communities who then went in search of labour markets. Subsequently the civil war of 1996-2006, and growing accessibility to Southeast Asia and the Gulf, put in train a genuine outpouring, challenging the viability of domestic subsistence practices and food-growing regimes.

Whether this loss of labour from village subsistence and the increased cash calculus lead to households becoming more insular, more acquisitive, and less interested in wider kin or solidarities is not so easy to say. Anthropological studies of work in 'the domestic domain' have tended to search too readily for dichotomous transitions (Spittler 2009) between kinship reciprocities and the market. The long-term research behind this essay has revealed 'the domestic' to be a far more malleable and interestingly worked set of social forms than the concretization of a primary household 'unit' suggests in the canonical literature (Gudeman & Rivera 1990; Hann 2009: 270; Sahlins 1974). Looking at subsistence practice a generation ago revealed a non-dichotomous working of moral economy oscillating between autonomy and co-operation in different institutional and strategic contexts. The operations of subsistence livelihood were far from determined by kin ties. An often-overlooked seam of anthropological literature on informal practices of labour co-operation recognizes variety in ways people get things done under different categories of reciprocity (Bloch 1973; Donham 1981; Harvey, this volume). The Tamang – with reciprocal reflexivity – evaluate expectations of benefit against the social offence that might be caused in not attending particular reciprocal work parties, or requests from NGOs to contribute labour for supposed community benefit.

This reciprocal problematic informed Tamang perceptions of their historical relations to state power and the forms of coercive labour demanded of them. Repetitive seasonal labour tasks of portering and pathbuilding were performed as service tax for rights to residence and landholding. Seasonal trans-Himalayan trade offered some labour opportunities for cash income, later enabling the trekking industry to grow from the 1960s with a subsistence-fed labour force. The tributary moral economy meant that village headmen who organized and personally benefitted from corvée labour turned a blind eye when households ran out of food and resorted to barter or sale of forest products.[10] This agro-ecological moral economy requiring silences, and misrecognition[11] broke down when state environmentalism targeted the inappropriately productive mountain peasant as a scourge of the environment.

If social forms of household and community are in danger of reification, so are notions of instituted moral orders setting the room for manoeuvre in scenarios of practice. Hierarchies project ordered complementarities of difference and conceal dissonant interpretation. In the three ethnographic vignettes discussed in this essay, the transition from peasant producers to migrant labourers has been explored by listening to people's articulations of the social gaps this transformation has created. For those left at home, people's conflicted reflections about maintaining relational worlds with absent kin (and the absence of their promised money) lead to uncertainties about what to do. Reputations of patrilineal provisioning require symbolic gifts of money by clansmen whose absence as migrants actually makes it more difficult to satisfy the traditional role that money played in rituals that once anchored livelihoods in gendered complementarity. The second vignette visited dilemmas faced by ageing herders, who see local cash incentives that worked for their generation now failing to keep their children interested in the herding enterprise. If the old patterns of kinship ritual, and property devolution, are facing novel threats, the third example was selected for its less pessimistic storyline. A ritual specialist of chthonic deities finds a dignity he never previously had thanks to his children's remittances from abroad. He cares for the therapeutic needs of families with absent menfolk by domestic convocation of beneficial spirits and expulsion of malign influences. He dispels the anxieties of migrants' dependants in chants of ancestral trails leading through the cosmos, and remakes order and regulation of the homestead, removing bad spirits attracted to the human hearth.

What kinds of persons will these new labourers become? Is the pathway of migrant labour more about masculinity and a rite of passage in modern personhood than about calculating returns from different employment options? These questions need to be approached ethnographically and with the active scepticism of these communities, who have conceded the fight for subsistence productivism in favour of a global reorientation. In doing so, they confront dislocation. Struggling to sustain meanings of money as gift, human-livestock viability, and the hearth as ritual microcosm, they deploy indigenous resources for reimagining plausible worlds of home and abroad.

South Asian migrants are not lone figures transacting in the labour market, but are relational actors. They carry relatives' and financiers' interests, which amplifies the exploitative characteristics of employment that does not match the contracts that lure them. Becoming migrant labourers with minimal workers' rights and no formal identity other than as a unit of labour leads to multiple senses of dislocation among these persons, and back among their families. This provides a strong example of the contemporary global economy taking on an 'uninstituted' character, as Gregory (2009) proposes. In the affective circumstances of such dislocation, ethnic belonging and religious affiliation take root. For those who return to Nepal, they find a homeland nation that struggles not to be labelled a failed state. The earthquakes of 2015 destroyed the material fabric of rural life for half a million people around its Tamang epicentre. The national economy in 2016 was officially listed as dependent for over 30 per cent of GDP on foreign remittances – the highest in Asia (ADB 2016). People are at a loss regarding what to do as the prospects for reshaping rural-urban asymmetries and achieving devolved government through a federal constitution were substantially blocked in 2016.

Capital has nonetheless been channelled into infrastructure projects such as roads and hydropower in select locations, giving opportunities for returnee migrants with relevant skills, such as truck-driving. However, people who were raised in conditions of labour-intense subsistence farming and then went abroad struggle to find work in their natal country using the skills they acquired as migrant labourers. The potential transition from subsistence agriculture to cash economy is deferred, much to the benefit of the economies employing temporary migrant labour. The collection *Global Nepalis* (Gellner & Hausner in press) clearly shows that Nepal has exported its poverty as labour since its encounter with the British Empire. The dislocated and uninstituted character of contemporary labour regimes abandons migrant labourers to non-productive roles back in their home communities, thwarting the desired transition from subsistence to more capitalized forms of local livelihood. In this failed transition to post-peasant modernity, within a poorly performing national economy, and with a state that has not served its indigenous citizens' aspirations to federalism, global capital parasitically exploits a reserve of labour power (Narotzky, this volume) that is reproduced by people's resourcefulness to reinvent subsistence in pathways of migratory livelihood.

NOTES

I acknowledge the generous patience of the editors of this volume and the apposite critical comments of the reviewers. Ph.D. (1989-92) and postdoctoral (1997-8) research was carried out with awards from the ESRC. Filmwork for *The way of the road* was thanks to my brother Cosmo Campbell, and was funded by an award in 2007 from the Williamson Fund (Cambridge Haddon Museum). I owe a huge debt to my undergraduate supervisors at Cambridge, Caroline Humphrey and Alan MacFarlane, and my postgraduate supervisors at Norwich (UEA), Piers Blaikie and David Seddon, for my training in cultural economy, inequality, and labour regimes in Nepal. The community of scholarship on Nepal centred on SOAS and Michael Hutt in particular, two generations of Gellners, and the remarkable dedication of the research team at CNRS (Centre d'études himalayennes, UPR 299) have been indispensable for the broader contexts to the development of my understanding of socioeconomic and environmental change in Nepal. The Tamang and Ghale clanspeople of Dhunche and Bharku Village Development Committees in Rasuwa district especially need thanking for never forgetting the *meme kyekpa* (old grandfather) who keeps returning like an improvident labour migrant for new ethnographic sustenance.

[1] *Parma* in Nepali.

[2] If for some reason a household experienced a crisis and could not commit a member for a whole task cycle to a *nangba* group, an alternative was to call a *gohar*. This involved providing a full meal on the day with rice, local beer, and regular snacks in the fields. Households could not rely on *gohar* except the village headman's, as this form of work mobilization blended into tributary obligation.

[3] The role of inter-household labour has tended to be given more prominence by feminist anthropologists and theorists in their recognition of co-operative work teams and informal reciprocities (Gibson-Graham 2007; Guyer 1991; Harris 1981; March & Taqqu 1986; H. Moore 1988).

[4] This is a point Bourdieu recognized: 'The archaic economy cannot escape the opposition between ordinary and extra-ordinary occasions, between regular needs, which can be satisfied by the domestic community, and the exceptional needs ... which require the voluntary assistance of a more extended group' (1990: 118).

[5] Sharma (2008) makes comparable points in relation to men from Western Nepal working in Delhi.

[6] Obviously, the motivations to go abroad are not ethnically unique, and the national picture of the growth of remittance economy needs to be mentioned. Graner (2010) locates the search for foreign labour markets for former carpet industry workers in the mid-1990s. Malaysia opened conveniently for Nepali labourers at the height of the civil war. Bruslé (2010) and Gardner (2012a; 2012b) give accounts of Qatari labourers' camps and their restrictive working conditions. Gardner (2012b) discusses people maintaining fictions of beneficial outcomes from their work, clearly beyond any cost-benefit analysis.

[7] This conversation features in my 2009 film *The way of the road* (*https://vimeo.com/35818236*, accessed 25 January 2018).

[8] March (in press) has described the loss of point of view for Tamang women, who take on men's subsistence roles, or move to the city to await remittances, subverting the life expectations that their mothers raised them for.

[9] Sahlins pithily observed that 'everywhere in the world the indigenous category for exploitation is "reciprocity"' (1974: 134).

[10] Similarly disrupted expectations concerning corvée labour were at the heart of resistance to British colonial interventions in the Indian Himalaya, described in Guha (1989).

[11] Bourdieu brings subtlety and ambivalence to the guises of embedding strategies:

> The discovery of labour presupposes ... the disenchantment of a natural world henceforward reduced to its economic dimensions alone; ceasing to be the tribute paid to a necessary order, activity can be directed towards an exclusively economic end ... This means the end of the primal undifferentiatedness which made possible the play of individual and collective misrecognition (1977: 176).

REFERENCES

ADB 2016. *Asian economic integration report.* Asian Development Bank (available on-line: *https://www.adb.org/publications/asian-economic-integration-report-2016*, accessed 25 January 2018).

BARBER, P. & W. LEM 2008. Introduction: migrants, mobility, and mobilization. *Focaal: Journal of Global and Historical Anthropology* **51**, 3-12.

BLOCH, M. 1973. The long term and the short term: the economic and political significance of the morality of kinship. In *The character of kinship* (ed.) J. Goody, 75-88. Cambridge: University Press.

BOURDIEU, P. 1977. *Outline of a theory of practice* (trans. R. Nice). Cambridge: University Press.

——— 1990. *The logic of practice* (trans. R. Nice). Cambridge: Polity.

BRUSLÉ, T. 2010. Who's in a labour camp? A socio-economic analysis of Nepalese migrants in Qatar. *European Bulletin of Himalayan Research* **35-6**, 154-70.

CAMPBELL, B. 1994. Forms of cooperation in a Tamang community. In *The anthropology of Nepal: peoples, problems and processes* (ed.) M. Allen, 3-20. Kathmandu: Mandala.

——— 2013. *Living between juniper and palm: nature, culture and power in the Himalayas.* Delhi: Oxford University Press.

DESCOLA, P. 1996. Constructing natures: symbolic ecology and social practice. In *Nature and society: anthropological perspectives* (eds) P. Descola & G. Pálsson, 82-102. London: Routledge.

——— 2013. *Beyond nature and culture* (trans. J. Lloyd). Chicago: University Press.

DONHAM, D. 1981. Beyond the domestic mode of production. *Man* (N.S.) **16**, 515-41.

ERASMUS, C. 1956. Culture structure and process: the occurrence and disappearance of reciprocal farm labour. *Southwestern Journal of Anthropology* **12**, 444-69.

GARDNER, A. 2012a. Rumour and myth in the labour camps of Qatar. *Anthropology Today* **28: 6**, 25-8.

——— 2012b. Why do they keep coming? Labor migrants in the Gulf States. In *Migrant labor in the Persian Gulf* (eds) M. Kamrava & Z. Babar, 41-58. London: Hurst.

GELLNER, D. & S. HAUSNER (eds) in press. *Global Nepalis.* Delhi: Oxford University Press.

GIBSON-GRAHAM, J.K. 2007. Surplus possibilities: postdevelopment and community economies. In *Exploring post-development* (ed.) A. Ziai, 145-62. London: Routledge.

GRAEBER, D. 2009. Debt, violence and impersonal markets: Polanyian meditations. In *Market and society: the great transformation today* (eds) C. Hann & K. Hart, 106-32. Cambridge: University Press.

GRANER, E. 2010. Leaving hills and plains: migration and remittances in Nepal. *European Bulletin of Himalayan Research* **35-6**, 24-42.

GREGORY, C. 2009. Whatever happened to householding? In *Market and society: the great transformation today* (eds) C. Hann & K. Hart, 133-59. Cambridge: University Press.

GUDEMAN, S. & A. RIVERA 1990. *Conversations in Colombia: the domestic economy in life and text.* Cambridge: University Press.

GUHA, R. 1989. *The unquiet woods.* Delhi: Oxford University Press.

GUYER, J. 1991. Female farming in anthropology and African history. In *Gender at the crossroads of knowledge* (ed.) M. di Leonardo, 257-77. Berkeley: University of California Press.

HANN, C. 2009. Embedded socialism? Land, labour and money in eastern Xinjiang. In *Market and society: the great transformation today* (eds) C. Hann & K. Hart, 256-71. Cambridge: University Press.

HARRIS, O. 1981. Households as natural units. In *Of marriage and the market: women's subordination internationally and its lessons* (eds) K. Young, C. Wolkowitz & R. McCullough, 49-68. London: Routledge.

HART, K. & C. HANN 2009. Introduction: learning from Polanyi. In *Market and society: the great transformation today* (eds) C. Hann & K. Hart, 1-16. Cambridge: University Press.

MARCH, K. in press. Tamang gendered subjectivities in a migrating world. In *Global Nepalis* (eds) D. Gellner & S. Hausner. Delhi: Oxford University Press.

———— & R. TAQQU 1986. *Women's informal associations in developing countries.* Boulder, Colo.: Westview Press.

MOORE, H. 1988. *Feminism and anthropology.* Cambridge: Polity.

MOORE, M. 1975. Cooperative labour in peasant agriculture. *Journal of Peasant Studies* **2**, 270-91.

NAROTZKY, S. 2015. The payoff of love and the traffic of favours: reciprocity, social capital, and the blurring of value realms in flexible capitalism. In *Flexible capitalism: exchange and ambiguity at work* (ed.) J. Kjaerulff, 173-206. Oxford: Berghahn Books.

SAHLINS, M. 1974. *Stone Age economics.* London: Tavistock.

SALLNOW, M. 1989. Cooperation and contradiction: the dialectics of everyday practice. *Dialectical Anthropology* **14**, 241-57.

SHARMA, J.R. 2008. Practices of male labor migration from the hills of Nepal to India in development discourses: which pathology? *Gender, Technology and Development* **12**, 303-23.

SPITTLER, G. 2009. Contesting *The great transformation*: work in comparative perspective. In *Market and society: the great transformation today* (eds) C. Hann & K. Hart, 160-74. Cambridge: University Press.

STEINMANN, B. 2016. Confrontations between Maoists and Buddhists in Nepal: historical continuities, flux, and transformations in collective myth and practice. In *Religion, secularism, and ethnicity in contemporary Nepal* (eds) D. Gellner, S. Hausner, & C. Letizia, 353-402. Delhi: Oxford University Press.

Écologies morales de la subsistance et du travail dans une communauté du Népal affectée par les migrations

Résumé

La migration de main-d'œuvre issue des communautés de langue tamang du nord du Népal annonce la transition de ceux-ci d'une économie agraire à une économie d'envoi de fonds par les émigrés. La migration implique l'abandon de processus de travail de subsistance qui tissaient autrefois des liens de mutualité réciproque entre les maisonnées. Elle détache ainsi les personnes des institutions et des normes économiques morales, et la réciprocité est remplacée par des logiques calculatrices concernant les systèmes alimentaires. Cela étant, la migration est une réponse socioculturelle plus large aux précarités historiques et à la lutte contre les effets déterritorialisants du développement de l'État. Au-delà des formes standard d'analyse de « l'économie paysanne », notamment de l'autarcie domestique, cet essai explore les zones négligées de l'anthropologie comparative du travail de subsistance et situe l'ethnographie du travail et les relations de pouvoir dans les critiques, indigènes et autres, du nationalisme du développement au Népal. La redirection de la main-d'œuvre vers l'étranger crée des tensions dans la reproduction domestique, qui se manifestent dans l'échange de dons au sein du clan, la gestion de la viabilité agropastorale et le maintien rituel de l'ordre parmi les humains et les non-humains, qui invoque les migrations ancestrales pour gérer les dilemmes liés aux dispersions contemporaines.

10

State, labour, and kin: tensions of value in an egalitarian community

Ingjerd Hoëm *University of Oslo*

This essay discusses the effects of a state apparatus and new forms of labour in a kin-based egalitarian distributive economy. The atoll society of Tokelau is currently establishing a modern state, largely financed by aid, but also through revenue from Tokelau's fisheries zone. The new labour regime associated with the introduction of a state administration is in practice entangled with an egalitarian distributive system of production and reproduction. The local kin-based leadership is able to incorporate and use the system of capital in an egalitarian fashion. Whether it will be able over time to accommodate social inequality – that is, the division of villagers into skilled and unskilled workers with potentially qualitatively different access to livelihoods – is, however, an open question. Where comparative studies from Aboriginal Australia describe unequal access to work and standards of livelihoods by reference to ontology, and hence by implication to ethnicity, the tensions experienced in Tokelau take place *within* one social network in which new forms of labour contribute to a devaluation of skills associated with gendered patterns of livelihoods. From this devaluation follows a potential loss of sustainability for the atoll society should the capital flow move elsewhere.

In this essay I discuss the effects of a state apparatus and new kinds of labour in a kin-based egalitarian community where a distributive economy is still dominant. Tokelau is situated in the middle of the Pacific Ocean, at a considerable distance from its closest neighbour, Samoa, 505 kilometres away. Tokelau has often found itself out of sync with the world at large. This is also true of the situation discussed below: as the era of nation building and decolonization draws to a close, this Pacific atoll society is currently in the early stages of establishing a modern state.

During the last three decades, Tokelau has gone from being a small-scale society, geographically remote from the centres of political dominance in the region, and with infrequent contact with representatives of such centres and their associated institutions as, for example, New Zealand, Australia, the United Nations, and others, to becoming an admittedly small but active player in the arenas of global politics.

From a situation, lasting up till the mid-1980s, where livelihoods were predominantly reliant on subsistence activities, and where all forms of production and reproduction were regulated by kinship, today waged labour has come to take up an increasingly dominant role. Opportunities for (more or less) well-paid jobs in the public sector and administration of the atolls pull non-kin and diasporic Tokelauans to Tokelau at present. These new forms of labour have consequences for the kin-based kinds of subsistence activities (subsumed under the Tokelauan term *galuega*, loosely translated as 'work') that are still common on the islands. Effects of the new forms of occupations on the way of life characterized by the egalitarian ethos and distributive economy are many and far-reaching.

In the following, I discuss the increasingly troublesome differentiation between waged and unwaged labour that has emerged in the three atoll societies of Tokelau: Atafu, Nukunonu, and Fakaofo. Access to qualitatively different kinds of livelihoods and career opportunities, also reflected in the introduced categories of skilled and unskilled labour, has emerged as a potentially divisive factor in the communities.

In other words, the monetary economy is clearly now in a position that threatens to undermine the egalitarian ethos of the communities. However, in reality things are not so simple. The ways in which the values of the egalitarian economy articulate with increasing economic differences deserves further scrutiny. In particular, the issue of how the rules and regulations that govern the modern administration's work environment become entangled with the local gender and leadership patterns common across the Pacific region leaves the outcome more ambiguous.

Tensions of value

Central to our understanding of this kind of emerging social differentiation associated with the distinction between skilled and unskilled labour is the exploration of how conceptual differences, and associated differences in perspectives between people with different life-experiences, relate to and play out in local arenas of practice (e.g. in the villages, and in state institutions such as the schools) (Graeber 2013: 229-33). To bring out the particularities and tensions of what locals often describe as an increasingly problematic social differentiation in Tokelau, I draw on Sylvia Yanagisako's perspective on kinship and gender (2002). The effects of the new state and associated labour regime on the egalitarian value system are discussed in relation to conceptualizations and negotiations of moral value related to traditionally gendered occupations such as fishermen and weavers, and to other practices of kinship and leadership. What I call 'tensions of value' is based on my reading of David Graeber's perspective on value as generative of what he calls 'universes' (Graeber 2013). By 'universe' he refers to the totality of a system of production and reproduction, and central to his understanding of how such totalities emerge is value. Value is defined as human creativity or 'production', and as 'a mode of coordinating projects of human action' (2013: 220). By my adding to this approach the aspect of 'tension', I want to point to typical characteristics of situations where such 'universes' generated by different kinds of value (or values, as it has commonly been called in comparative cultural anthropology) meet and engage on the ground. Anna Tsing's concept of 'friction' is an attempt to describe similar characteristics (Tsing 2004). However, as I wish here to focus on the entanglement of two different systems of production, an egalitarian subsistence economy and a monetary one, by placing value at the centre of my analysis, tension seems more fitting for the empirical situation that I present. In short, the term 'tension' serves to highlight the moral dilemmas that people experience in their daily efforts to negotiate the sometimes deeply contradictory logics of the two systems.

Journal of the Royal Anthropological Institute (N.S.), 166-179
© Royal Anthropological Institute 2018

A relevant contrast and comparison to the New Zealand- and UN-related state situation of Tokelau is that of Aboriginal Australia. I shall make brief references to descriptions of tensions between subsistence activities and waged labour by Lorraine Gibson (2010) and Elizabeth Povinelli (1995) from New South Wales and the Northern Territory, respectively, in order to highlight the effects of the state apparatus on the socioeconomic and political institutions in the atolls, but mainly to point to a similarity when it comes to a striking invisibility of difference of value (or 'culture blindness', as Yanagisako [2002] calls it) between what I for the sake of simplicity call the local and the outsider perspective.

Between subsistence and new forms of labour

If we go back but a short period to a feature article in the periodical *New Internationalist* on Tokelau from 1994 (Buckley 1994), we can observe that the dominant common practice locally – that is, to engage in non-waged, but otherwise compensated (in goods, such as food) communal work for the village – is suddenly described in the international press as amounting to a 'high level of unemployment'. This description of village work as synonymous with unemployment is so much at loggerheads with the local perspective that it warrants investigation. Taking this gap – between an outsiders' perspective on what they see as the labour situation and the actual work-related practices found on the ground – as our starting-point, therefore, the first important thing to note is that the concept of 'unemployment' is not locally used or seen as relevant to describe the situation. Different kinds of work-related activities are, however, commonly divided into two main types: for the village and in the offices of the public service. Secondly, and as mentioned above, we find that this recent and not fully realized separation of what only decades ago was one kin-based system of political and economic practice follows from a social division with its roots in the international labour market into two kinds of labour. This division became institutionalized in the mid-1980s and has gained increasing importance since that time. This is the locally significant division of village people into skilled and unskilled labourers. The terms of skilled and unskilled labour are of foreign origin, but in contrast to the equally foreign concept of unemployment, this distinction has gained conceptual salience in everyday discourse in the atolls.

To return to the *New Internationalist* article, the favourable condition of easy access for the Tokelauan economy to the New Zealand market is mentioned, but it is also added that what it sees as Tokelau's isolation and lack of resources makes little room for locally generated economic development. It is important to notice at this point that this seemingly neutral depiction is tendentious in its framing of Tokelau as remote and as lacking in resources. Firstly, it raises the question as to what it is that Tokelau is remote from, seeing as, from the perspective of the Pacific, it is a central node on a large-scale network that covers the entire ocean. Secondly, the framing of Tokelau as poor in resources belies the fact that its marine resources are among the most abundant in the world. In other words, this framing reflects the ethnocentric perspective of its authors, whose mental maps of the Pacific are of European origin, and who associate wealth with money. Turning to the issue of money on the atolls (which excludes all that is locally counted as wealth), this is described as in the main coming from remittances from kin overseas.

> Tokelauans rely on aid from Aotearoa – over NZ$2,500 per head in 1992. They also have a guaranteed export market to that country. Atoll dwellers have dual nationality and there are now more of them living in Aotearoa, mainly around Wellington, than there are in Tokelau. Unemployment is high in

this community with 47 per cent of 15-29 year olds out of work … Communal farming and fishing are the basis of Tokelau's economy. The islets' isolation, lack of minerals and infertile soils leave little room for economic manoeuvre. Remittances from migrant workers, postage stamps and souvenir coins are major sources of foreign currency (Buckley 1994).

Today, the overall economic situation of Tokelau is very different from what we saw described for the mid-1990s. With the security of a substantial trust fund, the income of which is mainly generated from revenue from the 200-mile nautical zone surrounding Tokelau and negotiated by New Zealand, and with an income-generating national telephone-company (again built with aid donations and with the assistance of foreign labour from the Netherlands), Tokelau is comparatively well off, even with a recent US plan for withdrawal from the fisheries zone agreement (Garrett 2016). The *CIA world fact book* from 2016 presents the economic situation of Tokelau in the following manner:

> The people rely heavily on aid from New Zealand – about $15 million annually in 2012-13 and 2013-14 – to maintain public services. New Zealand's support amounts to 80% of Tokelau's recurrent government budget. An international trust fund, currently worth nearly US$32 million, was established in 2004 to provide Tokelau an independent source of revenue (CIA 2016).

Currently, Tokelau finds itself in the surprising situation of being what is called the 'highest aided country ever', according to the Economic Support Arrangement Review ESA010 (2011: 25). Among the main findings in this economic review, of importance for our discussion is the following observation: 'Almost 50% of government expenditure is for employee compensation, which is extremely high in comparison to other countries' (2011: 30, see Fig. 7 in the report). Of importance, but not discussed in the review, is how this figure signifies a fantastic increase in jobs provided by state institutions, as the employee compensation referred to for the main part relates to administrative positions.

This transition from a kin-based subsistence economy mainly reliant on local resources to an aid-based monetary economy – that is, with a huge increase in reliance on outside economic support (see Hooper 1982) – makes demands on Tokelau's political institutions as well. How much the practices of leadership, the role of the Village Councils, and the running of everyday affairs really have changed in the process is a matter of debate (Hoëm 2015). It is possible to contend that the new state apparatus represents a radical break with former socioeconomic practices, but as I shall show, things are not that clear-cut as the two are entangled in the everyday reality of the villages.

The state apparatus deemed necessary (by agencies such as the United Nations and the New Zealand foreign service) for Tokelau to achieve self-determination has come, as we have learned, at the cost of a massive dependency on aid. It is also possible to observe a profound shift in the kinds of work in which people engage in a relatively short period – even to the extent that the ordinary everyday activities of twenty years ago are now described, admittedly by outside observers, as contributing to unemployment rates. The consequences of this shift from a reliance on subsistence activities to a reliance on aid is also noted and described in the report:

> At the same time, full-time work has limited people's ability to grow, gather and fish for local food thus increasing dependency on store bought food … There is also evidence of a growing disparity (in terms of income, expectations for health and education standards) and division between the salaried and waged workers, and between balancing family, community and work commitments. Tokelau will need to address these to avoid them *adversely impacting the society and culture*. Change will need to be balanced with productivity levels and the present guarantee of employment (ESA 2011: 9, emphasis added).

In other words, and again, according to an outside perspective, the egalitarian economy has been transformed to a degree where (formerly negligible) economic differences between people and families have emerged. While this observation agrees with empirical realities, the admonishment to Tokelau leaders to ensure that the recent economic development does not 'adversely impact' what they call the society and culture shows a blatant lack of understanding of the causal effects of the introduced, sectorized economy on the local system of production integral to what they call Tokelau's – presumably but not explicitly stated – egalitarian 'society and culture'. Most importantly, the local alternatives of livelihoods are challenged: by withdrawing a large proportion of the able-bodied population from subsistence activities and employing them in the growing public sector, Tokelau's self-sufficiency in terms of food security and local skills is gradually being undermined.

Kin and political leadership: the difficult issue of growth

As Sylvia Yanagisako (2002) has noted, the tendency in much economic theory to dismiss cultural factors and family-based production units from the analysis comes at the cost of a certain blindness. In order to rectify this, firstly, we need to see the stated increasing imbalance between families in terms of income in relation to measures taken by the political authorities in Tokelau to ensure that all have access to means of livelihood. Of particular importance among such measures is the *inati* system of village distribution of goods. The *inati,* to which I will return shortly, is the institutionalized distribution, in equal shares, to all villagers of all communally owned resources, mainly fish, but occasionally including other kinds of goods, for example such items as cement, wood, or cloth. Secondly, we need to see the demand for a balancing of 'family, community and work commitments' in light of local attitudes to social participation in order to gain a clearer perspective of the tensions and choices involved.

How people negotiate everyday life in the new work spaces provided by the expanding administration, where the knowledge possessed by younger people is more valid than that of their elders, and where men and women must relate as colleagues, despite being relatives bound by reciprocal patterns of etiquette, duties, and obligations, is a daily exercise in creativity and flexibility (see Hoëm 2015 for illustrations). Also, given Tokelau's relatively privileged economic and political position as compared to its neighbour states Tuvalu and Samoa, through its association with New Zealand, vacant positions in the Tokelau administration attract applicants from all over the world. In the hunt for potential for economic growth, non-monetary aspects of production in Tokelau, regulated through reciprocal relations of kin, are easily overlooked, undervalued, and, on occasion, risk being dismissed as corruption.

Present and future generations of Tokelauans face many consequences and effects of living with the tensions of value brought about by what I have elsewhere (Hoëm 2015) described as two languages of governance (or two 'universes', to use Graeber's term). On a general level, these tensions may be described as occurring as a result of the confrontation in local practice between two different systems of production and reproduction. This difference may, for the sake of simplicity, be described as one between an economic system based on the outsiders' definition of 'growth' as an exponential increase in imported material goods, measured by monetary value, and the local economic system, where the conceptual equivalent to growth is part of a semantically qualitatively different frame of thought. This local definition is the genealogical concept of growth, and according to this view, morally correct action generates fecundity. Fecundity, through its power (cf. the better-known concept of *mana*), is a necessary precondition for political competition over dominance, or '*tupu*', 'being on top'. This local practice of competitive, genealogically based leadership has historical roots across the Pacific (Fox 2006; Kirsch 2000), and is characterized by a dynamic merging of kinship-based production and political leadership.

The *inati* system of collective, equal distribution of communally held goods is an institutional expression of this system of production and social reproduction, the epitome of what is frequently referred to as 'the Tokelau way'. To this it is important to add that, as a model for political action, '*tupu*', or what one may call one-upmanship, creates social cohesion through its moulding of supporters into one group. However, it also fosters competition between leaders vying for dominance and has historically led to open conflict and a state of war between groups of supporters (see Hoëm 2005; also Huntsman & Hooper 1996).

Finally and importantly for our argument, from the current perspective of state-building, this local system of regulation of productive and reproductive activities is to an ever-increasing degree rendered invisible by the dominance of the aid-financed labour regime. This is particularly evident in administrative reports and outsiders' analyses of them, such as the one from the *New Internationalist* presented above.

Sharing (*inati*) and aid: incommensurable 'universes'?
As mentioned above, the *inati* is the Tokelau system of distribution of any communally owned resource, such as, for example, food prepared for a village feast, fish caught by any fishing crew which exceeds a specified number, but also imported goods such as cement, wood for house construction, and flour. The system of distribution follows the principle of equal shares to all, regardless of age and status.

A wide variety of goods, including items originating from aid-financed projects controlled by the administration, have also been distributed in this fashion. The *inati* is an efficient way of distributing goods, as all villagers on the atoll are registered by name by the local overseer (*tauvaega*) of the *inati*, as part of an *inati* group. The system promotes transparency in the sense of keeping a written record of all people currently residing on the islands, and of the goods that they receive. This tally, which is updated by the *tauvaega*, provides the leadership with a full overview in which every transaction is included.

In the early 1950s, co-operative stores were set up, one in each village. Under the control of the elders, basic goods such as soap, kerosene, sugar, tobacco, cloth, tinned fish, corned beef, and matches were on sale. As people gradually gained access to salaried work as church workers, teachers, nurses, telegraph operators, and other skilled or semi-skilled professions, the selection of goods in the stores increased. Occasionally an item would be distributed, and not sold through the store, as compensation to villagers for their participation in a village project, hence the examples of cement and flour being shared out through the *inati*. We see here a system of production where a small minority work as wage-labourers, and where livelihood security is provided for all, even if the resource situation is characterized by recurrent periods of scarcity. The *inati* taken on its own represents a system where transparency is in principle total, in the sense that all villagers and all goods are accounted for, known by all, and all are equally provided for. When seen from the vantage-point of today, however, including the increasingly dominant monetary sphere, the balance has shifted. In the new situation, only a few households are dependent on the *inati* for the main part of their livelihoods.

Journal of the Royal Anthropological Institute (N.S.), 166-179
© Royal Anthropological Institute 2018

In the period of transition from a predominantly subsistence to a predominantly monetary economy, throughout the 1980s, outside investment (i.e. aid channelled through the New Zealand Ministry of Foreign Affairs and Trade) in the local infrastructure was on the increase. The characteristics of the aid-financed labour regime, as it became entangled with the *inati* system, will be indicated through the following example. By the 1980s, a Department of Public Works was established, and it organized construction work on a large scale through what was called the Housing Scheme. Through this scheme, families were offered the opportunity to finance, through loans, a new house, built with cement and wood, and with a corrugated iron roof. A major attraction of this kind of construction is that it allows for water catchment, channelling the water from the roof into the basement, which is constructed as a water tank. This lessened the villagers' dependence on the (sometimes meagre) distributions from the communal water tanks and the village well, which was kept safely under guard. That this project also placed all kin groups in debt to the emergent Tokelau state administration was not much discussed at the time, however. The regime demanding accountability for the aid-based economy asked that the debt incurred by families be registered as debt to the aid donors, that is, the New Zealand state, through its Tokelau administration. However, and illustrative of a basic incommensurability between the two ways of practising social responsibility described above, as the years went by, the local ledgers of debt were erased. Discounted as no longer of political significance, the burden of debt was transformed into what to all intents and purposes amounted retrospectively to a distribution of housing material through the *inati*. In terms of the parameters of the aid system, this may be seen as corrupt practice. In terms of the *inati* economy, however, this amounts to treating people in a way that safeguards their livelihoods. Furthermore, it helped to uphold social equality.

In order to understand how pervasive the collective egalitarian ethos is, it is of significance that, until the end of the 1980s, a total ban on private enterprise was in force. This law was created and upheld by the Village Councils. Any individual (or family acting as a unit) who might have considered importing any kind of good, such as video films for rent or for sale, was prohibited from doing so. To sell food or alcohol, to let accommodation and similar activities that some people dreamed of engaging in, was out of the question.

Throughout the 1980s and 1990s, however, villagers saw the gradual return of the first generation of scholarship students who came back to take up positions in the by then expanding Tokelau state administration. In the early 1990s, the state administration included a department of finance, of health, of public works, of transport, and of education. Many of this first generation of scholarship students took up positions in these departments, for shorter or longer periods. Their administrative jobs required them to travel to Tokelau frequently, but at this stage, few of them actually took up residence in the atoll villages.

In the villages from the early 1980s, as noted by anthropologist Antony Hooper (1982), there was an emerging tension between unpaid work that was done for the village, and a new category, *galuega fakamua*. Charitably, it translates as 'work for the government'. More commonly, it was translated as 'work that takes precedence', that is, work that must come before any other activity. These 'other kinds of activities' then include all village work carried out by a multiplicity of groups, for example women, the *aumaga* ('untitled men'), and named task-orientated groups such as the Piula (in Fakaofo) who are responsible for all practical work related to funerals. This semantic creativity suddenly relegated to secondary status the category of village work, *galuega o te nuku*, which had until this time been almost all-dominant when work for monetary payment was scarce. In this period, and as mentioned above, remunerations even entered into the economy of redistribution within extended families. The new category of 'work that takes precedence' was in contrast dominantly time-regulated, wage-earning, office work – in other words, work that required skilled or semi-skilled labour. However, and importantly, over time it also increasingly included elements of village work, paying unskilled labourers by the hour for manual labour, such as was needed in the construction work instigated by the Housing Scheme, mentioned previously.

From this time on, in other words, a categorical distinction was introduced in the villages which was to become more and more significant in shaping people's life trajectories, namely that between skilled and unskilled labour. Importantly, the distributive egalitarian economy constituted a different form of livelihood security from that of the aid-driven waged work in the state administration. We also see how contradictions play out between qualitatively different principles of economy and accounting, exemplified through the distribution of aid resources through the *inati*. These examples represent creative solutions to what may in principle be incommensurable forms of kin-based production of livelihoods and the aid-financed governance economy. In practice, however, it is important to keep in mind that while people seek to obtain their livelihoods through whatever resources that are available, they also attempt to satisfy both systems of accountability and responsibilities.

Effects of the new labour regime on people's life trajectories

The new distinction of skilled and unskilled labour had most immediate impact on the lives of young men. Until its introduction as part of the new labour regime, a man's career path, and hence his value for society, relied on him acquiring skills that would make him an expert fisherman. To become an expert fisherman, a *tautai*, who could be trusted with open-ocean fishing required years of participating in fishing crews, learning from those elders who possessed the necessary knowledge. With seniority, and with acquiring a family and serving the village, a man's position would grow into ever-increasing positions of power. This trajectory was predictable and represented a real possibility for all, given that the person accepted the responsibilities for others that came with growing possibilities for leadership and influence. Physical strength and agility were valued, but were only admired if they were engaged in the service of the community, for example in public dancing or sporting competitions.

Fishermen, and all activities associated with fishing, are still appreciated (Hooper & Tinielu 2012). However, as the lives of the villagers are no longer solely dependent upon the skills of the *tautai* as people have access to money and hence to imported food, the attraction of fishing as a career path has waned. A profound shift has taken place, from a situation where *tautai* held the most prestigious knowledge and embodied the Tokelau way of life (*fakaTokelau*), to a situation where they are reduced to being unskilled labour. Unskilled labourers earn little, that is, in this case, men who only have their physical strength to offer. If they do not take part in political life, when as elders they may become members of the Village Council, they are dependent upon their extended family. It is the heads of the *kaiga* (family group) who decide whether a man in this position should stay in Tokelau and work for the family there, or if he should go and serve family members living overseas. If he is ordered to move overseas, as an unskilled labourer he can gather unemployment benefit, or if he is lucky, he might, as the first generation of migrants from Tokelau did, gain work as a manual labourer in New Zealand or Australia. Whereas that first generation were mainly employed in forestry and in car factories in New Zealand, as opportunities in the NZ labour market have reduced, more job seekers of this category have now moved to Australia to, for example, pick grapes, as laws regulating labour there have been relaxed.

The main difference between the former and the current situation is that previously while a man would expect to serve – albeit in different ways throughout his life – his family and the community, he could also expect to rise in status and increase the control he exercised over his life and over his family and community. It is the last factor that can no longer be counted on with any certainty. For this reason, more Tokelauan families see their future as connected with formal education (Huntsman 2007), and as education is free in Tokelau, this possibility is in principle open to all.

For women, the division between skilled and unskilled labour is also of major significance. The traditional trajectory also allows women more of a say in family and village affairs as they grow older, and the ways they are expected to serve change throughout life, from caretaking to more of an overseer role (see, e.g., Agee, McIntosh, Culbertson & Makasiale 2013).

In the pre-1990s economy of Tokelau, semi-skilled labour for women (as for men) included nurses' aides, teachers' aides, working in the village stores, and jobs in the new administration. Weaving skills become transformed around this time into 'traditional, cultural' skills, and the weaver-experts' knowledge underwent a loss of significance as they became unskilled workers on the same level as 'traditional fishermen'. Small-scale export of Tokelau handicraft exists but the income it generates cannot compete with even the most humble position as a clerk in the administration, despite the very high quality of the work involved.

As a result of consultations instigated by the United Nations, expert consultants came to the conclusion that what they called the traditional Tokelau society was highly conservative (see ESA 2011). To rectify what they saw as a lack of democratic representation in the political institutions by younger people and women, they encouraged among other things the establishment of a women's forum. This body was based on the already existing women's committees or sanitation committees (komiti tumamaa), established by the church missions (Hoëm 1995), and was given the name Fatupaepae, after the most important position women could hold within the kin group. In the nation-building process that followed from the efforts to move Tokelau into a position of political self-reliance, an important stage was reached in 1993 when the inter-atoll meeting forum, the General Fono, was transformed into a National Assembly. This assembly had the everyday support of a new administrative section, which was to serve a recently invented political institution called the Council of Faipule (CoF). This political institution became the governing executive body of Tokelau, running when the assembly was not in session, and consisted of the three previous 'foreign ministers' and their administrative support staff (Hoëm 2015). This new institution was founded on the premise that the previous political rivals would co-operate for the good of all Tokelau, and the National Assembly had for the first time one seat for each of the three atolls for a representative of the *Fatupaepae*. This national structure opened the door for women to participate in political life, and the administrative apparatus opened up new job opportunities for younger, educated people.

A labour action

In the late 1990s, some of the teachers in Tokelau took an unprecedented collective action and went on strike against their immediate leader, the Headmistress (see also Huntsman 2007: 186-7). The grounds for this labour action seem paradoxical as it was based not on work-related matters but on perceptions of proper behavioural codes among kin, according to gender and between age cohorts. In their experience of the tensions of value to which they responded, the teachers and teachers' aides expressed feelings of being treated disrespectfully according to norms of kinship. For this reason they stopped work. The Headmistress argued that other norms were the only relevant ones here: the public service manual regulating work performance and attendance had to be upheld. This leadership task arguably included admonishing people if they did not do their duty. These corrections, or reprimands as the employees on their side held, were experienced as demonstrations of disrespect. It is important to note that a public reprimand is a very serious matter in Tokelau, and most commonly such admonishments take place in relation to the Women's Committees and/or the Councils of Elders (see Hoëm 2015) as moral arbitraries.

In the context of the modern workplace, things are not so clear-cut, as this example shows. The Headmistress had already lost some authority before this strike occurred, for reasons related to the extended family to which she belonged and its position in the village. Both she and her husband had participated actively in the 'lifting up' (*hiki ki luga*) of Tokelau, and were seen as pro-modernizing: that is, they were in support of the new administration and proposed governmental changes. The Headmistress's higher educational background from Samoa set her apart from her contemporary peers, and she was perceived as feisty and more outspoken than is common for women of any age. Her husband had at the time taken up the newly created position of Work-Commissioner. This position was created as part of the new institutions deemed necessary for Tokelau to be able eventually to govern itself, and its main purpose was to ensure transparency in hiring processes. The then Director of Education, also female, was in the process of divorcing her husband. As divorce was relatively uncommon at the time, this fact had gradually been used against her to weaken her moral standing in the village as the situation became common knowledge. The more serious problems started as she hired one of the Work-Commissioners' sons as a teacher's aide. That he had no formal qualifications for the job was not an issue, as this was commonly the case for such aides. What made it into a contentious matter was that the aide and the Minister were suspected of having an affair. Villagers assumed that they were in a relationship already at the moment of employment and hence suspicions of favouritism were voiced. The hiring process, to make matters even more complicated, was sanctioned by the Work-Commissioner, who was the aide's father. The villagers' objections increased, and the extended family and all involved felt persecuted as the tide of sentiment in the village turned against them. As a result, the then Minister of Education, also occupying the position of *faipule* (i.e. one of the new national leaders), playing on traditional moral sentiments, saw his chance to increase his power (cf. the competitive leadership described above, *tupu*) by getting rid of a significant part of the troublesome modernizing fraction in the village. Finally, and as a direct result of the mounting pressure from her superior, the Director of Education abandoned her position and moved with her new partner to Australia. The Work-Commissioner lost his job, and the Headmistress's authority to reprimand her workers for poor work performance was eroded. The Minister as national leader had won a great victory, one that made sense in terms of local traditional leadership: that is, according to the way village politics has been conducted for a long time. In other words, his actions served to strengthen the traditional hierarchy of Tokelau, only now operating within the structures of the state administration. Equally it constituted a setback for the forces trying to build up a modern state administration: that is, to establish a management at a distance from the political leadership.

What we have here is a situation where tensions of value come to the fore. In the case of the teachers arguing on the basis of kinship morality, it was related to this backdrop of perceived breaches by members of the Headmistress's extended kin group. That the position held by the teachers did not make sense from the perspective of the rules and regulations laid out in the schools' work manual was not relevant from the strikers' point of view. The contested matter was one of moral value, related to issues of gender and kin and ultimately to norms governing social reproduction, and the strikers fought to uphold what they considered proper Tokelau etiquette. In the other case, the Director of Education used the possible breach of the public service code (in the case of the hiring) to erode the credibility of the modern administration, and thereby acquire power and support for his position as a village leader. His undermining of his director had the support of a majority of villagers, and while it was in line with the way village politics commonly is conducted (see Hoëm 1995), it is difficult to see how it was consistent with the demands of his ministerial role. To instigate an independent investigation would have been in line with his duty as minister, but to act on his own in this matter was questionable from the perspective of the public sector that he controlled.

Conclusion: tensions of value and livelihood security

That the once so familiar way of life in the villages should become equally distant and unfamiliar for the first generations of migrants and scholarship students after years of residence overseas was unexpected by most, and the loss of manual skills accompanied by a devaluation of gender identity is a process that is little understood and rarely discussed (but see Hoëm 2004). In my 2004 work on cultural relationships and identity work between the home and diasporic communities, I noted a cultural 'time-lag' that occurred between the New Zealand Tokelauan communities and the atoll villages. In short, the image of Tokelau held and cherished in New Zealand was of a Tokelau frozen in time, from the late 1950s and early 1960s. With the rapid transformations of infrastructure in the atolls during the 1980s and 1990s, travelling between the locations at that time was highly instructive. While the communities in New Zealand lacked the sovereignty over land and government that gave authority to the Councils of Elders in the atolls, the political changes in the atolls were such that the image held by most of Tokelau as a tightly knit subsistence-based community was out of sync with realities on the ground. As we have seen, many of the first group of scholarship students returned to Tokelau at various stages to take part in the process of building government there (Hoëm 2004; 2015; Huntsman 2007). After years of dreaming about Tokelau, and in particular cultivating the image of the great beauty of the natural environment and its ideal-typical gender roles (Hoëm 1992), the return to the realities of economic practices in the atolls was hard for many. In particular, a lack of age- and gender-appropriate skills, such as being able to climb a coconut tree, dive for clams, run an outboard motor, weave, prepare an earth oven (*umu*), and in some cases even speak the language, represented insurmountable challenges. In short, many found themselves without the basic skills needed to take a productive and active part in the life of their communities. As the mastery of such skills is part of what constitutes appropriate and sought-after gender roles as males and females, this situation is trying for those who experience it. On the positive side, the skills that they did possess, such as knowledge of English, and a broad spectrum of literacy ranging from accountancy to mastery of bureaucratic language and computing, were (and still are) of increasing importance.

Finally, and in a comparative perspective, this Tokelau situation is clearly different in some respects from that of local Aboriginal communities in Australia, such as described by Gibson (2010) and Povinelli (1995). The main difference from the situation described by Gibson is that the newly dominant labour market in Tokelau is primarily staffed by an indigenous workforce, even though the administration is not entirely locally controlled. In other words, the ethnic divide that exists *between* separate spheres of work and unemployment documented from multiple ethnographies from Australia is absent here. The situation in Tokelau, where the work institutions are mainly staffed by Tokelauans, is, rather, characterized by tensions of value taking place *within* work and political institutions, as we have seen exemplified by the entanglement of kin and labour in the teachers' strike.

There are, however, also some striking similarities to the situations described by Gibson and Povinelli. These we may find in the perceptual and conceptual gap that I have described above between qualitatively different systems of production and understanding. The conflicting descriptions of unpaid village work as valued or as amounting to unemployment exemplify this gap. As we have seen, the new labour regime represented by the introduction of a state administration is entangled with the egalitarian distributive system of production and reproduction. The local political kin-based leadership system of production and reproduction is able to incorporate and use the system of money (*tupe*). Whether it is able to accommodate the division of villagers into people with potentially qualitatively different access to livelihoods (based on the new labour regime's distinction between skilled and unskilled labour) is another matter. So far, the local preference seems to be to support whatever line of action maintains the egalitarian, collective orientation, as in the example above with the vanishing Housing Scheme debt.

One final reflection on the potential incommensurability or possible co-existence of the two entangled, and unequally powered, systems of social production and reproduction: Povinelli (1995) describes an Australian situation of unequal access to work and standards of livelihoods by reference to ontological differences. By choosing the ontological perspective, she also inadvertently comes to create an image of two incommensurable ways of being in the world. I admire her efforts at making visible what could in older terminology, with Edwin Ardener (2007 [1975]), be called a muted group's perspectives on their life-world. However, since the entanglements that I have described throughout demonstrate local people's capacity to incorporate difference into their way of living, I find this perspective of ontological difference less illuminating for the Tokelau case. Importantly, within this entanglement, as we have seen in this essay, people experience and express tensions of value. The division of skilled and unskilled labour is a clear expression of some important challenges that the labour situation on the islands presents to what is described in outsiders' reports as 'Tokelau culture'.

With the gradual shift towards a monetary economy and a state administration, the gendered and reciprocal organization of work is changing character to be of 'cultural' and not economic importance. The village/kin model of production and political leadership continues, however, as the case of the labour conflict shows; entangled with the state apparatus, it remains visible to those who know where to look. Finally, it is important to note yet again that the dominant source of livelihoods at present, and the job security it represents, is bolstered by an aid-driven economy. The skills needed to exploit local resources may still be of considerable importance, as the conditions of labour may shift with global economic fluctuations. Hence the knowledge and practices of subsistence activities and a sharing economy still provide a vitally important safety net for those making a living in the atoll environment.

ACKNOWLEDGEMENTS
I would like to thank the Norwegian Research Council for funding this research, which was conducted as part of the project 'Identity Matters: Movement and Place'.

REFERENCES

Agee, M.N., T. McIntosh, P. Culbertson & C.'O. Makasiale (eds) 2013. *Pacific identities and well-being*. London: Routledge.

Ardener, E. 2007 [1975]. Belief and the problem of women. In *The voice of prophecy and other essays* (ed. M. Chapman), 72-85. New York: Berghahn Books.

Buckley, A. 1994. Tokelau. *New Internationalist* **251** (available on-line: https://newint.org/features/1994/01/05/profile, accessed 22 January 2018).

CIA 2016. *The world fact book 2016* (available on-line: https://www.cia.gov/library/publications/download/download-2016/index.html, accessed 25 January 2018).

ESA 2011. *ESA 010 Tokelau, Economic Support Arrangement (ESA) review Final Report*. Narooma, N.S.W.: GHD Ltd.

Fox, J. 2006. Introduction. In *Origin, ancestry and alliance* (eds) J. Fox & C. Sather, 1-13. Canberra: ANU e-press.

Garrett, J. 2016. US announces withdrawal from crucial fisheries treaty with Pacific nations. ABC News, 20 January (available on-line: http://www.abc.net.au/news/2016-01-19/us-withdraws-from-crucial-treaty-with-pacific-nations/7099740, accessed 22 January 2018).

Gibson, L. 2010. Making a life: getting ahead, and getting a living in Aboriginal New South Wales. *Oceania* **80**, 143-60.

Graeber, D. 2013. It is value that brings universes into being. *HAU: Journal of Ethnographic Theory* **3: 2**, 219-43.

Hoëm, I. (ed.) 1992. *Kupu mai te Tutolu: Tokelau oral literature*. Oslo: Scandinavian University Press/The Institute for Comparative Research in Human Culture.

——— 1995. *A way with words*. Bangkok, Oslo: White Orchid Press/Institute of Comparative Research in Human Culture.

——— 2004. *Theatre and political process: staging identities in Tokelau and New Zealand*. Oxford: Berghahn Books.

——— 2005. Stealing the water of life. *History and Anthropology* Special Issue: Ethnographies of historicity (eds) E. Hirsch & C. Stewart **16**, 293-305.

——— 2015. *Languages of governance in conflict: negotiating democracy in Tokelau*. Amsterdam: John Benjamins.

Hooper, A. 1982. *Aid and dependency in a small Pacific territory* (Working Paper **62**). Department of Anthropology, University of Auckland.

——— & I. Tinielu (eds) 2012. *Echoes at Fishermen's Rock: traditional Tokelau fishing. By elders from Atafu Atoll* (Knowledges of nature, vol. **4**). Paris: Unesco.

Huntsman, J. 2007. *The future of Tokelau: decolonising agendas 1975-2006*. Honolulu: University of Hawai'i Press.

——— & A. Hooper 1996. *Tokelau: a historical ethnography*. Auckland: University Press.

KIRSCH, P.V. 2000. *On the road of the winds.* Berkeley: University of California Press.
POVINELLI, E.A. 1995. Do rocks listen? The cultural politics of apprehending Australian Aboriginal labor. *American Anthropologist* **97**, 505-18.
TSING, A.L. 2004. *Friction: an ethnography of global connection.* Princeton: University Press.
YANAGISAKO, S.J. 2002. *Producing culture and capital: family firms in Italy.* Princeton: University Press.

État, main-d'œuvre et parenté : tensions entre les valeurs dans une société égalitaire

Résumé

Cet essai discute des effets d'un appareil d'État et de nouvelles formes de travail sur une économie distributive et égalitaire fondée sur la parenté. La société insulaire de l'atoll de Tokelau est en train de mettre en place un État moderne, financé en grande partie par l'aide mais aussi par les recettes de ses zones de pêche. Dans la pratique, le nouveau régime du travail associé à l'introduction d'une administration étatique s'imbrique avec un système distributif égalitaire de production et de reproduction. La structure de pouvoir locale, fondée sur la parenté, peut incorporer et utiliser le système du capital de façon égalitaire. On ne sait toutefois pas encore si elle parviendra à gérer durablement les inégalités sociales, autrement dit la division des villageois en travailleurs qualifiés et non qualifiés, ayant potentiellement droit à des moyens de subsistance qualitativement différents. Alors que les études comparatives des Aborigènes australiens décrivent leurs inégalités d'accès au travail et aux niveaux de vie en faisant référence à l'ontologie, donc implicitement à l'origine ethnique, les tensions à Tokelau s'inscrivent dans un *même* réseau social, où de nouvelles formes de travail contribuent à une dévaluation des compétences associées à des schémas genrés de subsistance. Cette dévaluation menace à son tour la durabilité de la société de l'atoll, qui pourrait être compromise si le flux de capitaux se déplaçait ailleurs.

11

State against industry: time and labour among Dominican furniture makers

CHRISTIAN KROHN-HANSEN *University of Oslo*

This essay analyses time and labour among small Dominican furniture producers. The Dominican Republic's small workshops and firms experience much waiting – not speed and political-economic integration, but, instead, slowness, blockades, and marginalization. The national production of furniture has faced increasingly tough competition from imported commodities. In the early 1990s, the national finances were in crisis. Pressured by its international lenders, the state deregulated and opened the economy, while it has continued to spend little on the development of the country's workshops and industry. In addition, the country's electricity sector is in poor condition and long blackouts are the norm. Because of the situation, the country's small furniture makers are forced to live with contradictory and clashing social rhythms. The diversity among forms of time is navigated through concrete labour and in the everyday. Contemporary global capitalism ought to be understood as a contingent outcome of labour activity in the form of a myriad of localized, mundane efforts to 'fix' it. Such efforts always mirror a specific political and social history. By exploring contemporary capitalist time through a focus on particular forms of labour, we can analyse how global capitalism's discrepant rhythms help to give shape to, disrupt, and dislocate forms of labour in a given place. At the same time, we show how the involved agents seek to adapt to, and work on the effects of, the conflicts between rhythms.

Marx's explorations in *Capital* show that the abstract time-reckoning of capitalism in practice helps to produce a large number of contradictory social rhythms that must be mediated by social agents – capitalists, workers, financiers – through concrete activity in time. His studies of capitalist 'circulation time' in Volume 2 (1993 [1885]), for example, demonstrate that there is a contradiction between the rhythms of production and consumption and those of money markets – and that decisive infrastructures of production are often left vulnerable or jeopardized by the patterns and rhythms of credit markets. In turn, the diversity and clashes among rhythms have a bearing on both collective and individual experiences of time. At the level of the self, the navigation of capitalist time is replete with dilemmas and choices.

A basic anthropological task is consequently to examine ethnographically the various forms of labour through which inconsistent capitalist rhythms are mediated. As Laura Bear (2014*a*; 2014*b*) has recently underscored, in such work we should focus on labour

Journal of the Royal Anthropological Institute (N.S.), 180-197
© Royal Anthropological Institute 2018

practices.[1] It is through specific encounters with the material world and creative use of the body, technology, and time that humans seek to reconcile disparate time-maps[2] and social rhythms. In the following essay, I examine forms of time and labour among a group of small entrepreneurs – owners and operators of what mainly represent small, precarious family businesses. These entities have in common that they produce and sell furniture and mattresses, and that they are situated in various areas of the Dominican capital, Santo Domingo.

The Dominican Republic's furniture industry is neither large nor powerful. On the contrary, its position today is fairly weak, not to say seriously threatened. Around 95 per cent of the production units constitute only *talleres* (workshops or small enterprises), with fewer than fifty workers, most often fewer than ten. In 2012, the national production of furniture constituted 1 per cent of the gross domestic product (Rodríguez Bencosme 2013: 16). A large proportion of these firms are situated in the capital – typically in its most popular and populous neighbourhoods. I underscore that most of my material is derived from examples of small, precarious operations that employ few workers. In these firms, the owner has an office (or at least a desk and a couple of chairs pushed into a corner) where he or she attends to customers and paperwork – but the workshop is never far away; most owners spend the bulk of their time with the workers, making or repairing furniture.

Anthropological analyses of social time under contemporary capitalism are important for at least three reasons. Firstly, such analyses provide a window through which to comprehend power differentials and forms of inequality. We ought to be concerned with capitalism's forms of time because they express the constant negotiation of the power relationships in the capitalist system.

Secondly, we need an ethnographically driven critique of approaches that seem too general or abstract. Many explorations of the social time of capitalism work only at the scale of global processes – in almost complete isolation from studies of specific places. This applies, for example, to the works of Marxist thinkers like David Harvey (1989; 2005) and Noel Castree (2009). The problem with their – and many others' – discussions of capitalist circulation time is that they almost exclusively seek to account for capitalism's dynamics and 'fixes' in terms of large-scale processes, such as the advancing of credit through banking activity and financial operations. These analyses do not draw attention to the everyday forms of labour that constantly make global capitalism possible. Real, contemporary capitalist circulation has to be understood as a contingent outcome of labour activity in the form of a myriad of localized, prosaic, and creative efforts to 'fix' it according to manifold ideas about time, well-being, useful help, advantage, and profit. Such efforts always articulate particular moral and affective forms and a particular history. By studying contemporary capitalist time through a focus on concrete (in other words, localized) labour, we can discover and reveal how global capitalism's discrepant rhythms help disrupt and dislocate forms of labour in a given place (Harvey & Krohn-Hansen, this volume). Simultaneously, we show how the involved agents seek to adapt to, and work on the effects of, the contradictions between rhythms.

Thirdly, anthropological examinations of contemporary capitalist time are significant because they can help us better understand the sustained, tremendous role of the state. The world's nation-state systems and global capitalism are entangled in one another. This continues to apply notwithstanding the fact that most states since the 1980s have deregulated markets and trade and privatized assets in striking ways

(Graeber 2002; Pedersen 2013). In the following, I discuss especially the effects of state debt (Bear 2015). Like so many other states, the Dominican Republic has for a long time had significant debt. Debt relations are by definition about social shaping of time. In the words of Gustav Peebles, '[T]he crucial defining feature of credit/debt is its ability to link the present to the past and the future ... [C]redit is a method of lending concrete resources to an institution or an individual in the present and demanding (or hoping for) a return in the future' (2010: 226-7). A modern state's debt is bound to the calendar (Graeber 2011; Guyer 2012: 491). In the Dominican case, we shall see that the construction and reconstruction of the state's debt based on calendar time produces large amounts of unpredictability, delays, and waiting, and, more generally, clashes between forms of time. The other side of this is, of course, that the country's inhabitants, including the producers of furniture, are forced to seek to adapt. The adaptations take place in the everyday and in, and through, labour.

The labour of Dominican furniture makers is also political – or, put differently, their efforts to find solutions have a political dimension as well. How so? Firstly, the Dominican state, with its various institutions, is a crucial actor. Producers of furniture continually need to adjust to public laws and regulations – and many apply to state institutions for loans and credit. Many also attempt to sell their products to public agencies. The outcome is that most, if not all, in the industry find themselves in almost constant negotiation – struggles over rights and obligations, resources, documents, and meaning – with representatives of the state. Secondly, Dominican producers of furniture and mattresses have created their own interest organization, La Asociación Nacional de Industriales de Muebles, Colchones y Afines – or ASONAIMCO. Through this, they attempt to act collectively and fight for their interests. As we shall see, a vast majority of those in the industry are profoundly critical of the state. According to them, the Dominican state has rendered it increasingly difficult – almost impossible – for the national industry to survive and develop. In the following section, I outline some features of the general economic situation of the industry before looking in more detail at social time among Santo Domingo's furniture makers.

Trujillo's authoritarian legacy, structural adjustment, and the conditions of the Dominican industry

The timescape of today's Dominican industry is a product of the past. Two processes have been key: first, the nation's protracted authoritarian political history; and second, the country's adoption of an increasingly neoliberal political-economic model since the beginning of the 1990s. General Rafael Trujillo ruled the Dominican Republic dictatorially from 1930 to 1961. From 1966 to 1978, and from 1986 to 1996, the country was governed by Joaquín Balaguer. The latter had been one of Trujillo's close collaborators, and his first twelve years in power were violently repressive. After 1978, the use of military repression was discontinued, and the nation has celebrated presidential and congressional elections every four years.

In 1990, the Dominican economy was in deep crisis, and the government was unable to pay its debts (Greenberg 1997: 87-8). This period, between 1990 and 1993, saw the beginning of a marked opening of the Dominican economy under IMF stabilization programmes backed by a large number of neoliberal reforms. The 1990 tax reforms opened national markets to foreign competition by lowering tariffs and getting rid of most import quotas and licensing requirements. The Foreign Investment Law, passed in 1995, opened significant parts of the economy to foreign investment, and removed all restrictions on profit remittances (Moya Pons 2010: 444-8, 458-9). Leonel Fernández, who came to power in 1996, only intensified this whole process of neoliberal restructuring. Fernández was president first from 1996 to 2000 and subsequently for eight years from 2004 to 2012.

Since the mid-1980s, tourism, export manufacturing, and migrant remittances have been the country's most important sources of foreign exchange (Gregory 2014). Whereas tourism and export manufacturing have enjoyed state support and special incentives and privileges, traditional industry, such as the furniture industry, has felt opposed and marginalized, as illustrated by the following two examples.

The bulk of the Dominican production of furniture is for the domestic market. There is a tiny export market, but it is highly limited (and goes almost exclusively to Haiti, Puerto Rico, and Jamaica). With the opening of the Dominican economy, Dominican production of furniture for the national market has faced increasingly tough competition from imported commodities – forms of furniture made in China, Indonesia, the United States, and Europe. Many of these imported products are cheap, or relatively so. For example, Denny Reynoso, a spokesperson for the Dominican furniture makers, declared in May 2009, 'Today … the problem is that the demand for local furniture has gone down more than 40 per cent because people buy more furniture made in China, Indonesia, and Malaysia' (Listín Diario 2009). Those I met in the industry underscored that they do not oppose free trade or stronger economic competition. But what frustrated them was that the changes, according to them, had happened so quickly and that domestic producers in practice had received no help – not even, as they put it, in a brief, limited transition period.

The tourist companies constantly erect hotels, and these need furniture: beds, chairs, tables, cupboards. But the access to this possible market has been undermined and blocked through the state's tax policies. This is how Santo Domingo's producers of furniture explained it. For the owners in the tourist industry, it is economically favourable to import. If hotel owners in the tourist industry purchase furniture from local producers, they have to pay the country's normal 18 per cent value-added tax (VAT, or ITBIS). But if they instead import the furniture directly from abroad, they do not have to pay this tax. In this situation, most choose to import, not to buy locally.

The timescape of the production of furniture in Santo Domingo – and a history of entrepreneurship and labour

A number of Santo Domingo's small furniture makers underscored that a part of their basic survival strategy, given the context of a rapidly growing import of furniture made in Asia and elsewhere, consisted in seeking to offer 'Dominican', not foreign, products. What kind of mapping and navigation of time does this strategy express? While the first part of this section provides answers to this question, the second part examines the following question: how did these workshops and firms work in order to secure sufficient access (a) to electricity (for production) and (b) to the market? Although the main theme of temporality recurs throughout the analysis, the specific, ethnographically driven intervention explaining the connections between historically constituted structures of power, labouring practices, exploitation, and forms of time features as a shifting and contingent picture that refracts differently in each part. The explanation is, as I have said, that I seek to formulate a bottom-up and anthropological account of capitalist labour and its value(s). Specifically, I seek to develop a perspective with the aid of material on just a few firms. Social time and capitalist time may appear as elusive categories, a bit slippery, vague, mystical. Ethnography is replete with mundane stuff, prosaic and concrete realities. Ethnography from the level of the individual workshop or enterprise can show examples of how society's and capitalism's framings of time and diverse rhythms are reflected in the most ordinary and trivial occurrences, or the biographies and everyday life and labour of flesh-and-blood citizens.

Power, timber, time

Before the Dominican economy started to transform through trade liberalizations from the early 1990s onwards, only highly limited amounts of furniture made abroad entered the country – and then mostly only through diplomatic and/or 'occult' (illegal) channels. The regimes of Trujillo and Balaguer protected the domestic industry through prohibitions against import of commodities that could be made in the country: beverages, shoes, furniture, and a long list of other products. As one furniture maker put it in a conversation, in the early 1990s 'suddenly the restrictions and prohibitions were abolished and the country was hit by an avalanche'.

Dominican furniture products, Santo Domingo's furniture makers maintain, are different from most of the imported products in terms of at least three criteria: (a) the use of materials, (b) the production process, and (c) forms of time. In the following paragraphs, I will explain this, and in so doing I hope to be able to demonstrate that many ordinary Dominicans, representatives of the large popular classes and members of the middle class, continue to want, and prefer, 'Dominican' furniture. The bulk of the small firms live by these groups. My argument is this: the government's loans tied to IMF and World Bank conditionalities became decisive. Pressured by its financial difficulties and international lenders, the state deregulated and opened the economy, while it has continued to spend little on the development of the nation's workshops, small firms, and industry. The combination of contemporary global capitalism's (technical, social, and economic) ability to compress time and space and the Dominican opening and liberalization gave us the last twenty-five years of import growth. In a large number of cases, the outcome for Santo Domingo's small furniture makers is that to which I have referred: difficult or precarious conditions and experiences of conflicts between social rhythms and forms of time. The firms seek to get by through their labour. As we shall see, one strategy is important: continuing to offer forms of furniture that are in tune with a certain historically constituted tradition and a widespread Dominican (popular) taste. This taste expresses a way of thinking about furniture and time, and is linked to memories. Put differently, these Dominican furniture makers' labour is a labour on forms of time and history.[3]

The Dominican furniture market today can be divided into three categories (Rodríguez Bencosme 2013: 93). The first of these represents what may be summarized as more or less traditional forms of furniture. The preferred colours are dark and the style is classic – or corresponds to a fusion of classic styles. Large parts of the population prefer this 'classic' design to rustic or more contemporary (straight) lines. The furniture is made from wood, preferably mahogany (or materials that somehow resemble mahogany). Desirable chairs, sofas, and tables have lavish carvings. The second category represents furniture of a more 'contemporary' type – often with straight lines. Very few in the Dominican Republic make these products; instead, most are imported. In 2002, this type corresponded to about 16 per cent of the value of the national consumption of furniture (Rodríguez Bencosme 2013: 93). The third category contains products that do not fit the two others, owing to the use of materials or the typical places where the furniture is used. Examples are forms of furniture made of iron or rattan, modular kitchens, and furniture for gardens, offices, and hotels. These parts of the market have registered an increasing number of imports.

In addition to mahogany, Dominican firms use other wood, especially pine, oak, and to a smaller extent acacia. Almost all the timber used by Dominican furniture makers is imported. In 2000, in an attempt to prevent deforestation, the country passed a law – Law 64-00 on the Environment and Natural Resources – that prohibits the use of native forests for commercial purposes. The labour in the workshops is anchored in carpentry traditions. Firms take the measurements of kitchens and bedrooms, receive small orders, and do repair work.

Small Dominican furniture makers argue that many ordinary Dominicans prefer Dominican furniture to imported furniture. They are of the opinion that the familiar national products last longer – they are more solid and hence better. Dominican furniture is made from solid wood, not from wood veneer, plywood, or other less robust materials. This is how Rafael Estévez, a furniture maker in the eastern part of the city, put it. He and his father had sought to diversify and develop an extra source of income by importing some furniture in addition to continuing to make and sell their own products:

> We wanted to experiment, attempt to import and sell furniture made in China. We sold a little before we imported a bit more and sold a bit more. But as I see it, our audience prefers the furniture made here, the wood, to know that it's wood and not a type of compressed cardboard or something similar, which will get damaged rapidly. People remain traditional concerning this.

María Paulino, who runs a tiny workshop in the popular *barrio* of Los Mina, explained:

> The creole furniture made here (*El mueble criollo de aquí*) in the Dominican Republic is the furniture that lasts. The imported furniture doesn't last, isn't equally good, I think. Here, people want their furniture to be durable – and the furniture lasts for many years, which isn't a good business for us [*laughing*] … But the furniture that we make is furniture that lasts – owing to the materials, the way of working. Because we use wood; abroad they often use cardboard or plywood, materials that immediately are damaged if they get wet. Wood veneer is fine in a country with a lot of resources, where people change furniture each year, but not here. We don't change our furniture so quickly.

Dominicans with limited means do not treat furniture as disposable. On the contrary, when they invest in furniture, they want it to be durable. The life of a piece of furniture can be long. In popular *barrios*, there are usually stores selling used furniture. The desire for solid furniture made from whole wood, not plywood, has to do with typical Dominican (bourgeois and working-class) domestic rituals. As María said, imported products are often made from materials that are easily damaged if they get wet. When Dominicans clean their homes (typically every Saturday), they empty buckets of water and soap onto the floor. Furniture with legs or plinths of veneer does not stand up to this treatment.

As previously mentioned, the preferred type of wood among large groups is mahogany, or *caoba*. For a long time, this has been the most culturally valued material – good furniture is made from or with mahogany. Aldo Núñez, one of two owners of a firm in the *barrio* Casa Vieja in the north of the city, put it in this manner:

> We Dominicans have always said that mahogany is the best wood. I'm from the countryside and grew up with this: mahogany is mahogany (*la caoba es la caoba*) … It's like a culture. The Dominican is so fond of mahogany that he even is fooled or swindled! Yes! Because you take a piece of wood and paint it and tell him that it's mahogany and he buys it.

Mahogany is more expensive; people with less money purchase furniture with less mahogany or with only the colour of mahogany – or they purchase furniture made from pine or rattan. Yuri Chez, who headed ASONAIMCO until late 2012, explained:

> Trujillo planted a lot of mahogany, and in the past, people planted a lot of mahogany. But in those days, a lot of mahogany was felled without any control and without any reforestation programmes. Even exceedingly old trees were cut, forests which had been made by the Spaniards after they had arrived to colonize – the Spaniards used mahogany precisely to make furniture, and for shipbuilding and housebuilding.[4] Mahogany was precious wood that was sold at low prices as if it were a cheap wood, owing to the abundance. This is the background to the tradition that we still see today, that people prefer furniture made from mahogany, that it's viewed as better than any other wood.

Dominican workshops and firms that make furniture from and with mahogany work in a tradition. Through their products, they elicit and sell emotions, notions, and memories – historically produced affective forms filled with a sense of history. Today, *la caoba*, or mahogany, is the national tree of the Dominican Republic. The builder of the twentieth-century Dominican nation-state was General Trujillo (1930-61). Trujillo was a ruthless dictator, but his protracted rule transformed Dominican society in important ways, for better or worse (Derby 2009; Turits 2003). A man of modest background and with thoroughly popular taste, the dictator incarnated the state. The regime built roads, irrigation canals, homes, schools, and hospitals across the territory. One of the rule's most central idioms was patronage. In the most important public buildings and offices that the regime constructed, it placed furniture made from high-quality mahogany. In his native community of San Cristóbal, Trujillo built what became his favourite country house, La Casa de Caoba, or Mahogany House, as early as 1940. Mahogany was the principal material used in the building, hence the name.

Today, the Dominican Republic is among the world's largest mahogany importers, only behind nations like the United States, China, and the United Kingdom. The largest exporter today is Peru, which surpassed Brazil after the country banned mahogany exports in 2001. A depressingly large proportion of exported Peruvian mahogany is illegally harvested (Gordon 2016). Illegal logging and its destructive environmental and social effects led to mahogany's incorporation in 2003 into Appendix II of the Convention on International Trade in Endangered Species (CITES). Other suppliers of genuine mahogany today are commercial plantations in India, Bangladesh, Indonesia, and Fiji.

The Dominican furniture makers I know adapt to their clientele and are flexible. Take Lorenzo Ortiz and Aldo Núñez, for example. When they started their firm in the north of the city in 2002, they made upholstered furniture – chairs, sofas – and tables in slightly different styles. Their customers belonged to the popular strata and the lower middle class. The chairs and sofas were, as said, upholstered, but had legs of mahogany; under the textiles, the makers used Chilean pine. The small tables were of mahogany.

In offering Dominican furniture, and especially products of and with *caoba*, workshops and firms help give form to experiences of time. Through the mundane use of objects with mahogany, people inscribe themselves and their families into the national past and present narratives of the island, of the national territory with its vegetation and resources, and of the building of the Trujillo dictatorship and today's Dominican Republic. The construction (or the remembering) of the nation and the making and the remaking of the self and the family are woven together, work together. The sight of familiar furniture evokes personal memories – of one's own adolescence, of family and neighbours, of homes, kitchens, sitting rooms. Additionally, the consumption of *caoba* operates as a language for measurement of relative success: through purchases and uses of furniture and other objects in mahogany, it is possible to experience time as a form of personal growth and individual mobility – or as a form of spectacular political-economic triumph, as Trujillo must have experienced when he luxuriated in mahogany at La Casa de Caoba.

As we have seen, the picture is dynamic and the growing import of furniture a reality. Well-to-do Dominicans purchase furniture made in Europe or the United States. Younger, educated couples, and Dominicans who grew up or used to live in New York or Spain, may opt for a more 'contemporary' style: objects with straight lines, made from cardboard or plywood. The tourist sector imports the furniture it needs. Furthermore, public institutions and the mass public purchase imported products. In this landscape, small Dominican furniture makers attempt to get by and survive. Their efforts are generated from particular affective and moral ideas about workmanship, materials, furniture objects, and time. Dominican furniture of solid wood is considered to be long-lived. In addition, the products are part of a history – or a variety of concepts of the past and the present. The manufacture and the use of the objects help sustain and modify memories, produce roots, and anchor and authorize self-understandings, including notions of growth and mobility.

Capitalism as speed, capitalism as foot-dragging

In the real capitalist world, the rhythms of credit and money markets frequently imperil the health of important infrastructures of production. Infrastructure has to be kept in repair and renewed. Not least, it has first to be created and constructed. But these tasks require the withholding of significant capital from circulation for the long term, and in so many states today this is difficult to manage. It is especially hard to manage for a state that already struggles with debt problems (Mains 2012; Schwenkel 2015). The best example in today's Dominican Republic is probably the nation's power sector. In most parts of Dominican society, access to electricity has for decades been unreliable, and short and long blackouts have been – and continue to be – part of everyday experience. As a consequence of the protracted, apparently chronic crisis in the country's power sector, Dominicans experience a number of discrepant social and economic rhythms. The lasting contradictions are an effect of the dominant use of abstract time in global capitalism. But, and this is important to recognize, they are also a product of something more delimited, namely Dominican political and social history – or features of a particular historically constituted state system and of a particular historically produced political culture. Below, I show ways in which small furniture makers seek to cope and find solutions, or 'fix' the contradictions, through their forms of labour. But I must first say a bit more about the history of the Dominican power sector.

Electricity rates in the Dominican Republic are among the highest in Latin America. As with so many other nations, high prices are a consequence of the country's reliance on oil for electricity generation. But the industry also suffers from low collection rates and considerable electricity theft. A massive reform implemented by the Fernández administration in the late 1990s led to the privatization of the largest of the state enterprises. The state's companies, which had been confiscated from Trujillo and his associates in 1961, had been a heavy financial burden on the state for years, as mismanagement and corruption had left them more or less in a shambles. As a result of the changes, the formerly state-owned Corporación Dominicana de Electricidad (which until then owned all of the commercial electricity generation, transmission,

Journal of the Royal Anthropological Institute (N.S.), 180-197
© Royal Anthropological Institute 2018

and distribution assets in the country) was split up and sold. Nearly fifteen years later, or at the time of my fieldwork, much of the nation's generating system was owned by American corporations, while the Dominican state continued to control and operate the bulk of the distribution sector; the state owned two of the country's distribution companies, EdeSur and EdeNorte, and it also maintained a 50 per cent ownership of the third one, EdeEste. The government owed large amounts to the IMF and other international lenders, and in July 2012 the state's distribution companies' total debt to the foreign generation companies broke the earlier record when it was estimated to be around US$1 billion (*Hoy* 2012*b*). The outcome was *apagones*, or blackouts, across much of the national territory: the generators reduced the electricity to the country's distribution grid, and/or the distribution companies sought to discipline a recalcitrant population (and the government) into paying the electricity bills through shutting down service to *barrios* in the capital and other places where too few paid for the electricity that they consumed. In May 2012, for example, owners of stores and workshops in Villa Consuelo, one of the capital's populous working-class *barrios* with a number of furniture workshops, protested loudly, telling reporters that the power in the area was gone each day from seven in the morning to eight in the evening (*Hoy* 2012*a*).

In the meantime, some are far better prepared to deal with the chronic crisis. Tourist enclaves, free zones, and large companies have their own generators and solutions in order to secure permanent access to electricity. Most wealthy Dominicans have backup generators to provide power when the lights go out – transforming the capital into a hodgepodge upon nightfall, with some leafier districts brightly lit up while much of the city smoulders in the dark.

As an outcome of the historical-political-economic-cultural production and reproduction of *apagones*, Santo Domingo's small producers of furniture are compelled to seek to work with, and on, time – or put another way, are driven to seek to produce time that can be put to use to produce and make money. Let us briefly look at how a couple of them get by.

María Paulino's small workshop is, as said, located in Los Mina, in the eastern part of the city. She is in her late fifties, married, and has a grown daughter who is a student. María's husband, a retired teacher, assists her in the workshop – he buys materials, runs errands, and visits the bank. María runs the workshop, takes part in production, and deals with customers. Most of the work is manual. The workshop uses machines, but no heavy equipment. María has two permanent workers who have worked with her for years. Before she established her own workshop over two decades ago, in 1992, she worked for many years in different furniture factories in the capital. In one of these, she learned how to make furniture from rattan: rattan chairs, rattan sofas, and rattan garden furniture. Ever since she started in 1992, she has specialized in the production of rattan furniture.

One of the biggest challenges remains *la luz*, or the electricity. Sometimes the power is gone all day – or for two or three whole days, María said. In addition, it is unpredictable. As she put it, 'When I arrive in the morning and there is power, I begin to work, filled with energy. But when the workers have arrived but wish to leave because we lack electricity and can't work, I'm at the point of despair'. How have they worked to seek to limit the loss of time? María has a small backup generator to provide power when it is needed; she cannot afford a large one. If the day begins without electricity, the first thing she has to do is send someone out to purchase petrol for the generator. Sometimes she doesn't have the money, and they are unable to get to work – and sometimes the generator suddenly stops working and needs repair. Since she began, she has had to buy three different generators. Two have collapsed. 'When you have to use the generator without intermission eight hours a day for long periods, it ends up breaking down', she explained, showing me the remains of the two earlier ones in a corner of the workshop. The one she uses now was made by a workshop in the vicinity from a used car engine.

The other firm is situated about 8 kilometres to the north of the city centre, in the *barrio* Casa Vieja in Villa Mella, as noted above. Lorenzo Ortiz and Aldo Núñez are in their late forties and *socios*, or business partners. Together they run an economic venture that makes furniture from wood and fabric. Before they joined forces and established their own firm, they had for many years worked together as employees in the same furniture making business. Lorenzo is the salesman and administrative head; Aldo is the furniture maker and spends most of his time in the workshop with the workers. In 2012, the firm had thirty-two workers, mainly young men in their early twenties; some years earlier, the number of workers had varied between eight and twenty. The workshop had seven simple machines – the production activities far more closely resembled craft than industry.

The two had not even tried to work with the power supplied by the companies. Ever since they started in 2002, they had exclusively relied on their own generator. As Lorenzo put it,

I've never used the power from the street [*la energía de la calle*], because in this neighbourhood where we operate they supply only four or five hours of electricity, and only in the night when I don't work – I work in the day. In brief, if I were to work with those lines, I would never be able to work.

He went on to emphasize that this was expensive and that their petrol costs were high, but that it nevertheless was an easy choice: 'Without the generator, we would have depended on the power from the street and that wouldn't have worked, because, in this area, there is never electricity!' When they created the firm, they began in Aldo's home and backyard in the *barrio* Cristo Rey, a bit closer to the centre of the city. After only three months, they relocated the firm to the *barrio* Casa Vieja on a piece of property of about 1,000 square metres that Aldo's family owned. The property was just a field that lay fallow. In those days, the area had few houses and was without electricity; on the contrary, it was still mainly fields and vegetation. Within a month, Lorenzo and Aldo constructed a simple workshop building themselves and installed a used generator on the property. Subsequently, they gradually invested more and constructed a storehouse, offices, and a high, solid wall towards the street as protection against theft. Today, Casa Vieja is a poor, populous *barrio* – with many homes, a few small stores, and a labyrinth of narrow streets, both paved and unpaved.

Again, Dominican furniture makers run different types of enterprises, and their technical, economic, cultural, and political strategies and solutions vary a great deal. But what all of them, and their workers, have in common is that they are forced to live with the consequences of the crisis that for years has haunted the country's power industry. As an outcome of the crisis, they experience lasting contradictions between forms of social and economic time. It is with their labour that they develop solutions.

If the sale of Dominican furniture to families and households is undermined as an effect of imports of foreign products, and if owners of tourist complexes, hotels, and other types of companies choose foreign furniture, there is nevertheless another possibility: supplying furniture to parts of the Dominican state apparatus – ministries, the armed forces, the police, hospitals, universities, and schools. In the remainder of this section, I discuss Dominican furniture makers' work on securing contracts with government agencies. This activity shows the same basic thing: that there is no uniform contemporary capitalist time. As we have already seen, the Dominican state system is diverse, a relatively fragmented structure of institutions and practices – and as a result, it produces a wide range of forms of political-economic time, including, for example, delays, waiting, and full stops or blockades.

Cristian Nolasco heads the firm Industrias Colón in Villa Consuelo – a *barrio* situated not far from downtown Santo Domingo. His father is a trader, with a store in another part of the city, and formerly owned Industrias Colón with a partner. The latter had created the firm in the late 1980s. In 1996, Cristian's father bought his partner's share and became sole owner. Cristian has run the firm since 1994. The enterprise makes furniture of wood and metal, in addition to mattresses. Industrias Colón has always been a small venture, but in the period from 1996 to 2000 the firm went well and the workshop employed around fifteen workers. After these promising years, however, Industrias Colón experienced stagnation and decline before production in the workshop dried up in 2012. When I met Cristian for the first time, the workshop had essentially been without production for six months. He said that he would call some of his workers if he got a small order. But Cristian is diligent, a hard worker. He works hard in order to try to breathe new life into the family firm, and in late 2012 he was elected ASONAIMCO's new president. A last major task for Cristian is to make some money and take care of his family. When the situation of Industrias Colón worsened, Cristian decided to create a small enterprise that imports and sells cosmetics. In his office in Industrias Colón, there are boxes of samples, and he sells and distributes to hair salons and beauty parlours in different parts of the city.

Industrias Colón's customers had mainly been a series of different furniture stores, but Cristian's firm had also produced furniture for the state. However, Cristian recalled that some of these contracts were challenging. One day in his office, he took out a set of documents and three invoices and put them on his desk, explaining that the invoices referred to supplies from Industrias Colón to public institutions. Two were dated from 1997 and 2003 and concerned supplies of a type of simple bed to a part of the armed forces; the amounts were significant, but had never been paid. The third unpaid invoice was from 1994 and concerned a smaller amount. Cristian's father's partner, the man who had originally established the firm, had relatives who were officers and worked for the government, and contracts with public institutions had been secured through these contacts. Through the years, Cristian had tried many times to collect the debts, but without result. After having experienced these difficulties, he said, he and the family had got a bit scared and had for a number of years – at least until 2005 or 2006 – sought to avoid selling to the state.

Industrias Colón's and Cristian's labour had a political dimension. This is representative of the larger situation: often, contracts with – and services from – public institutions must be obtained by firm owners with the aid of personal connections, kinsmen, and friends. Moral bonds, or kinship and friendship, have various faces. Such ties may secure assistance or favours, but they may also be a source of experiences and feelings of treason (Yanagisako 2002: 110-44).

ASONAIMCO is a member of the umbrella organization La Confederación Dominicana de la Pequeña y Mediana Empresa – or CODOPYME, a union of a series of the country's small business associations. Furniture and mattress makers act politically through both organizations. In late 2012, Yuri Chez was elected president of CODOPYME. For many years, Chez had run a furniture firm and was, as mentioned, head of ASONAIMCO before he advanced and became head of CODOPYME.

In December 2008, Dominican authorities promulgated a new law: Law 488-08: Regulatory Regime for the Development and Competitiveness of Micro, Small, and Medium Enterprises – MSMEs. This was viewed as a great victory by CODOPYME. Through the law, the Fernández government sought to render stronger support to the development of the nation's myriad of small- and medium-sized firms. The organizations had fought for such a law for many years – some said it had taken two decades. A central component of Law 488-08 says that all state institutions' purchases of goods and services must include a minimum proportion of 15 per cent of the total purchase supplied by small and medium-sized domestic firms, provided that the goods and services in question are supplied in the country. Needless to say, this was met with enthusiasm. However, when I began fieldwork almost four years after the promulgation of the law, it had yet not been put to use. In late 2011, a newspaper headline declared sarcastically that Law 488-08 had gone to bed. According to the article, the entity in charge of elaborating and formulating the rules and directives for the implementation of the law, the Programa de Promoción y Apoyo a la Micro, Pequeña y Mediana Empresa (PROMIPYME), had not yet managed to execute the task; instead, the law had travelled back and forth between PROMIPYME and the office of the president (*Listín Diario* 2011). Organizations, activists, and small business owners were disappointed and bitter, but continued fighting. Cristian pointed to a copy of Law 488-08 in his office: 'Look! The 15 per cent rule is great! But almost four years have passed since the law was ready, and it has still not been put to use. The 15 per cent rule isn't used'.

Delays and waiting are one thing; being stopped is quite another. The Dominican state's purchases are driven and governed by merciless power struggles: one outcome is that small domestic producers (like Cristian and his colleagues) not only experience delays and that things take time, but also that they are blocked and excluded – stopped outright. To be able to support and explain this, I shall round off this essay by looking at a further example: I will outline the furniture makers' fight for the opportunity to deliver school furniture, particularly *butacas,* or tablet-arm chairs, to public educational institutions.

A number of Dominican firms produce tablet-arm chairs; Cristian's firm, Industrias Colón, used to supply them to private schools and universities. The bulk of the sales occur during a limited period of the year – in June, July, and August, before the start of a new school year or academic year. Industrias Colón used to make 1,500 tablet-arm chairs in wood and metal during this period; the rest of the year, it made about 100 a month.

The state continued to purchase *butacas* from domestic producers for its schools and universities until 2006, but in 2007 it began exclusively to purchase imported products. In 2007, a *Listín Diario* headline announced, 'Foreign tablet-arm chairs outcompete the national: The domestic producers say the Ministry of Education does not buy from them'.

Representatives of the industry protested in the media and demanded that the state again start buying tablet-arm chairs made in the country. But with a minor exception in 2010 (when the state bought a small number from local firms, including Cristian's), the Ministry of Education continued to import them. All the tablet-arm chairs which it bought for public schools and universities in 2011 and 2012 had been made abroad in China, Mexico, Panama, and elsewhere.

Journal of the Royal Anthropological Institute (N.S.), 180-197
© Royal Anthropological Institute 2018

In August 2012, the country got a new president. Danilo Medina took over after Fernández, and although Medina represents the same political party as Fernández, and Medina's vice-president is Fernández's wife, leaders and activists in the industry felt a certain qualified hope. For a long time, Medina had underscored his will to strengthen the state's support for the development of the small economic ventures, or the popular economy. In September 2012, the Medina administration passed a measure that declared that all public purchases must include a minimum proportion of 20 per cent of the total purchase supplied by small and medium-sized domestic firms. The measure therefore increased the previous proportion as expressed in Law 488-08 by 5 per cent. The implementation was scheduled to take effect in January 2013, and in June and July 2013 it was again time for the Ministry of Education's annual considerable purchase of tablet-arm chairs. After having received bids from a series of local firms, the Ministry chose to offer contracts to thirty-three firms; twenty-five, it announced, were small firms, while eight were large. But this was immediately and loudly dismissed by representatives of the small enterprises. Chez spoke on behalf of all in the press: 'The small firms had in reality not been given anything', he concluded. Instead, he went on, the Ministry had committed forgery; it had offered contracts to a series of fictive – or only apparently small – ventures that in reality had been established and were controlled by a handful of large firms. This, he concluded, not only violated Law 488-08, but was also an insult against the will of President Medina (*Hoy* 2013). Although the accusations were harsh, they were not always repudiated, not even among the state's own representatives. In August 2013, for example, Director of Public Procurement Yocasta Guzmán Santos recognized frankly in the press that 'There are large companies that create small firms in order to take advantage of the programmes and projects devoted to the small enterprises' (*DiarioLibre.com* 2013*a*).

I confess: I continued to be unforgivably naïve. I asked Chez about this situation in his office one day, and he explained to me that the state, like the country's tourist enclaves, increasingly purchased imported products, and not from the domestic industry.

'But *why*?' I asked. 'Are the increased amounts of state imports due to the tax policy?'

'No', he said, 'let's be frank – this occurs because of corruption'.

Cristian supported Chez's interpretation:

> The reason is the corruption. Let me give you an example. Let's say that the price of a locally made product – for example, a tablet-arm chair – is 1,000 pesos. The importer gets the product for 500 pesos from a free zone or a special economic zone in Asia – because in China, they produce thousands, millions. You sell the product to the state for 900 apiece – which means that you, as importer and the representative of the state, have the difference of 400 to play with; both make good money. Or they buy in Mexico or Asia for 500, and the state is invoiced at 750 or 800. They still make a good profit. Government officials and owners of import firms make money – and the two are not infrequently relatives or friends.

Cristian went on:

> You can't prove it – but there is far too much circumstantial evidence. Because, when you check, like I have done many times, when you go through the lists of the firms, study documents, and invoices, you find that the owner of the import operation is the cousin – or the brother-in-law, or the husband of a daughter – of the civil servant. For example, last year we found out that one of the firms that had been offered a contract by the ministry in order to import tablet-arm chairs was a hardware store. Look! A hardware store doing business with furniture! But it turned out that the owner of the hardware store was married to a daughter of the government official.

As I see it, this pretty much sums up a key dimension of capitalist time in the field. On the one hand, the Dominican furniture makers experience contemporary capitalism's tremendous capacity to compress time and space and to transport and deliver goods from far away at an accelerated pace – the constantly growing competition from imported furniture testifies to these processes, these dimensions of modern global capitalism as it unfolds in today's Dominican society. On the other hand, or simultaneously, they experience conspicuous slowness, or constant delays and loss of time, when they seek to do business with, and sell their products to, representatives of the state apparatus. Although both processes, or sets of processes, must be viewed as products of today's neoliberal global capitalist system, both have a Dominican shape; both mirror and embody a specific Dominican political-economic-cultural history and reality (see in addition Gregory 2014: 4-6; Tsing 2013). Small Dominican furniture makers seek to produce and act at the intersection of these forces, or in the gap and the tension between the pace of the imports and the delays or blockades of state and non-state political-economic agents. The opening of the Dominican economy and the accompanying trade liberalization made it feasible and far easier to import. The last decades' development of export processing zones and special economic zones across the world made it easier to continue to obtain and deliver cheap commodities.[5] The year 1978 put an end to a protracted Dominican authoritarian history, in a sense. But the Dominican state system continues to mirror the many decades under Trujillo and Balaguer, and to be deeply shaped by uses of kinship and friendship, or forms of patronage and forms of corruption (Krohn-Hansen 2009). Today, powerful groups and networks in the country make more money by importing than by doing business with national producers.

Organizations, activists, and others struggle indefatigably for small enterprises' rights and interests. Chez and the organization he heads are visible in the national press and on television, negotiate with politicians, and organize workshops and seminars; this is likewise the case with ASONAIMCO. In July 2013, Cristian investigated and analysed the thirty-three firms that had been offered contracts by the Ministry for supplies of tablet-arm chairs. In September and October of the same year, he and ASONAIMCO mapped and investigated the results of a long list of processes in which the state had recently selected firms for deliveries of different types of furniture to public institutions. In a large open meeting organized by CODOPYME on 12 November 2013, Cristian presented the findings and decried unlawfulness and injustice. None of the examined processes had in reality, he said, been good or valid. On the contrary, he continued, the usual process enables a small group of individuals or large enterprises to get most of the contracts with the aid of a set of front firms (*DiarioLibre.com* 2013*b*).

Conclusion

Capitalism encourages time economy and the social acceleration of time; it condenses or elides temporal and spatial distances and advances through this global social integration. Capitalism and speed are consequently virtually synonymous terms – at least this is what we typically tell one another (in the social sciences and in many parts of society). But as we have seen, in today's Santo Domingo this picture corresponds to only half the story. The nation's small workshops and enterprises experience lots of delays and waiting – instead of speed and incorporation, they encounter slowness, blockades, and exclusion. The state's debt and financial crisis, and the accompanying negotiations with the IMF and other lenders, have resulted in (enforced) deregulations and free-trade agreements – and a massive increase in the country's imports, an entirely new export-import regime. Today, it is largely the same political-economic (often kinship- and/or friendship-based) networks and groups in Santo Domingo that produce and reproduce both the accelerated velocity and the shameless delays, both the compression of time and space and the braking and the foot-dragging – or the marginalization.

The production and the distribution of *la luz*, or electricity, remain driven and permeated by power struggles. At the core of the battle today remains the management of the consequences of the state debt – or the question of who must pay what to whom when. In a way, the system appears to be based on calendar time *and* a pattern of belated and barely co-ordinated or unpredictable repayments of debt: The foreign energy companies limit or reduce the power to the national distribution grid, and/or the state-controlled distribution companies seek to discipline the citizens and the government into paying their electricity bills through production of blackouts. One result is that small and marginalized producers, like María and the rest of the owners and operators of firms in the popular *barrios*, experience much wasted time – or lasting vulnerability and doubt. The condition for production is structured by contradictions between rhythms or times, or as Lorenzo put it: 'I've never used the power from the street, because in this neighbourhood where we operate, they supply only four or five hours of electricity, and only in the night, when I don't work – I work in the day'.

Again, the timespaces of contemporary capitalism are heterogeneous. In their efforts to co-ordinate activities, and to produce and sell, my informants (Lorenzo and Aldo, María, and the others) draw heavily on a tradition – or particular notions of workmanship, materials, and history. María summed it up by saying, 'The creole furniture ... is the furniture that lasts ... Because we use wood ... We don't [wish to] change our furniture so quickly'. But we ought to go further. Important aspects of the activity of many of the Dominican furniture makers are part of more comprehensive (historically, politically, and culturally produced) forces, a form of collectively shaped everyday politics of self-understanding and belonging. As we have seen, many Dominicans continue to be fond of *caoba*, or mahogany. The history of mahogany logging and mahogany use on the island is linked inextricably to the history of Spanish colonialism. Prized originally by European furniture makers for its dark colour, stability, and other qualities, mahogany was first targeted shortly after Columbus 'discovered' Hispaniola and the New World. With the emergence of an independent Dominican Republic in the nineteenth and twentieth centuries, excessive *caoba* logging and conspicuous *caoba* use were nationalized, but remained inseparably connected to the history of the political and economic hierarchies, and the central power, in society. *Caoba* continued to function as a sign of authority and as a source of experience of success and esteem. The less wealthy and powerful strata sought to mimic the practices and forms of consumption at the top of society. Today, things have changed once again. Members of the Dominican elite have shifted in taste and habit and increasingly purchase foreign products, made not of mahogany, but of other materials. However, many in the middle and lower parts of the social hierarchy continue, as before, to seek social acknowledgement and respect, or a stake in the networks of power (however small it might be), through obtaining objects made of *caoba* and/or *caoba* imitations.[6] Furniture made of true mahogany is politically incorrect, nearly a bad word, in significant parts of the world today. But this is not the case among many in today's Dominican society.

In the mid-1930s, 82 per cent of the Dominican population lived in rural areas. In 1960, 70 per cent remained rural, still one of the highest percentages in Latin America and the Caribbean (Turits 2003: 265). Trujillo's strategies to increase agricultural production and secure peasant access to land helped make the dictator's Dominican Republic 'a virtually self-sufficient country in agricultural terms (save wheat), in contrast to the rest of the twentieth-century Caribbean and much of Latin America' (Turits 2003: 20). After the end of the dictatorship, the country witnessed massive urbanization and international migration. But the large Dominican cities continue to house fairly few factories. Put differently, large parts of today's Dominican capital, not least its many popular *barrios*, are both urban and rural – they are cosmopolitan, and apparently industrialized, but mainly without factories. They represent a particular form of modern urban landscape: not particularly industrialized, not pre-industrial, and not post-industrial, and with limited public welfare and a state in debt. Many run their own small or tiny enterprises, and many work in the so-called 'informal economy'. It is in this type of capitalist reality that I have examined some forms of navigation of time through labour.

NOTES

Special thanks go to Penny Harvey, Elisabeth Schober, and two anonymous reviewers for their extremely valuable comments on earlier versions of this essay. In the essay, I have used the real names of politicians and familiar leaders and activists in Santo Domingo. All other names of persons have been changed.

[1] In this essay, I am inspired by Bear's stimulating thinking (2014a; 2014b).

[2] For discussions of the notion of 'time-maps', see Bear (2014a: 15-16) and Gell (1992: 235-41).

[3] For a relevant comparative perspective, see Michael Herzfeld's (2004) study of the production of a tradition through an analysis of small-town Cretan artisans' workshops with their labour forms.

[4] Mahogany, the reddish-brown timber of the genus *Swietenia*, is indigenous to the Americas. The wood first came to the notice of Europeans with the beginning of Spanish colonization.

[5] For a history of the creation and the emergence of the world's export processing zones, see Neveling (2015).

[6] For classic works on power, memories, and mimicry, see Stoller (1995) and Taussig (1993).

REFERENCES

BEAR, L. 2014a. Doubt, conflict, mediation: the anthropology of modern time. *Journal of the Royal Anthropological Institute* (N.S.) Special Issue: Doubt, conflict, mediation: the anthropology of modern time (ed.) L. Bear, 3-30.

——— 2014b. For labour: Ajeet's accident and the ethics of technological fixes in time. *Journal of the Royal Anthropological Institute* (N.S.) Special Issue: Doubt, conflict, mediation: the anthropology of modern time (ed.) L. Bear, 71-88.

——— 2015. Beyond economization: state debt and labor. Fieldsights – Theorizing the Contemporary. *Cultural Anthropology* (available on-line: *http://culanth.org/fieldsights/659-beyond-economization-state-debt-and-labor*, accessed 24 January 2018).

CASTREE, N. 2009. The spatio-temporality of capitalism. *Time and Society* **18**, 26-61.

DERBY, L. 2009. *The dictator's seduction: politics and the popular imagination in the era of Trujillo*. Durham, N.C.: Duke University Press.

DIARIOLIBRE.COM 2013a. Denuncian empresas grandes crean Pymes. 8 August (available on-line: *http://www.diariolibre.com/noticias_print.php?id=396612&s=*, accessed 24 January 2018).

——— 2013b. Mipymes cuestionan política del Poder Ejecutivo para impulsar ese sector. 13 November (available on-line: *http://www.diariolibre.com/noticias_print.php?id=410736&s=*, accessed 24 January 2018).

GELL, A. 1992. *The anthropology of time: cultural constructions of temporal maps and images*. Oxford: Berg.

GORDON, S.M. 2016. The Foreign Corrupt Practices Act: prosecute corruption and end transnational illegal logging. *Boston College Environmental Affairs Law Review* **43**: 1 (available on-line: *http://lawdigitalcommons.bc.edu/ealr/vol43/iss1/5=*, accessed 24 January 2018).

GRAEBER, D. 2002. The anthropology of globalization (with notes on neomedievalism, and the end of the Chinese model of the nation-state). *American Anthropologist* **104**, 1222-7.
———— 2011. *Debt: the first 5,000 years*. Brooklyn, N.Y.: Melville Publishing House.
GREENBERG, J.B. 1997. A political ecology of structural-adjustment policies: the case of the Dominican Republic. *Culture and Agriculture* **19: 3**, 85-93.
GREGORY, S. 2014. *The devil behind the mirror: globalization and politics in the Dominican Republic*. Berkeley: University of California Press.
GUYER, J.I. 2012. Obligation, binding, debt and responsibility: provocations about temporality from two new sources. *Social Anthropology* **20**, 491-501.
HARVEY, D. 1989. *The condition of postmodernity: an enquiry into the origins of cultural change*. Oxford: Blackwell.
———— 2005. *A brief history of neoliberalism*. Oxford: University Press.
HERZFELD, M. 2004. *The body impolitic: artisans and artifice in the global hierarchy of value*. Chicago: University Press.
HOY 2012a. Comerciantes Villa Consuelo se quejan por tanda de apagones. 8 May, 5E.
———— 2012b. Deuda con generadores sube a US$1,000 millones, 26 July, 1E.
———— 2013. Desmiente Educación escogiera pymes para pupitres. 6 July, 1A, 4A.
KROHN-HANSEN, C. 2009. *Political authoritarianism in the Dominican Republic*. New York: Palgrave Macmillan.
LISTÍN DIARIO 2007. Las butacas extranjeras 'sientan' a las nacionales. Economía y Negocios, 28 July.
————2009. Se reducen las ventas de muebles. Economía y Negocios, 13 May.
———— 2011. La ley 488-08 se acostó a dormir junto al Disdo. Economía y Negocios, 11 November.
MAINS, D. 2012. Blackouts and progress: privatization, infrastructure, and a developmentalist state in Jimma, Ethiopia. *Cultural Anthropology* **27**, 3-27.
MARX, K. 1993 [1885]. *Capital*, Vol. 2 (trans. D. Fernbach). London: Penguin.
MOYA PONS, F. 2010. *The Dominican Republic: a national history* (Third edition). Princeton: Markus Wiener Publishers.
NEVELING, P. 2015. Export processing zones and global class formation. In *Anthropologies of class: power, practice and inequality* (eds) J. Carrier & D. Kalb, 164-82. Cambridge: University Press.
PEDERSEN, D. 2013. *American value: migrants, money, and meaning in El Salvador and the United States*. Chicago: University Press.
PEEBLES, G. 2010. The anthropology of credit and debt. *Annual Review of Anthropology* **39**, 225-40.
RODRÍGUEZ BENCOSME, A.M. 2013. *El mueble de madera Dominicano*. Santo Domingo: Instituto Tecnológico de Santo Domingo/Editora Búho, S.R.L.
SCHWENKEL, C. 2015. Spectacular infrastructure and its breakdown in socialist Vietnam. *American Ethnologist* **42**, 520-34.
STOLLER, P. 1995. *Embodying colonial memories: spirit possession, power, and the Hauka in West Africa*. London: Routledge.
TAUSSIG, M. 1993. *Mimesis and alterity*. New York: Routledge.
TSING, A.L. 2013. Sorting out commodities: how capitalist value is made through gifts. *HAU: Journal of Ethnographic Theory* **3: 1**, 21-43.
TURITS, R.L. 2003. *Foundations of despotism: peasants, the Trujillo regime, and modernity in Dominican history*. Stanford: University Press.
YANAGISAKO, S. 2002. *Producing culture and capital: family firms in Italy*. Princeton: University Press.

État contre industrie : temps et travail parmi les ébénistes dominicains

Résumé

Le présent article analyse le temps et le travail parmi de petits producteurs de meubles dominicains. Les petits ateliers et les petites entreprises de République Dominicaine passent beaucoup de temps à attendre : pas de voie rapide ni d'intégration politico-économique pour eux, mais des lenteurs, des blocages et une marginalisation. La production nationale de meubles affronte la concurrence de plus en plus rude des articles d'importation. Les finances nationales ont connu une crise dans les années 1990. Pressé par ses créanciers internationaux, l'État a déréglementé et ouvert l'économie, sans dépenser davantage pour le développement de l'artisanat et de l'industrie du pays. En outre, le secteur de l'électricité ne se porte pas bien dans le pays et les longues coupures de courant sont la norme. De ce fait, les petits producteurs de meubles sont obligés de vivre selon des rythmes sociaux contradictoires et conflictuels. Ils naviguent à travers les diverses formes de temps dans leur travail concret et leur quotidien. Il faudrait envisager le capitalisme global contemporain comme un résultat contingent de l'activité du travail, à travers une myriade d'efforts localisés et quotidiens pour le « fixer ». Ces efforts reflètent toujours une histoire politique et sociale spécifique. L'exploration du temps capitaliste contemporain, concentrée sur des formes particulières de travail, peut analyser la manière dont les rythmes discordants du capitalisme mondial ont aidé à donner forme au travail, à le perturber et à le disloquer dans un lieu donné. Dans le même temps, l'auteur montre comment les agents concernés cherchent à s'adapter à des rythmes contradictoires et à travailler sur leurs effets.

Index

activation, 22, 40; 105–19; and complicity, 112–13; and dislocation, 106; and poverty, 108–9; organization, 109–11; selection for, 116; status, 114–15

actor-network theory, 32

affect, 10, 22–3, 76, 135–6, 141; and emotion, 136

affective labour, 13, 31, 59, 76, 85

age, 16, 76

agrarian economies, 10, 15

agricultural labour, 120–33

agriculture, 31, 33, 49, 64, 82; subsistence, 122, 151, 163

aid money, 14, 23, 166, 169

alienation, 14, 18, 32–3

ambiguity, 29, 32, 35, 41, 68, 85, 96, 115

anthropology, and craft, 61, 62, 71; and work, 17; economic, 15, 151; of labour, 10, 11, 13, 19, 20, 41, 71, 75, 86, 151

Apple iPhones, 12; production process, 12

Argentina, 15, 21, 77–8, 86; agrarian leagues, 77–8, 81, 83, 86

artisanal workshops, 21, 61–74

autarky, 14, 151

authorship, 61, 65, 66–71

Bear, Laura, 16, 19, 180

Besnier, Niko, 19, 76

Bourdieu, Pierre, 35, 163

Breman, Jan, 38, 39, 132, 137

Burawoy, Michael, 39–40

Campbell, Ben, 7, 12, 14, 23, 40, 151–65

Cant, Alanna, 7, 13, 21, 32, 61–74, 83

capital, accumulation, 14, 20, 31, 33; and labour, 10, 11, 13, 16, 20, 34–5, 48–51; mobility, 11; movements, 10

capitalism, 13, 14, 16, 30; and culture, 63, 71; and speed, 187–93; global, 15, 30, 180, 181; instability, 19; neoliberal, 40, 152; transnational, 10, 15, 23–4, 58

carbon emissions, 12

care work, 13, 32

cash economies, 11, 163

caste, 160

Castree, Noel, 181

China, 20–1, 47, 51–7, 138, 183; managers, 54, 58–9; workers, 54, 56, 58–9

citizens' rights, 13, 154

citizenship, 11, 16, 22, 76, 108, 116, 121

class, 16, 62, 126

collectives, 22, 120, 121, 123–6; in future, 130–1, 132

colonialism, 30, 152, 194

Journal of the Royal Anthropological Institute (N.S.), 198-202
© Royal Anthropological Institute 2018

Journal of the Royal Anthropological Institute (N.S.), 198-202
© Royal Anthropological Institute 2018